POLICE
PRE-DISASTER
PREPARATION

POLICE
PRE-DISASTER
PREPARATION

By

V. A. LEONARD, B.S., M.A., Ph.D.

Professor Emeritus of Police Administration
Washington State University
Pullman, Washington

CHARLES C THOMAS • PUBLISHER
Springfield • Illinois • U.S.A.

Published and Distributed Throughout the World by
CHARLES C THOMAS • PUBLISHER
Bannerstone House
301-327 East Lawrence Avenue, Springfield, Illinois, U.S.A.

*With THOMAS BOOKS careful attention is given to all details of
manufacturing and design. It is the Publisher's desire to present books that are
satisfactory as to their physical qualities and artistic possibilities and
appropriate for their particular use. THOMAS BOOKS will be true to those
laws of quality that assure a good name and good will.*

Printed in the United States of America
R-1

PREFACE

T HIS book could save many lives, prevent many injuries and reduce property loss and destruction, if it encourages police departments and the communities they serve to prepare themselves for action in advance of the hour when calamity strikes.

The unexpected is a fact of life; it can come anytime, anywhere. No city or community can be certain that it will not be the scene of the next disaster. One such disaster, the New Madrid, Missouri, earthquake of 1811, ranks as one of the twenty great earthquakes in recorded history. It rocked the United States all the way from the Canadian border to the Gulf Coast, from the headwaters of the Missouri River to the Atlantic Ocean. Who can say when the next one will come?

In this book will be found the blueprints for police pre-disaster preparation and planning. Included are specific plans that have stood the test and have carried the police and their communities through the strains of disaster — the hurricane, the tornado, the earthquake and civil disorder — at a time when no plan at all would have been catastrophic.

I wish to acknowledge the cooperation and assistance of others in the preparation of the manuscript for this book. I am especially indebted to Executive Director Quinn Tamm of the International Association of Chiefs of Police and Assistant Director Horace S. Webb for permission to use the *IACP GENERAL EMERGENCY PLAN - Unit 4A11, Supplement 1* and *IACP GUIDELINES FOR CIVIL DISORDER AND MOBILIZATION PLANNING;* to Chief R. C. Loranger of the Burbank (California) Police Department for letting me use the *BURBANK UNUSUAL OCCURRENCE CONTROL PLAN;* to Civil Defense Director R. T. Runyan and Chief J. H. Avant of the Corpus Christi (Texas) Police Department for giving me the authority to include the *CORPUS CHRISTI*

HURRICANE AND EMERGENCY PLAN; and to Chief J. M. Towle of the Bakersfield (California) Police Department for authorization to use the *BAKERSFIELD MANUAL ON RIOT AND CIVIL DISTURBANCES.*

I am also grateful to Meyer Mathis, Director, Office of Systems Analysis, Information and Statistics Headquarters, The American National Red Cross; Elizabeth Thole, Administrative Assistant for the *Reader's Digest;* and V. P. Bannan, Editorial Office of the *World Almanac,* for permission to use their important materials.

If this book becomes a factor in the protection of life and property in this country, it will have been well worth the research and effort that it represents.

V.A.L.

CONTENTS

Page

Preface v

Chapter

I. THE ANATOMY OF DISASTER 3
Chronology of disaster 3
Natural disasters 5
Earthquakes 5
Winds, hurricanes and tornadoes 11
Floods 21
Fires 21
Volcanic eruptions 26
Railroad wrecks 28
Mine disasters 28
Explosions 28
Aircraft disasters 28
Man-made emergencies 37
Riot and mob situations 37
Nuclear attack 40
II. WHEN DISASTER STRIKES 46
Camille . . . the incredible 46
Her name was Celia 47
Planning – vital, indispensable 48
The Lubbock tornado 49
The IACP General Emergency Plan 51
III. THE BURBANK UNUSUAL OCCURRENCE
CONTROL PLAN 68
Organization chart 72
Definitions 72
Functions 72
Organization and command 73

Chapter   *Page*

    Tactical procedure 73

    Operational procedure 74

    Reporting procedure 75

    Directory 75

    References 75

IV. THE CONTAINMENT OF CIVIL DISORDER 163

    Guidelines for Civil Disorder and Mobilization Planning 164

        Purpose 164

        Administrative policy 165

        Organizational policy 167

        Operational policy 167

        Planning 168

        Legal considerations 176

        Intelligence 177

        Logistics 183

        Strategy 189

        Control tactics 196

        Miscellaneous tactics 202

        The command post 206

        Establishment of emergency control center 209

        Arrest procedures 211

        Recovery after disturbance 219

V. THE RESERVE FORCE CONCEPT 238

    The auxiliary police unit 238

        The Highland Park (Michigan) operation 241

    The tactical unit or mobile task force 241

        General operations 241

        Special operations 242

VI. TWO MAJOR DISASTER-ORIENTED ORGANIZATIONS ... 250

    The National Civil Defense System 250

        Responsibilities and programs 251

        Organization 251

        National fallout shelter program 252

        Emergency operating capability of state and

        local governments 255

Chapter *Page*

    Civil Defense warning and communications 257
    Military support of Civil Defense 258
    Support activities 260
    Financial assistance 262
    Fallout and radiation 263
    Fallout shelters, public and private 265
    Local Civil Defense 267
  The American Red Cross 270
    The Red Cross Disaster Relief Program 272
    Red Cross-government teamwork 275
    Red Cross Chapter responsibility 275
  The role of the federal government in
  natural disasters 277
    Disaster services under federal agencies' own
    statutory authority 278
    Assistance available following a major disaster
    declaration 279
    Requests for federal disaster assistance 280
    Requesting a major disaster declaration 281
    Procedures for providing federal assistance 282
VII. COLLATERAL ASPECTS OF PRE-DISASTER PLANNING . . 286
  Mobile emergency headquarters 286
  Increasing apprehension capability 289
    The alarm system 289
    The police roadblock 291
    Disaster and the computer sciences 294
  Developing emergency medical services 296

Appendix
  A. THE CORPUS CHRISTI HURRICANE
    AND EMERGENCY PLAN 299
  B. AMERICAN NATIONAL RED CROSS
    — DENTON COUNTY (TEXAS) CHAPTER PLAN 315
Bibliography 325
Index 329

POLICE
PRE-DISASTER
PREPARATION

CHAPTER I

THE ANATOMY OF DISASTER

POLICE departments are usually so busy administering current business that they give little thought to the planning of police procedures for times of disaster or catastrophe, such as earthquakes, fires, floods or tornadoes, or for times of acute social disturbance, including· demonstrations, mob situations, riots, strikes and political unrest. Furthermore, they may function for years without ever being faced by the pressing problems which a great earthquake, fire or flood may bring; this tends to lull them into a false sense of security — false because no community can be certain that it will not be the scene of the next disaster. The unexpected is a fact of life; it can come anytime, anywhere.

Chronology of Disaster

Disaster follows a definite time sequence which is about the only compensation it offers in terms of an opportunity to at least confront the challenge. The literature is in general agreement concerning the division of time elements in a disaster situation — the threat, the warning, the impact and the response. *

Thus, the chronology of disaster offers the opportunity for planning in advance of the catastrophe in order to implement prevention in some instances and to effect a reduction in the number of casualties. The threat and the warning are virtually absent in the case of an earthquake. But seismologists have developed concrete information concerning fault lines in the earth's crust which germinate into this form of disaster. The San

---

*Garb, Solomon, and Eng, Evelyn: *Disaster Handbook*. New York, Springer Publications, 1969, p. 12.
Healy, Richard J.: *Emergency and Disaster Planning*. New York, John Wiley and Sons, 1969, p. 275.

Andreas fault line along the Pacific Coast, for example, is well known. Here the threat and the warning are actually continuous from hour to hour, from day to day, from month to month. The threat phase is easily identifiable in most disaster situations by such indicators as a low barometric reading, heavy rains and melting snow, excessive drought in forest areas and the identification of a hurricane far out to sea and may last from minutes to weeks.

Garb and Eng point out that the warning phase is usually much shorter, varying from seconds to hours, and accompanied by a high degree of certainty that disaster will strike. The nature of the warning in many disaster situations is familiar to most people. An extremely low reading on the barometer, for example, is a sufficient indication to be on the alert for high winds, thunderstorms and even a tornado.

In Denton, Texas, alert periods known as *tornado watches* are a common feature of the weather scene between about April 15 and June 15. Currently, since April 15 and the present date (May 17), a dozen or more tornado watches have been announced by the United States Weather Service for this area. A tornado watch usually involves a rectangular area from one to three hundred square miles in which the Weather Service predicts a strong degree of probability for a tornado strike. These warnings are broadcast by radio and television. The sighting of a funnel cloud is an immediate indication of such a strike.

Today, the United States Weather Service routinely pinpoints and plots the course of hurricanes in the Carribean. Hurricane warnings give the coastal areas an opportunity to *batten down the hatches* and prepare for a blow and possible high tide conditions. Similarly, a marked decrease in the water level along the coast would indicate the possibility of an impending tsunami or tidal wave. A violent earthquake may constitute more advanced warning of tidal wave possibilities. Rising river levels and, as previously indicated, severe drought conditions may offer the forecast of flood or forest fire.

The impact phase is the crisis itself and marks the period — less than a minute in earthquakes and explosions — when the fury of the strike makes its destructive contact. The response involves taking stock of the loss of life and the number of injured persons, application of first aid and medical attention and planning for a return to normal conditions in the community or area.

Natural Disasters

It is relevant at this point to consider the various types of natural disasters that may occur in virtually any community.

Earthquakes

It is generally believed that earthquakes are caused by gradual changes in the weight distribution of the earth's crust, resulting in enormous strains and stresses in the rock layers. When the strain exceeds the strength of the rock, a slippage occurs along a fault line, such as the San Andreas fault previously mentioned. The slippage generates a series of shock waves or convulsions which are transmitted outward at a speed of several miles per second to the surface of the earth's crust. They are felt and observed as earthquake tremors, occasionally violent in nature and causing widespread loss of life and property damage.

Although the great majority of earthquakes in the United States have been mild in nature, eleven of them were major disturbances of the earth's surface, including the New Madrid, Missouri, earthquake of 1811-1812, which ranks as one of the twenty great earthquakes in recorded history. Although it did little damage because of the unpopulated condition of the territory in which it occurred, it is alarming to speculate upon the tremendous social and economic losses it would have caused had it happened a century later.

Three shocks of greatest intensity were felt during December, 1811, and in January and February of 1812. Topographic changes occurred over an area of 30,000 to 50,000 square miles, and the territory shaken was at least a million square miles in area. The disturbance was felt from Canada to New Orleans and from the headwaters of the Missouri River to the Atlantic Ocean. The ground moved in great rolls over a wide area; great blocks of the earth were uplifted and others sunk; islands disappeared in the rivers and new lakes were formed.* Earthquakes are not unusual in the United States. As recently as 1948, Helena, Montana, reported that it had experienced its 2,888th recorded tremor since 1935! Who can tell us where the next one will strike? Everyday, they occur somewhere on the earth's surface.

Two methods have been developed for the measurement of earthquakes. One known as the Richter Magnitude Scale, developed by Dr. Charles F. Richter of the California Institute of Technology in Pasadena (1935), is designed for the measurement of energy released or magnitude and is calculated from instrumental data recorded on the seismograph.

The other, the Modified Mercali Intensity Scale, is a measure of the intensity of an earthquake at various points in the impact area and is based upon personal observation of its effect on people and objects such as buildings. The original scale was developed in 1902 by the Italian seismologist Mercali and was based upon a series of twelve measurement criteria, graduating in severity. The scale was modified in 1931 by Harry O. Wood and Frank Newmann, two American seismologists, as shown in Table I.

TABLE I

MODIFIED MERCALI INTENSITY SCALE†

By Wood and Neumann (abridged)

   I. Not felt except by a very few under especially favorable conditions.
  II. Felt only by a few persons at rest, especially on upper floors of buildings. Delicately suspended objects may swing.
 III. Felt quite noticeably especially on upper floors of buildings, but many people do not recognize it as an earthquake. Standing motor cars may rock slightly. Vibration like that of passing truck.
  IV. During the day felt indoors by many, outdoors by few. At night some awakened. Dishes, windows, doors disturbed; walls made cracking sound. Sensation like heavy truck striking building. Standing motor cars rocked noticeably.
   V. Felt by nearly everyone; many awakened. Some dishes, windows, and so forth broken; a few instances of cracked plaster; unstable objects overturned. Disturbances of trees, poles and other tall objects sometimes noticed.

---

*Heck, H. N.: *Earthquake History of the United States.* U. S. Geodetic Survey, Special Publication No. 49.
†Leonard, V. A., and More, Harry W., Jr.: *Police Organization and Management,* 3rd ed. Mineola, Foundation Press, Inc., 1971, p. 496.

   VI. Felt by all; many frightened and ran outdoors. Some heavy furniture moved; a few instances of fallen plaster or damaged chimneys. Damage slight.

  VII. Everybody runs outdoors. Damage negligible in buildings of good design and construction; slight to moderate in well-built structures; considerable in poorly built or badly designed structures; some chimneys broken; noted by persons driving motor cars.

 VIII. Damage slight in specially designed structures, considerable in ordinary substantial buildings with partial collapse; great in poorly built structures. Paneled walls thrown out of frame structures. Fall of chimneys, factory stacks, columns, monuments, walls. Heavy furniture overturned. Sand and mud ejected in small amounts. Changes in well water. Persons driving motor cars disturbed.

   IX. Damage considerable in specially designed structures; well designed frame structures thrown out of plumb; great in substantial buildings, with partial collapse. Buildings shifted off foundations. Ground cracked conspicuously. Underground pipes broken.

    X. Some well-built wooden structures destroyed; most masonry and frame structures destroyed with foundations; ground badly cracked. Rails bent. Landslides considerable from river banks and steep slopes. Shifted sand and mud. Water splashed (slopped) over banks.

   XI. Few, if any (masonry) structures remain standing. Bridges destroyed. Broad fissures in ground. Underground pipe lines completely out of service. Earth slumps and land slips in soft ground. Rails bent greatly.

  XII. Damage total. Waves on ground surfaces. Lines of sight and level distorted. Objects thrown upward into the air.

Table II indicates the major earthquakes that have occurred on the earth's surface since the year 1057, showing the date, location and loss of life.

The largest known earthquakes anywhere in the world have been close to 8.5 magnitude on the Richter scale. The San Francisco earthquake of April, 1906, occurred before Dr. Richter of the California Institute of Technology had developed the Richter scale. A study of its effects, however, has led seismologists to set its magnitude at 8.3. The Good Friday earthquake in Alaska in 1964 was magnitude 8.4. The February, 1971, earthquake in the Los Angeles area was 6.5 (the same as the Anza-Borrego, California, earthquake of April 8, 1968), slightly stronger than the 6.3 of the Long Beach earthquake of March 10, 1933, and considerably weaker than the 7.7 of the Tehachapi, California, earthquake of July 21, 1952.

A comparison of these magnitudes and the damage caused by these earthquakes provides a clear illustration of the difference between earthquake magnitude and earthquake intensity. The

TABLE II*

MAJOR EARTHQUAKES

Source: United States Coast and Geodetic Survey

Year	Place	Deaths	Year	Place	Deaths
1057	China, Chihli	25,000	1783 Feb. 4	Italy, Calabria	50,000
1268	Asia Minor, Silicia	60,000	1797 Feb. 4	Ecuador, Quito	41,000
1290 Sept. 27	China, Chihli	100,000	1811 Dec. 16	U.S. New Madrid, Mo.	
1293 May 20	Japan, Kamarkura	30,000	1822 Sept. 5	Asia Minor, Aleppo	22,000
1531 Jan. 26	Portugal, Lisbon	30,000	1828 Dec. 28	Japan, Echigo	30,000
1556 Jan. 24	China, Shensi	830,000	1868 Aug. 13-15	Peru and Ecuador	25,000
1667 Nov.	Cancasia, Shemaka	80,000	1875 May 16	Venezuela, Colombia	16,000
1693 Jan. 11	Italy, Catania	60,000	1896 June 15	Japan, Sea wave	22,000
1737 Oct. 11	India, Calcutta	300,000	1906 Apr. 18	Calif. San Francisco	700
1755 June 7	Persia, northern	40,000	1906 Aug. 16	Chile, Valparaiso	1,500
1755 Nov. 1	Portugal, Lisbon	60,000	1905 Dec. 28	Italy, Messina	75,000
1915 Jan. 13	Italy, Avezzano	29,970	1954 Sept. 9-12	Northern Algeria	1,657
1920 Dec. 16	China, Kansu	180,000	1956 June 10-17	Northern Afghanistan	2,000
1923 Sept. 1	Japan, Tokyo	143,000	1957 July 2	Northern Iran	2,500
1932 Dec. 26	China, Kansu	70,000	1957 Dec. 4	Outer Mongolia	1,200
1933 Mar. 10	Long Beach, Calif	115	1957 Dec. 13	Western Iran	2,000
1935 May 31	India, Quetta	60,000	1960 Feb. 29	Morocco, Agadir	12,000
1939 Jan. 24	Chile, Chillan	30,000	1960 May 21-30	Southern Chile	5,700
1939 Dec. 27	Turkey, Erzincan	23,000	1962 Sept. 1	Northwestern Iran	10,000
1946 May 31	Eastern Turkey	1,300	1963 July 26	Yugoslavia, Skopje	1,100
1946 Dec. 21	Japan, Honshu	2,000	1964 Mar. 27	Alaska	131
1948 June 28	Japan, Fukui	5,131	1966 Aug. 19	Eastern Turkey	2,529
1949 Aug. 5	Ecuador, Pelileo	6,000	1968 Aug. 31	Northeastern Iran	11,588
1950 Aug. 15	India, Assam	1,500	1970 Mar. 28	Western Turkey	1,068
1953 Mar. 18	Northwestern Turkey	1,200	1970 May 31	Central Peru	50,000

*Reproduced through the courtesy of The World Almanac, 1971. New York, Newspaper Enterprise Association, 1971.

Richter scale is a measurement of the earth movement at the epicenter, which is that part of the earth's surface directly above the focus of an earthquake. The older Mercali scale measures intensity at specific places; an earthquake could be intensity X in one place, intensity V at another.

On the Mercali scale, the Long Beach earthquake of March 10, 1933 was XI, a rating near the top of the scale. Richter classified it as 6.3, which is not a great earthquake, even though the Long Beach quake destroyed hundreds of buildings in southwest and central Los Angeles County and killed more than one hundred people.

California has its quota of fault lines and has had its quota of earthquakes. In addition to the previously mentioned San Andreas fault, which is the best-marked and -mapped fault in the world, there are the Garlock, San Jacinto, Hayward and Calaveras fault lines. The San Gabriel fault, along which the 1933 earthquake in Long Beach apparently occurred, had been quiescent in recent decades.

According to the U. S. Coast and Geodetic Survey, the following are the great California earthquakes that have occurred in historic times:

The Southern California temblor of December 21, 1812, that destroyed La Purisma Mission and severely damaged the San Fernando, Santa Barbara and San Buenaventura Missions, is said to have caused the biggest tidal wave ever reported on the Pacific Coast. It was even greater than those that hit northern California's Crescent City after the 1964 earthquake in Alaska. Contemporary accounts say the greatest of the sea waves of 1812 was 50 feet above sea level at Gaviota Beach, north of Santa Barbara, and 35 feet above sea level at Santa Barbara.

A second California earthquake, also in December of 1812, killed more people, but it is not believed to have been a great or even major temblor. It knocked down the north tower of San Gabriel Mission and caused the transept at San Juan Capistrano to collapse, killing 40 persons attending mass.

The Monterey earthquake of June, 1838, in which the missions at Yerba Buena (San Francisco), Santa Clara and San Jose were damaged, was another great quake, though it is thought that the greatest California earthquake of all took place on January 9, 1857, in Southern California. It is believed to have been as strong as the 1906 San Francisco temblor. The ground surface was broken and displaced along the San Andreas fault from San Luis Obispo county in northern California to San Bernardino. According to Richter, this was the most recent great earthquake in Southern California. He wrote in a contemporary issue of the bulletin of the Seismological Society that water in the bed of the Los Angeles River was thrown out of the stream, and in the San Gabriel Valley, where the ground was cracked and fissured, water gushed out.

In the Owen's Valley, California, earthquake of March 26, 1872, the shock was felt throughout the state. Huge masses of granite and ice were dislodged from the face of the eastern escarpment of California's Sierra Nevada Mountains. In the San Francisco earthquake of 1906, 450 people died, 28,000 buildings were destroyed and 100,000 persons were made homeless. The Imperial Valley earthquake in May, 1940, caused enormous damage to highways, canals and buildings. Displacement along the San Andreas fault was 15 feet at some locations.

The Coast and Geodetic Survey lists almost 500 earthquakes that have caused loss of life and damage to property in California since 1759. Among the best known of these damaging earthquakes are the Santa Barbara temblor of June, 1925, in which 12 died and the Santa Barbara Mission lost its beautiful facade and the Long Beach earthquake of 1933, the third most destructive in the history of the United States.

Looking at the Pacific Basin as a whole, the earthquake-prone zone resembles a giant inverted horseshoe beginning in the Straits of Magellan at the southern tip of South America, coming on up the Pacific Coast to Alaska where it crosses the Pacific Ocean and then comes on down the coast of the Orient.

There are more than 1,200 seismograph stations around the world which detect 500,000 temblors a year, according to the National Geographical Society. Of these, 100,000 can be heard or felt, and some 1,000 cause damage and loss of life. Apparently, earthquakes perform a necessary function. Scientists assert that this repeated uplifting of the earth's crust, with the earthquakes that go with it, is essential to life. With mountains constantly eroding, the world would become a place of stagnant seas and swamps if they were not raised again.

Winds, Hurricanes and Tornadoes

Ordinary gales and squalls are responsible for about 80 percent of all wind damage and injury, and storms of this type can and do occur in every part of the United States.* But it is the hurricane and tornado with their awesome and destructive force that meet all the specifications of disaster and catastrophe.

In 1806, Sir Francis Beaufort, a British Admiral, developed a scale for the classification of wind velocity which is still used today by the United States Weather Service in their official weather forecasts. It is shown in Table III.

TABLE III

BEAUFORT WIND SCALE

Number	Title	Description	Miles per hour
0	calm	Smoke rises vertically	Less than 1
1	light air	Smoke drifts	1 to 3
2	slight breeze	Leaves rustle	4 to 7
3	gentle breeze	Leaves and twigs in motion	8 to 12
4	moderate breeze	Small branches moved; dust and light paper lifted	13 to 18
5	fresh breeze	Small trees sway; wavelets form on inland lakes	19 to 24
6	strong breeze	Wind whistles in telegraph wires; large branches move.	25 to 31
7	high wind	Whole trees in motion; walking difficult	32 to 38
8	gale	Twigs broken off trees; traffic slowed	39 to 46
9	strong gale	Chimneys down; roofs damaged	47 to 54
10	whole gale	Trees uprooted; damage considerable	55 to 63
11	storm	Damage widespread	64 to 75
12	hurricane		Above 75

*Healy, Richard J.: *Emergency and Disaster Planning.* New York, John Wiley and Sons, 1969, p. 153.

TABLE IV

SPEED OF WINDS IN THE UNITED STATES*

Stations	Avg.	High	Stations	Avg.	High	Stations	Avg.	High
Albany, N.Y.	8.8	71	Helena, Mont.	7.9	73	Pensacola, Fla.	7.9	(b) 91
Albuquerque, N.M.	8.8	90	Jacksonville, Fla.	8.9	82	Philadelphia, Pa.	9.5	73
Atlanta, Ga.	9.3	70	Key West, Fla.	11.5	122	Pittsburgh, Pa.	9.4	(b) 51
Bismarck, N.D.	10.8	72	Knoxville, Tenn.	7.5	73	Portland, Ore.	7.7	88
Boston, Mass.	12.9	65	Little Rock, Ark.	8.2	65	Rochester, N.Y.	9.7	73
Buffalo, N.Y.	12.6	91	Louisville, Ky.	8.3	61	St. Louis, Mo.	9.4	(b) 91
Cape Hatteras, N.C.	11.6	(b) 110	Memphis, Tenn.	9.2	56	Salt Lake City, Utah	8.7	71
Chattanooga, Tenn.	6.3	82	Miami, Fla.	8.9	(a) 80	San Diego, Calif.	6.5	51
Chicago, Ill.	10.2	60	Minneapolis, Minn.	10.7	92	San Francisco, Calif.	10.4	62
Cincinnati, Ohio	7.1	49	Mobile, Ala.	9.7	(b) 98	Savannah, Ga.	8.5	66
Cleveland, Ohio	11.0	74	Montgomery, Ala.	6.9	60	Spokane, Wash.	8.2	56
Denver, Colo.	9.3	56	Nashville, Tenn.	7.7	73	Toledo, Ohio	9.5	72
Detroit, Mich.	10.2	77	New Orleans, La.	8.5	(b) 98	Washington, D.C.	9.5	78
Fort Smith, Ark.	7.7	58	New York, N.Y. (c)	9.6	70	Mt. Washington, N.H.	35.6	231
Galveston, Texas	11.0	(d) 100	Omaha, Nebr.	11.1	73			

(a) Highest velocity ever recorded in Miami area was 132 mph, at former station in Miami Beach in September, 1926. (b) Previous location. (c) Data for Central Park. Battery Place data through 1960, avg. 14.5, high 113. (d) Recorded before anemometer blew away. Estimated high 120.

WINDS, THEIR FORCE AND OFFICIAL DESIGNATIONS

Designation	Miles per hour	Designation	Miles per hour	Designation	Miles per hour	Designation	Miles per hour
Calm	Less than 1	Moderate breeze	13 to 18	Near gale	32 to 38	Storm	55 to 63
Light air	1 to 3	Fresh breeze	19 to 24	Gale	39 to 46	Violent storm	64 to 73
Light breeze	4 to 7	Strong breeze	25 to 31	Strong gale	47 to 54	Hurricane	74 and above
Gentle breeze	8 to 12						

*Reproduced through the courtesy of *The World Almanac, 1971*. New York, Newspaper Enterprise Association, p 298.

TABLE V

HURRICANES, TYPHOONS, BLIZZARDS, OTHER STORMS*

Date, Locations, Number of Deaths

Date	Event	Deaths	Date	Event	Deaths
1888 Mar. 11-14	Blizzard, East U.S.	400	1959 Sept. 26-27	T. *Vera*, Honshu, Japan	4,466
1926 Sept. 16-22	Hurricane, Fla., Ala.	372	1960 Sept. 4-12	H. *Donna*, Caribbean,e. U.S.	148
1926 Oct. 20	Hurricane, Cuba	600	1961 Sept. 11	H. *Carla*, Tex., La.	40
1928 Sept. 12-17	Hurricane, W. Indies, Fla.	4,000	1961 Oct. 31	H. *Hattie*, Br. Honduras	400
1930 Sept. 3	Hurricane, San Domingo	2,000	1963 May 28-29	Windstorm, E. Pakistan	22,000
1938 Sept. 21	Hurricane, New England	600	1963 Oct. 4-8	H. *Flora*, Cuba, Haiti	6,000
1942 Oct. 15-16	Hurricane, Bengal, India	11,000	1964 Oct. 4-7	H. *Hilda*, La., Miss., Ga.	38
1944 Sept. 12-16	Hurricane, N. C. to N. Eng.	1,300	1965 May 11-12	Windstorm, E. Pakistan	17,000
1953 Sept. 25-27	Typhoon, Vietnam, Japan		1965 June 1-2	Windstorm, E. Pakistan	30,000
1954 Aug. 30	H. *Carol*, northeast U.S.	68	1965 Sept. 7-10	H. *Betsy*, Fla., Miss., La.	74
1954 Sept. 11	H. *Edna*, n.e. U. S., Canada	23	1965 Dec. 15	Windstorm, E. Pakistan	10,000
1954 Oct. 12-16	H. *Hazel*, east U. S., Haiti	347	1966 June 4-10	H. *Alma* Honduras, s.e. U.S.	51
1955 Aug. 12-13	H. *Connie*, Carolinas, Va., Md.	43	1966 Sept. 24-30	H. *Inez*, Carib., Fla., Mex.	293
1955 Aug. 18-19	H. *Diane*, eastern U.S.	400	1967 July 9	T *Billie*, Japan	347
1955 Sept. 19	H. *Hilda*, Mexico	200	1967 Sept. 5-23	H. *Beulah*, Carib, Mex., Tex.	54
1955 Sept. 22-28	H. *Janet*, Caribbean	500	1967 Dec. 12-20	Blizzard, southwest U. S.	51
1956 Feb. 1-29	Blizzard, western Europe	1,000	1968 Nov. 18-28	T. *Nina*, Phillipines	63
1957 June 27-30	H. *Audrey*, La., Tex.	430	1969 Aug. 17-18	H. *Camille*, Miss.	132
1958 Feb. 15-16	Blizzard, n.e. U. S.	171	1969 July 4-5	Flooding, wind, and electrical storms, N. Ohio	41
1959 Sept. 17-19	T. *Sarah*, Far East	2,000			

*Reproduced through the courtesy of *The World Almanac, 1971.* New York, Newspaper Enterprise Association, 1971.

Table IV indicates the speed of winds in different sections of the United States in terms of average miles per hour and the high through the year 1970:

Table V indicates the hurricanes, typhoons, blizzards and other major atmospheric disturbances that have struck the United States and other countries since 1888.

Hurricanes have battered the southern and eastern coasts of the nation since the beginning of recorded history. The hurricane, a great mass of rotating air, may vary from 50 miles to 500 miles in diameter. They revolve in a counter-clockwise direction in the northern hemisphere and in a clockwise direction in the southern hemisphere. They develop over ocean areas and cause maximum destruction when they strike coastal territory with speeds up to 200 miles per hour.

Their forward movement is usually from 10 to 15 miles per hour, but this may increase up to 25 miles per hour or more. It has been estimated that a single hurricane releases forces much greater than would be released by all the hydrogen bombs in the world and equal to all the electric power generated in the United States in one year. The hurricane and the tornado, to be considered shortly, are the most gigantic and powerful storms that the atmosphere produces.

Plate I

HURRICANE SAFETY RULES

Hurricane Advisories will Help You Save Your Life . . . . But You Must Help. Follow These Safety Rules During Hurricane Emergencies:

1. *Enter each hurricane season prepared.* Every June through November, recheck your supply of boards, tools, batteries, nonperishable foods, and the other equipment you will need when a hurricane strikes your town.

2. *When you hear the first tropical cyclone advisory,* listen for future messages; this will prepare you for a hurricane emergency well in advance of the issuance of watches and warnings.

3. *When your area is covered by a hurricane watch,* continue normal activities, but stay tuned to radio or television for all ESSA Weather Bureau advisories. Remember: a hurricane watch means possible danger within 24 hours; if the danger materializes, a hurricane warning will be issued. Meanwhile, keep alert. Ignore rumors.

4. *When your area receives a hurricane warning:*

Plan your time before the storm arrives and avoid the last-minute hurry which might leave you marooned, or unprepared.

Keep calm until the emergency has ended.

Leave low-lying areas that may be swept by high tides or storm waves.

Moor your boat securely before the storm arrives, or evacuate it to a designated safe area. When your boat is moored, leave it, and don't return once the wind and waves are up.

Board up windows or protect them with storm shutters or tape. Danger to small windows is mainly from wind-driven debris. Larger windows may be broken by wind pressure.

Secure outdoor objects that might be blown away or uprooted. Garbage cans, garden tools, toys, signs, porch furniture, and a number of other harmless items become missiles of destruction in hurricane winds. Anchor them or store them inside before the storm strikes.

Store drinking water in clean bathtubs, jugs, bottles, and cooking utensils; your town's water supply may be contaminated by flooding or damaged by hurricane floods.

Check your battery-powered equipment. Your radio may be your only link with the world outside the hurricane, and emergency cooking facilities, lights, and flashlights will be essential if utilities are interrupted.

Keep your car fueled. Service stations may be inoperable for several days after the storm strikes, due to flooding or interrupted electrical power.

Stay at home, if it is sturdy and on high ground. If it is not, move to a designated shelter, and stay there until the storm is over.

Remain indoors during the hurricane. Travel is extremely dangerous when winds and tides are whipping through your area.

Monitor the storm's position through ESSA Weather Bureau advisories.

BEWARE OF THE EYE OF THE HURRICANE
If the calm storm center passes directly overhead, there will be a lull in the wind lasting from a few minutes to half an hour or more. Stay in a safe place unless emergency repairs are absolutely necessary. But remember, at the other side of the eye, the winds rise very rapidly to hurricane force, and come from the opposite direction.

---

5. *When the hurricane has passed:*

Seek necessary medical care at Red Cross disaster stations or hospitals.

Stay out of disaster areas. Unless you are qualified to help, your presence might hamper first-aid and rescue work.

Drive carefully along debris-filled streets. Roads may be undermined and may collapse under the weight of a car. Slides along cuts are also a hazard.

Avoid loose or dangling wires, and report them immediately to your power company or the nearest law enforcement officer.

Report broken sewer or water mains to the water department.

Prevent fires. Lowered water pressure may make fire fighting difficult.

Check refrigerated food for spoilage if power has been off during the storm.

Remember that hurricanes moving inland can cause severe flooding. Stay away from river banks and streams. ESSA Weather Bureau advisories will keep you informed on river flood stages.

HURRICANE WATCHES MEAN A HURRICANE MAY THREATEN AN AREA WITHIN 24 HOURS
HURRICANE WARNINGS MEAN A HURRICANE IS EXPECTED TO STRIKE AN AREA WITHIN 24 HOURS

Hurricane Carla which struck the Texas Coast and left a path of destruction during the period September 3-14, 1961, was designated *the greatest hurricane in recorded coastal history.* The following description of this killer, released by the Office of Civil Defense, indicates the deadly characteristics of this type of storm:

Carla's winds, tides and barometer readings were to break all records in coastal history. It size was near-incredible, with its circulation filling the entire Gulf of Mexico, its eye thirty miles across and hurricane force winds extending 300 miles from the center.

Around 3:45 P. M., winds at Port Lavaca dropped, the barometer leveled off and skies became almost sunny. Exhausted Yucatan birds plopped into the courthouse square. The gigantic eye of the hurricane was moving over the city.

Disaster workers ventured out briefly for a quick survey of the shocking damage. In less than two hours, at about 5:45 P. M., black clouds and squalls returned and howling winds began again, this time from the southwest. "How much longer can this last?" asked one who remained. It lasted approximately seven hours more. Winds rose to 100 miles per hour and throughout the night tore at weakened buildings, inflicting further damage.

Plowing almost straight across Texas, Carla passed between Victoria and Edna, some twenty-five miles inland, with winds in excess of 150 miles per hour. At Edna, roofs blew off three shelters, and scarcely a roof was left in town which would not require replacement.

For more than a hundred miles inland, giant oaks, which had seen the coming of Texas' pioneers, crashed to the ground, not broken but torn up by the roots. Trees, signboards, shingles, telephone and power lines went down.

Plate II

STORM SURGE
KILLER FROM THE SEA

A hurricane causes sea level to rise above normal tidal heights, with giant wind-driven waves and strong, unpredictable currents. These are the hurricane's worst killer.

If you live in a coastal area, be prepared.
Know the elevation of your property above mean sea level. This information is available
    from city and county engineers.
Have a safe evacuation route planned. Your community's hurricane preparedness plan
    should include designated safe areas, areas to be evacuated during a hurricane
    emergency, and safe evacuation routes to shelter.
Learn the storm surge history for your area.

*During the hurricane emergency, stay tuned to your radio or television for the latest
ESSA Weather Bureau advisories, and follow hurricane safety rules.*

The tornado, an inland phenomenon, is the most intense and violent of all storms generated in the atmosphere. Usually 200 yards to one mile in width and with a forward movement from 30 to 70 miles per hour, they are generally local in character. Estimated from 400 to 500 miles per hour, the velocity of the rotating winds within a tornado is so great that they have never been accurately measured. Although every section of the United is vulnerable, the Gulf and mid-western states are particularly tornado-prone.

Although tornadoes may occur at any hour of the day, the records indicate that they appear generally between 4:00 P. M. and 6:00 P. M., normally between March and July.

Table VI reveals the principal tornadoes occuring in the United States during the period from 1900 through 1969.

The Texas Department of Public Safety, recognizing the dangerous threat and aftermath of a tornado, instructed its Division of Defense and Disaster Relief to issue the following safety rules:

If You Are Near a Tornado Cellar

When time permits, go to a tornado cellar, cave or underground excavation which should have an air outlet to help equalize the air pressure. It should be kept fit for use, free from water, gas or debris and preferably equipped with pick and shovel. *There is no universal protection against tornadoes except underground excavations.*

TABLE VI

THE TORNADO RECORD SINCE 1900*

Date	Place	Dead
1900 Nov. 20	Ark., Miss., Tenn.	73
1903 June 1	Gainesville, Ga.	98
1905 May 10	Snyder, Okla.	87
1908 April 24	Lamar Co. and Wayne Co., Miss.	100
1913 Mar. 23	Omaha, Neb.	95
1916 June 5	Ark. (series of tornadoes)	83
1917 Mar. 23	New Albany, Ind.	45
1917 May 26	Mattoon-Charleston, Ill.	101
1917 May 27	Tennessee, Kentucky	70
1918 Aug. 21	Tyler, Minn.	36
1919 June 22	Fergus Falls, Minn.	59
1920 Mar. 28	Ala., Ga.	50
1920 Apr. 20	Mississippi, Alabama	87
1920 May 2	Oklahoma	64
1921 Apr. 15	Texas, Arkansas	61
1924 Apr. 30	Central South Carolina	67
1924 June 28	Lorain, Sandusky, Ohio	85
1925 Mar. 18	Mo., Ill., Ind	689
1926 Nov. 25	Belleville to Portland, Ark.	53
1927 Apr. 12	Rock Springs, Tex.	74
1927 May 9	Arkansas, Poplar Bluff, Mo.	92
1927 Sept. 29	St. Louis, Mo.	72
1929 Apr. 25	S.E.-Central Ga.	40
1930 May 6	Hill & Ellis Co., Tex.	41
1932 Mar. 21	Ala. (series of tornadoes)	268
1936 Apr. 5	Tupelo, Miss.	216
1936 Apr. 6	Gainesville, Ga.	203
1938 Sept. 29	Charleston, S. C.	32
1942 Mar. 16	Central to N.E. Miss.	75
1942 Apr. 27	Rogers & Mayes Co., Okla.	52
1944 June 23	Ohio, Pa., W. Va., Md.	150
1945 Apr. 12	Okla.-Ark.	102
1946 Jan. 4	N. E. Texas	30
1947 Apr. 9	Texas, Okla. & Kans.	169
1948 Mar. 19	Bunker Hill & Gillespie, Ill.	33
1949 Jan. 3	La. & Ark.	58
1952 Mar. 21	Ark., Mo., Tenn. (series)	208
1953 May 11	Waco, Texas	114
1953 June 8	Flint to Lakeport, Mich.	116
1953 June 9	Central & Eastern Mass.	90
1953 Dec. 5	Vicksburg, Miss.	38
1955 May 25	Udall, Kans.	80
1957 May 20	Williamsburg, Kans. to Ruskin Heights, Mo.	48
1958 June 4	Northwestern Wisconsin	30
1959 Feb. 10	St. Louis, Mo.	21
1960 May 5, 6	S. E. Oklahoma, Arkansas	30
1965 Apr. 11	Ind., Ill., Mich., Wis.	271
1966 Mar. 3	Jackson, Miss.	57
1966 Mar. 3	Mississippi, Alabama	61
1967 April 21	Illinois	33
1968 May 15	Arkansas	34
1969 Jan. 23	Mississippi	32

*Reproduced through the courtesy of the *World Almanac, 1971.* New York, Newspaper Enterprise Association, 1971.

If You Are in Open Country

Move at right angles to the tornado's path. Tornadoes usually move ahead at about 25 to 40 miles per hour. If there is no time to escape, lie flat in the nearest depression, such as a ditch or ravine.

If in a City or Town

Seek inside shelter, preferably in a strongly reinforced building. *Stay away from windows.* In your home, the corner of the basement toward the tornado usually offers the greatest safety, particularly in frame houses. People in houses without basements can sometimes be protected by taking cover under heavy furniture against inside walls. Doors and windows on the sides of the house away from the tornado may be opened to help reduce damage to the building. Standing against the inside wall on a lower floor of an office building offers some protection.

If in Schools

If the school building is a strongly reinforced construction, stay inside, away from windows, and remain near an inside wall on the lower floors when possible. Avoid auditoriums and gymnasiums with large, poorly-supported roofs. In rural schools that do not have strongly reinforced construction, remove children and teachers to a ravine or ditch if a storm shelter is not available.

If in Factories and Industrial Plants

On receiving a tornado warning, a lookout should be posted to keep safety officials advised of the tornado's approach. Advance preparation should be made for moving workers to sections of the plant offering the greatest protection.

No matter where you are, keep calm; it will not help to get excited. People have been killed by running out into streets and by turning back into the path of a tornado. Even though a warning is issued, chances of a tornado striking one's home or location are very slight. Tornadoes cover such a small zone, as a rule, that only a few places in a warned area are directly affected. You should know about tornadoes though, just in case.

Also keep tuned to your radio or television station for latest tornado advisory information. Do not call the Weather Bureau, except to report a tornado, as your individual request may tie up telephone lines urgently needed to receive special reports or to relay advisories to radio and television stations for dissemination to thousands in the critical area.

Plate III

TORNADO SAFETY RULES

**When a Tornado Approaches – Your Immediate
Action May Mean Life or Death**

A TORNADO WATCH means tornadoes are expected to develop. Keep a battery-operated radio or television set nearby, and listen for weather advisories – even if the sky is blue.

A TORNADO WARNING means a tornado has actually been sighted or indicated by weather radar. Seek inside shelter (in a storm cellar or reinforced building) and stay away from windows. Curl up so that your head and eyes are protected. Keep a battery-operated radio or television nearby, and listen for further advisories.

In Shopping Centers, go to a designated shelter area (*not* to your parked car).
In Homes, the basement offers the greatest safety. Seek shelter under sturdy furniture if possible. In homes without basements, take cover in the center part of the house, on the lowest floor, in a small room such as a closet or bathroom, or under sturdy furniture. Keep some windows open, but stay away from them.
In Office Buildings, go to an interior hallway on the lowest floor, or to the designated shelter area.
In Schools, follow advance plans to an interior hallway on the lowest floor. If the building is not of reinforced construction, go to a nearby one that is, or take cover outside on low, protected ground. Stay out of auditoriums, gymnasiums, and other structures with wide, free-span roofs.
In Open Country, move away from the tornado's path at right angles. If there is not time to escape, lie flat in the nearest ditch or ravine.
Mobile Homes are particularly vulnerable to overturning during strong winds, and should be evacuated when strong winds are forecast. Damage can be minimized by securing trailers with cables anchored in concrete footing. Trailer parks should have a community storm shelter and a warden to monitor broadcasts throughout the severe storm emergency. If there is no shelter nearby, leave the trailer park and take cover on low, protected ground.

Tornadoes are only one of a thunderstorm's killers.

Lightning is the Worst Killer. Stay indoors and away from electrical appliances while the storm is overhead. If you are caught outside, stay away from the lower than high, conductive objects.

Thunderstorm Rains cause flash floods. Be careful where you take shelter.

Floods

Consisting of an overflow of water beyond normal confines, floods occur in every part of the world. Floods may be the result of inundation from the sea such as a tidal wave *(tsunami),* a storm surge of water above tidal heights, the overflow of land waters such as rivers and lakes or the bursting of dams. Inland floods are generally predictable because they occur each year during the same seasonal period; on occasion, they follow a sporadic pattern. Table VII shows the principal world floods that have occurred since 1228, together with the cause and loss of life. It will be noted that in some instances, there was a staggering loss of life; property damage is usually on a heavy scale. In fact, Healy notes that floods cause a greater loss to life and property throughout the world than any other type of disaster.*

Somewhat related to flood conditions are tidal waves, as water is involved in both situations. They are occasionally referred to as seismic waves. More frequent in the Pacific than in the Atlantic, they are caused by earthquakes on the ocean floor. These waves are extremely dangerous because of their speed of travel — about 400 miles per hour — and the tremendous volume of water involved in the wave, which may attain a height of fifty feet as it strikes the shoreline. The tidal wave of May 23 and 24, 1960, traveled 8,000 miles through the Pacific, and it was felt in the Hawaiian Island, Japan and Okinawa, resulting in 237 deaths.

Fires

Fire is conceded to be the greatest single factor in the destruction of property.† It often accompanies disaster but may constitute the disaster itself. Most fire deaths result from exposure

---

*Healy, Richard J.: *Emergency and Disaster Planning.* New York, John Wiley and Sons, 1969, p. 167.
†Healy, Richard J.: *Emergency and Disaster Planning.* New York, John Wiley and Sons, 1969, p. 36.

TABLE VII

PRINCIPAL WORLD FLOODS*

Date	Place	Deaths†	Explanation
1228	Holland	100,000	Sea flood in Friesland
1642	China	300,000	Kaifeng seawall destroyed
1787	Eastern India	10,000	Storm drove seawater inland 20 miles
1887	Honan, China	900,000	Yellow River overflowed
1889	Johnstown, Pennsylvania	2,000	Flood
1900	Galveston, Texas	6,000	Tidal wave
1903	Heppner, Oregon	247	Flood destroyed town of Heppner
1911	China	100,000	Yangtze River overflowed
1913	Ohio and Indiana	467	Ohio and Indiana rivers flooded
1928	Santa Paula, California	450	Collapse of St. Francis Dam
1939	China	1 million	Floods in north; extensive drownings and starvation
1947	Honshu Island, Japan	2,000	Flooding after typhoon
1948	Foochow, China	1,000	Flood
1950	Southern and eastern China	500	Flooding left one million homeless
1951	Manchuria	1,800	Flood
1953	Northwest Europe	1,794	Storm and floods devastated North Sea coastal areas
1954	Iran	2,000	Flash flood
1955	Pakistan and India	1,700	Flood
1956	China	2,000	Three provinces flooded after typhoon
1957	Kyushu Island, Japan	513	Flood
1957	Ceylon	300	Flood
1959	Western Mexico	2,000	Flood
1959	Frejus, France	412	Collapse of dam and flood
1960	East Pakistan	10,000	Tidal wave

Date	Place	Deaths	Explanation
1962	German North Sea coast	343	Flood
1963	Barcelona, Spain	445	Flash flood, west and north of city
1963	Northern Italy	2,000	Vaiont Dam collapsed
1963	Haiti	500	Flood
1966	Arno Valley, Italy	112	Arno River overflowed; Florence, Venice hit
1966	Rio de Janeiro, Brazil	405	Floods and landslides left 50,000 homeless
1967	Brazil	600	Heavy rains in Rio de Janeiro and Sao Paulo states
1967, Nov. 26	Lisbon, Portugal	457	Record rainfall caused heavy flooding
1968, Aug. 7-14	Western India	1,000	Widespread flooding killed 80,000 cattle
1968, Oct. 3-7	Northeastern India	900	Torrential rains caused flooding
1968, Nov. 3-6	Northwestern Italy	104	Extensive flooding and landslides
1969, Jan. 18-26	Southern California	91	Floods and mudslides left 9,000 homeless
1969, March 16	Northeastern Brazil	218	Flash floods
1969, Aug. 20-22	Virginia and West Virginia	114	Rains from Hurricane Camille caused extensive flooding
1970, May-June	Romania	161	Flooding destroyed 40,000 homes
1970, July	Uttar Pradesh, India	600	Buses swept away by flooding of Alaknanda River

*Reproduced through the courtesy of Reader's Digest Almanac, 1971. Pleasantville.
†Estimated.

TABLE VIII

FIRES*

Date, Location and Number of Persons Killed

Date	Location	Killed
1871 Oct. 8	Chicago, $196,000,000 loss	250
1871 Oct. 9	Peshtigo, Wis., forest fire	1,182
1876 Dec. 5	Brooklyn (N.Y.) Theater	295
1877 June 20	St. John, N. B., Canada	100
1881 Dec. 8	Ring Theater, Vienna	850
1883 Jan. 10	Milwaukee, Newhall Hotel	71
1887 May 25	Opera Comique, Paris	200
1887 Sept. 4	Exeter, Eng., theater	200
1894 Sept. 1	Hickley, Minn., forest fire	413
1897 May 4	Charity bazaar, Paris	150
1899 Mar. 17	Windsor Hotel, New York	45
1900 June 30	Hoboken, N. J., docks	326
1902 Sept. 20	Church, Birmingham, Ala.	115
1903 Dec. 30	Iroquois Theater, Chicago	602
1904 Feb. 7	Baltimore, Md.	none
1905 Mar. 20	Brockton, Mass., shoe factory	50
1908 Jan. 13	Rhoads Thea., Boyertown, Pa.	170
1908 Mar. 4	School, Collinwood, Ohio	176
1911 Mar. 25	Triangle factory, New York	145
1913 July 22	Binghamton, N. Y., factory	35
1914 Mar. 9	Mo. Athletic Club, St. Louis	37
1918 Apr. 13	Norman, Okla., state hospital	38
1918 Oct. 12	Cloquet, Minn., forest fire	400
1919 June 20	Mayaguez Theater, San Juan	150
1923 May 17	School, Camden, S.C.	76
1924 Dec. 24	School, Hobart, Okla.	35
1957 Nov. 16	Niagara Falls, N.Y., tenement	18
1958 Mar. 19	New York City loft building	24
1958 Nov. 8	Tenement, Montreal, Can.	21
1958 Dec. 1	Parochial school, Chicago	95
1959 Mar. 5	Store, Bogota, Colombia	83
1959 June 23	School near Little Rock, Ark.	24
1960 Mar. 12	Resort hotel, Stalheim, Norway	34
1960 June 11	Pusan, Korea, chemical plant	68
1960 July 14	Liverpool, Eng., store	22
1960 Nov. 13	Mental hospital, Guatemala City	225
1961 Jan. 6	Movie theater, Amude, Syria	152
1961 May 15	Thomas Hotel, San Francisco	20
1961 Dec. 8	Tenement, Hong Kong	25
1961 Dec. 17	Hospital, Hartford, Conn.	16
1963 May 4	Circus, Niterol, Brazil	323
1963 Nov. 18	Theater, Diourbel, Senegal	64
1963 Nov. 23	Surfside Hotel, Atlantic City, N.J.	25
1963 Dec. 29	Rest home, Fitchville, Ohio	63
1964 May 8	Roosevelt Hotel, Jacksonville, Fla.	22
1964 Dec. 18	Apartment building, Manila	30
1965 Mar. 1	Nursing Home, Fountaintown, Ind.	20
1965 Dec. 20	Apartment, LaSalle, Canada	28
1966 Mar. 11	Jewish center, Yonkers, N.Y.	12
1966 Aug. 13	Numata, Jap., 2 ski resorts	31
	Melbourne, Austr., hotel	29

Date, Location and Number of Persons Killed

Date	Location	Killed
1929 May 15	Crile Hospital, Cleveland, Ohio	124
1930 Apr. 21	Penitentiary, Columbus, Ohio	320
1931 July 24	Pittsburgh, Pa., home for aged	48
1936 Apr. 6	Gainesville, Ga., hardware co.	57
1938 May 16	Atlanta, Ga., Terminal Hotel	35
1940 Apr. 23	Dance hall, Natchez, Miss.	198
1942 Nov. 28	Cocoanut Grove, Boston	491
1943 Sept. 7	Gulf Hotel, Houston	55
1944 July 6	Ringling Circus, Hartford	168
1946 June 5	LaSalle Hotel, Chicago	61
1946 Dec. 7	Winecoff Hotel, Atlanta	119
1946 Dec. 12	New York, ice plant, tenement	37
1949 Apr. 5	Hospital, Effingham, Ill.	77
1950 Jan. 7	Davenport, Iowa, Mercy Hospital	41
1953 Mar. 29	Largo, Fla., nursing home	35
1953 Apr. 16	Chicago, metalworking plant	35
1957 Feb. 17	Home for Aged, Warrenton, Mo.	
1966 Sept. 12	Anchorage, Alaska, hotel	14
1966 Oct. 17	N. Y. City bldg. (firemen)	12
1966 Dec. 7	Erzurum, Turkey, barracks	68
1967 Feb. 7	Restaurant, Montgomery, Ala.	25
1967 May 22	Store, Brussels, Belgium	322
1967 July 16	State prison, Jay, Fla.	37
1968 Jan. 9	Brooklyn, N.Y., tenement	13
1968 Feb. 11	Franklin, Pa., residence	11
1968 Feb. 16	Moberly, Mo., tavern	12
1968 Feb. 26	Shrewsbury, Eng., hospital	22
1968 May 11	Vijayawada, Ind., wedding hall	58
1968 Nov. 18	Glasgow, Scotland, factory	24
1969 Jan. 26	Victoria Hotel, Dunnville, Ont.	13
1969 Feb. 25	Office Building, New York City	11
1969 April 6	Tenement, Bridgeport, Conn.	11
1969 Dec. 2	Nursing Home, Notre Dame, Quebec	54

*Reproduced through the courtesy of the *World Almanac, 1971*. New York, Newspaper Enterprise Association, 1971.

to smoke and toxic gases rather than by flames. The records show that hospitals, nursing homes, hotels and schools, including public, private and parochial schools from the elementary grades to the university level, are particularly vulnerable to fire, often with fatal results. The tragedy is that most fires are preventable. Table VIII indicates the major fires that have occurred in the United States and other countries since 1871.

The following organizations are in a strong position to furnish information concerning fire prevention and protection:

National Fire Protection Association
    60 Batterymarch Street
    Boston, Massachusetts
Factory Insurance Association
    85 Woodland Street
    Hartford, Connecticut
Factory Mutual
    1151 Boston-Providence Turnpike
    Norwood, Massachusetts
American Insurance Association
    85 John Street
    New York, New York
Federation of Mutual Fire Insurance Companies
    20 North Wacker Drive
    Chicago, Illinois
Underwriter's Laboratories, Inc.
    P. O. Box 247
    Northbrook, Illinois
International Association of Fire Chiefs
    232 Madison Avenue
    New York, New York

Volcanic Eruptions

The violence of an explosive eruption of a volcano can be disastrous if located near populated areas. Volcanoes are described as active, dormant or extinct. The Hawaiian Islands have a number of active volcanoes; in fact, the Islands are volcanic in origin. In the continental United States, there are several volcanoes

TABLE IX

MAJOR VOLCANIC ERUPTIONS*

Date	Place	Deaths	Remarks
79 A.D., Aug. 24-26	Pompeii, Herculaneum, and Stabiae, Italy	16,000	Mount Vesuvius erupted; destroyed these towns
1169	Sicily	15,000	Mount Etna erupted
1631, Dec. 16	Italy	4,000	Mount Vesuvius erupted; destroyed five towns
1669	Sicily	–	Mount Etna erupted for 40 days
1772	Java	3,000	Mount Papapadayang erupted
1783	Iceland	9,000	Mount Hekla erupted; 20 villages obliterated by lava and many more flooded by water
1815	Java	12,000	Tamboro exploded, followed by violent whirlwinds and tidal waves
1883, Aug. 26-28	East Indies	35,000	Krakatau erupted; most of the island destroyed; Java and Sumatra heavily damaged by tidal wave
1902, April 8	Guatemala	1,000	Santa Maria erupted
1902, May 8	Martinique, West Indies	40,000	Mount Pelee erupted, wiping out the city of St. Pierre
1911	Philippines	1,400	Mount Taal, on Luzon, erupted
1919	Java	5,000	Mount Kelud erupted; 100 villages destroyed
1951, Jan. 18-21	New Guinea	3,000	Mount Lamington erupted
1963, Feb.	Bali	1,500	Mount Aguing erupted, leaving 85,000 homeless
1964, March and April	Chile	–	Villarrica erupted, routing 30,000 persons and causing heavy damage
1965, Sept. 28	Philippines	500	Mount Taal, on Luzon, erupted
1966, April 28	Java	1,000	Mount Kelud erupted; nine villages destroyed
1968, July 29	Costa Rica	100	Mount Arenal erupted for first time in 500 years

*Reproduced through the courtesy of *Reader's Digest Almanac, 1971.* Pleasantville.

considered dormant or extinct, including Mt. Ranier and Mt. Baker in Washington, Mt. Shasta and Lassen Peak in California and Mt. Hood in Oregon. It is reported that Mt. Baker and Lassen Peak have shown signs of activity within the past 150 years. Geologists are of the opinion that down beneath the Cascade Range on the Pacific coast, there is a smoldering holocaust.*

Major volcanic eruptions since A.D. 79 are shown in Table IX.

Railroad Wrecks

Although railroads are probably the safest form of travel, railroad wrecks do occur on occasion, as shown in Table X.

Mine Disasters

Mine disasters continue to haunt the front pages on occasion, although the number appears to be decreasing. Generally caused by a cave-in or explosion, the number of miners killed per accident is also decreasing due to the fact that modern mining equipment and methods have reduced the number of personnel required in a mining operation. Table XI reveals the principal mine disasters in the United States since 1869.

Explosions

Explosions, the sudden conversion of an explosive material into a hot, rapidly expanding gas, are always a threat to life and property. Table XII lists major exposions in the United States and other countries since 1910.

In recent years, the home-made bomb, together with the bomb threat and hoax, have plagued American society. The major airlines have proven to be somewhat vulnerable in this respect.

Aircraft Disasters

In Table XIII are listed the major aircraft disasters that have

---

*From a televised address on Station KHQTV, Spokane, Washington, by Dr. Rohm of the Department of Geology, Washington State University, 1963.

TABLE X

MAJOR RAILROAD WRECKS IN THE UNITED STATES

Date	Location	Deaths	Date	Location	Deaths
1876 Dec. 29	Ashtabula, Ohio	92	1922 Aug. 5	Sulphur Springs, Mo.	34
1880 Aug. 11	Mays Landing, N. J.	40	1922 Dec. 13	Humble, Tex.	22
1887 Aug. 10	Chatsworth, Ill.	81	1923 Sept. 27	Lockett, Wyo.	31
1888 Oct. 10	Mud Run, Pa.	55	1925 June 16	Hackettstown, N. J.	50
1896 July 30	Atlantic City, N. J.	60	1925 Oct. 27	Victoria, Miss.	21
1903 Dec. 23	Laurel Run, Pa.	53	1926 Sept. 5	Waco, Colo.	30
1904 Aug. 7	Eden, Colo.	96	1928 Aug. 24	I. R. T. subway, N. Y., Times Sq.	18
1904 Sept. 24	New Market, Tenn.	56	1938 June 19	Saugus, Mont.	47
1906 Mar. 16	Florence, Colo.	35	1939 Aug. 12	Harney, Nev.	24
1906 Oct. 28	Atlantic City, N. J.	40	1940 Apr. 19	Little Falls, N. Y.	31
1906 Dec. 30	Washington, D. C.	53	1940 July 31	Cuyahoga Falls, Ohio	43
1907 Jan. 2	Volland, Kans.	33	1942 Dec. 27	Almonte, Ontario	36
1907 Jan. 19	Fowler, Ind.	29	1943 Aug. 29	Wayland, N. Y.	27
1907 Feb. 16	New York City	22	1943 Sept. 6	Frankford Junction, Philadelphia	79
1907 Mar. 23	Colton, Calif.	26	1943 Dec. 16	Bet. Rennert and Buie, N. C.	72
1907 July 20	Salem, Mich.	33	1944 July 6	High Bluff, Tenn.	35
1907 Sept. 15	Canaan, N. H.	24	1944 Aug. 4	Near Stockton, Ga.	47
1910 Mar. 1	Wellington, Wash.	96	1944 Sept. 14	Dewey, Ind.	29
1910 Mar. 21	Green Mountain, Ia.	55	1944 Dec. 31	Bagley, Utah	50
1911 Aug. 25	Manchester, N. Y.	39	1945 Aug. 9	Michigan, N. Dak.	34
1912 July 4	East Corning, N. Y.	39	1946 Apr. 25	Naperville, Ill.	45
1912 July 5	Ligonier, Pa.	23	1947 Feb. 18	Gallitzin, Pa.	24
1913 Sept. 2	North Haven, Conn.	21	1950 Feb. 17	Rockville Centre, N. Y.	31
1914 Aug. 5	Tipton Ford, Mo.	43	1950 Sept. 11	Coshocton, Ohio	33
1914 Sept. 15	Lebanon, Mo.	28	1950 Nov. 22	Richmond Hill, N. Y.	79

Date	Location	Deaths	Date	Location	Deaths
1916 Mar. 29	Amherst, Ohio	27	1951 Feb. 6	Woodbridge, N. J.	84
1917 Feb. 27	Mount Union, Pa.	20	1951 Nov. 12	Wyuta, Wyo.	17
1917 Sept. 28	Kellyville, Okla.	23	1951 Nov. 25	Woostock, Ala.	17
1917 Dec. 20	Shepherdsville, Ky.	46	1953 Mar. 27	Conneaut, Ohio	21
1918 June 22	Ivanhoe, Ind.	68	1956 Jan. 22	Los Angeles, Calif.	30
1918 July 9	Nashville, Tenn.	101	1956 Feb. 28	Swampscott, Mass.	13
1918 Nov. 2	Brooklyn, Malbone St. Tunnel	97	1956 Sept. 5	Springer, N. M.	20
1919 Jan. 12	South Byron, N. Y.	22	1957 June 11	Vroman, Colo.	12
1919 July 1	Dunkirk, N. Y.	12	1958 Sept. 15	Elizabethport, N. J.	48
1919 Dec. 20	Onawa, Maine	23	1960 Mar. 14	Bakersfield, Calif.	14
1921 Feb. 27	Porter, Ind.	37	1962 July 28	Steelton, Pa.	19
1921 Dec. 5	Woodmont, Pa.	27	1966 Dec. 28	Everett, Mass.	13

World's worst wreck occurred Dec. 12, 1917, Modane, France, passenger train derailed, 543 killed.

TABLE XI

PRINCIPAL MINE DISASTERS IN THE U. S.

All Coal Mines Unless Otherwise Designated   Source: Bureau of Mines

Date	Location	Killed	Date	Location	Killed
Sept. 6, 1869[1]	Plymouth, Pa.	110	Mar. 8, 1924	Castle Gate, Utah	171
Mar. 13, 1884	Pocahontas, Va.	112	Apr. 28, 1924	Benwood, W. Va.	119
Jan. 27, 1891	Mammoth, Pa.	109	May 19, 1928	Mather, Pa.	195
Jan. 7, 1892	Krebs, Okla.	100	Nov. 5, 1930	Millfield, Ohio	82
May 1, 1900	Scofield, Utah	200	Dec. 23, 1932	Moweaqua, Ill.	54
May 19, 1902	Coal Creek, Tenn.	184	Jan. 10, 1940	Bartley, W. Va.	91
July 10, 1902	Johnstown, Pa.	112	July 15, 1940	Portage, Pa.	63
June 30, 1903	Hanna, Wyo.	169	Feb. 27, 1943	Red Lodge, Mont.	74
Jan. 25, 1904	Cheswick, Pa.	179	Mar. 25, 1947	Centralia, Ill.	111
Feb. 20, 1905	Virginia City, Ala.	112	Dec. 21, 1951	West Frankfort, Ill.	119
Dec. 6, 1907	Monongah, W. Va.	361	Feb. 4, 1957	Bishop, Va.	37
Dec. 19, 1907	Jacobs Creek, Pa.	239	Oct. 27, 1958	Bishop, Va.	22
Nov. 28, 1908	Marianna, Pa.	154	Mar. 2, 1961	Terre Haute, Ind.	22
Nov. 13, 1909	Cherry, Ill.	259	Dec. 6, 1962	Carmichaels, Pa.	37
Apr. 8, 1911	Littleton, Ala.	128	Apr. 25, 1963	Dola, W. Va.	22
Oct. 22, 1913	Dawson, N. Mex.	263	Aug. 27, 1963[3]	Moab, Utah	18
Apr. 28, 1914	Eccles, W. Va.	181	Dec. 28, 1965	Redstone, Colo.	9
Mar. 2, 1915	Layland, W. Va.	112	June 1, 1966	Dora, Pa.	5
Apr. 27, 1917	Hastings, Colo.	121	July 23, 1966	Mt. Hope, W. Va.	7
June 8, 1917[2]	Butte, Mont.	163	Mar. 5, 1968[4]	Calumet, La.	21
Nov. 6, 1922	Spangler, Pa.	77	Aug. 7, 1968	Greenville, Ky.	9
Feb. 8, 1923	Dawson, N. Mex.	120	Nov. 20, 1968	Farmington, W. Va.	78

World's worst mine disaster killed 1,549 workers in the Honkeiko Colliery in Manchuria Apr. 26, 1942. (1.) Anthracite mine. (2.) Metal mine. (3.) Potash mine. (4.) Salt mine.

TABLE XII

EXPLOSIONS

Date, Location, Number of Deaths

Date	Location	Number of Deaths
1910 Oct. 1	Los Angeles Times Bldg.	21
1913 Mar. 7	Dynamite, Baltimore harbor	55
1915 Sept. 27	Gasoline tank car, Ardmore, Okla.	47
1916 July 22	San Francisco parade	10
1917 Apr. 10	Munitions plant, Eddystone, Pa.	133
1917 Dec. 6	Halifax Harbor, Canada	1,600
1918 July 2	Explosives, Split Rock, N. Y.	50
1918 Oct. 4	Shell plant, Morgan Station, N. J.	64
1919 May 22	Food plant, Cedar Rapids, Iowa	44
1920 Sept. 16	Wall St., New York, bomb	30
1924 Jan. 3	Food plant, Pekin, Ill.	42
1937 Mar. 18	New London, Tex., school	294
1940 Sept. 11	Hercules Powder, Kenvil, N. J.	51
1942 June 5	Ordnance plant, Elwood, Ill.	49
1944 Apr. 14	Bombay, India, harbor	700
1944 July 17	Port Chicago, Calif., pier	322
1944 Oct. 21	Liquid gas tank, Cleveland	135
1947 Apr. 16	Texas City, Tex., pier	561
1948 July 28	Farben works, Ludwigshafen, Ger.	184
1950 May 19	Munitionbarges, S. Amboy, N. J.	30
1956 Aug. 7	Dynamite trucks, Call, Colombia	1,100
1956 Dec. 3	Brooklyn, N. Y., pier	10
1957 Dec. 5	Villa Rica, Ga., gas line	17
1958 Apr. 18	Sunken munitions ship, Okinawa	40
1958 May 22	Nike missiles, Leonardo, N. J.	10
1959 Apr. 10	World War II bomb, Philippines	38
1959 June 2	Gas truck, Penn. Turnpike	10
1959 June 28	Rail tank cars, Meldrin, Ga.	25
1959 Aug. 7	Dynamite truck, Roseburg, Ore.	13
1959 Dec. 13	Dortmund, Ger., 2 apt. bldgs.	26
1960 Mar. 4	Belgian munition ship, Havana	100
1960 Oct. 4	Chemical plant, Kingsport, Tenn.	10
1960 Oct. 25	Gas, Windsor, Ont., store	11
1962 Jan. 16	Gas pipeline, Alberta, Canada	19
1962 Mar. 3	Gasoline truck, Syria	31
1962 Oct. 3	Telephone Co. office, New York	23
1963 Jan. 2	Packing plant, Terre Haute, Ind.	16
1963 Mar. 9	Dyn. plant, Modderfontain, S. Af.	45
1963 Aug. 13	Explosives dump, Gauhiti, India	32
1963 Oct. 31	State Fair Coliseum, Indianapolis	73
1964 July 23	Bone, Algeria, Harbor, munitions	100
1965 Mar. 4	Gas pipeline Natchitoches, La.	17
1965 Aug. 9	Missile silo, Searcy, Ark.	53
1965 Oct. 21	Bridge, Tila Bund, Pakistan	80
1965 Oct. 30	Marketplace, Cartagena, Col.	48
1965 Nov. 24	Armory, Keokuk, Iowa	20
1966 Oct. 13	Chemical plant, La Salle, Que.	11
1967 Feb. 17	Chemical plant, Hawthorne, N. J.	11
1967 Dec. 25	Apartment bldg., Moscow	20
1968 Apr. 6	Sports store, Richmond, Ind.	43

TABLE XIII

SOME NOTABLE AIRCRAFT DISASTERS SINCE 1937

Date	Aircraft	Site of accident	Deaths
1937 May 6	Ger. zeppelin Hindenburg	Burned at Mooring, Lakehurst, N. J.	36
1944 Aug. 23	U. S. Air Force B-24	Hit school, Freckelton, England	761
1945 July 28	U. S. Army B-25	Hit Empire State bldg. N. Y. C.	141
1946 May 20	U. S. Army C-45	Struck Manhattan Co. bldg., N. Y. C.	5
1949 Nov. 1	Eastern Air Lines DC-4	Rammed by Bolivian P-38, Wash., D. C.	55
1950 Mar. 12	Chartered Avro Tudor	Crashed near Cardiff, Wales	80
1950 June 24	Northwest Airlines DC-4	Exploded in storm over Lake Michigan	58
1951 Dec. 16	Miami Airlines C-46	Plunged into Elizabeth River, N. J.	56
1952 Jan. 22	American Airlines Convair	Crashed in Elizabeth, N. J.	30[1]
1952 Feb. 11	National Airlines DC-6	Crashed in Elizabeth, N. J.	33[1]
1952 Dec. 20	U. S. Air Force C-124	Fell, burned, Moses Lake, Wash.	87
1953 Mar. 3	Canadian Pacific Comet jet	Karachi, Pakistan	11[2]
1953 June 18	U. S. Air Force C-124	Crashed, burned near Tokyo	129
1954 Apr. 8	TCA North Star, RCAF trainer	Collided over Moose Jaw, Sask., Canada	36
1955 Aug. 11	2 USAF Flying Boxcars	Collided near Stuttgart, Germany	66
1955 Nov. 1	United Air Lines DC-6B	Exploded, crashed near Longmont, Colo.	44[7]
1956 June 20	Venezuelan Super-Const	Crashed in Atlantic off Asbury Park, N. J.	74
1956 June 30	TWA Super-Const., United DC-7	Collided over Grand Canyon, Arizona	128
1956 Dec. 9	Trans-Canada North Star	Crashed in mountains, British Columbia	62
1957 Mar. 21	Military Air Transport C-97	Disappeared over Pacific	67
1957 Aug. 11	Maritime, Central Airways DC-1	Crashed in swamp near Quebec	79
1958 Feb. 1	MATS C-118, USN P2V Neptune	Collided over Los Angeles	48
1958 Apr. 21	United Airlines DC-7, USAF Jet	Collided near Las Vegas, Nev.	49
1958 Aug. 14	KLM Super-Constellation	Plunged into sea 130 mi. w. of Ireland	99
1958 Oct. 17	Soviet TU-104 jet airliner	Crashed near Kanash, 400 mi. e. of Moscow	75

Date	Aircraft	Site of accident	Deaths
1959 Feb. 3	Amer. Airlines Lockheed Electra	Crashed in East River, New York City	65
1959 June 26	TWA Super-Constellation	Crashed in storm near Milan, Italy	68
1960 Feb. 25	USN transport & Arg. airliner	Collided in air near Rio de Janeiro	61
1960 Mar. 17	Northwest Airlines Electra	Exploded over Tell City, Ind.	63
1960 July 27	Sikorsky S-58 helicopter	Crashed in Chicago suburbs	135
1960 Oct. 4	Eastern Air Lines Electra	Crashed after takeoff from Boston	61
1960 Dec. 16	United DC-8 jet, TWA Super-Constellation	Collided over New York City	1346
1960 Dec. 17	U. S. Air Force C-131 Convair	Crashed into Munich street car	531
1961 Feb. 15	Sabena Airlines Boeing 707	Crashed at Berg, Belgium	731
1961 May 10	Air France Starliner	Crashed in Sahara Desert	79
1961 July 12	Czech Ilyushin-18	Hit power line, Casablanca	72
1961 July 19	Argentine Airlines DC-6	Crashed at Azul, Brazil	67
1961 Aug. 9	Cunard Eagle Airways Viking	Crashed in North Sea off Norway	397
1961 Sept. 1	TWA Constellation	Crashed at Hinsdale, Ill.	78
1961 Sept. 10	President Airlines DC-6	Crashed at Shannon, Ireland	83
1961 Nov. 8	Imperial Airlines Constellation	Crashed near Richmond, Va.	778
1962 Mar. 1	Amer. Airlines Boeing 707 jet	Crashed after takeoff, New York City	95
1962 Mar. 4	Br. Caledonian Airlines DC-7C	Crashed near Douala, Cameroun	111
1962 Mar. 16	Flying Tiger Super-Const	Vanished in western Pacific	107
1962 June 3	Air France Boeing 707 jet	Crashed on takeoff from Paris	130
1962 June 22	Air France Boeing 707 jet	Crashed in storm, Guadeloupe, W. I.	113
1962 July 7	Italian Alitalia airliner	Crashed in storm 50 miles n.e. of Bombay	94
1962 Nov. 27	Brazilian Varig-Boeing 707 jet	Crashed and burned in Lima, Peru	97
1963 Feb. 1	Mid. E. Viscount, Turk. AF C-47	Collided over Ankara, Turkey	95
1963 June 3	Chartered Northw. Airlines DC-7	Crashed in Pacific off British Columbia	101
1963 Sept. 2	Swissaire Caravelle Jetliner	Crashed after takeoff from Zurich, Switz.	80
1963 Nov. 29	Trans-Canada Airlines DC-8F	Crashed after takeoff from Montreal	118
1963 Dec. 8	Pan American Boeing 707	Crashed near Elkton, Md.	82

Date	Aircraft	Site of accident	Deaths
1964 Feb. 29	Br. Eagle Bristol Britannia	Crashed near Innsbruck, Austria	83
1964 Mar. 1	Paradise Airline Constellation	Crashed in snow storm, Lake Tahoe, Calif.	85
1964 May 7	Pacific Airlines F-27	Crashed near Doublin, Calif.	449
1964 May 11	U.S. MATS C-135 Stratolifter	Crashed at Clark AFB, Philippines	75
1965 Feb. 8	Eastern Air Lines DC-7B	Plunged into Atlantic after takeoff, New York	84
1965 May 20	Pakistani Boeing 720-B	Crashed at Cairo, Egypt, Airport	121
1965 Dec. 4	TWA Boeing 707, Eastern shuttle	Collided over Danbury, Conn.	4
1966 Jan. 24	Air India Boeing 707 jetliner	Crashed on Mont Blanc, Switzerland	117
1966 Feb. 4	All-Nippon Boeing 727	Plunged into Tokyo Bay	1334
1966 Mar. 5	BOAC Boeing 707 jetliner	Crashed on Japan's Mount Fuji	124
1966 Apr. 22	Military-chartered Electra	Crashed in storm near Ardmore, Okla.	82
1966 Sept. 1	Britannia 102 turboprop	Crashed near Ljubljana, Yugoslavia	97
1966 Nov. 24	Bulgarian Tabson Ilyushin-18	Crashed near Bratislava, Czechoslovakia	82
1966 Dec. 24	U. S. military-chartered, CL-44	Crashed into village in South Vietnam	129[1]
1967 Mar. 9	TWA DC-9, Beechcraft	Collided in air at Urbana, Ohio	26
1967 Apr. 20	Swiss Britannia turboprop	Crashed at Nicosia, Cyprus	126
1967 June 3	Chartered British DC-4	Crashed into Mont Canigon, France	88
1967 June 4	Chartered British Argonaut	Crashed at Stockport, England	72
1967 July 19	Piedmont Boeing 727, Cessna 310	Collided in air, Hendersonville, N. C.	82
1967 Oct. 12	British-Cypriot Mark IV Comet	Crashed into sea off Turkey	66
1967 Nov. 20	TWA Convair 880	Crashed in snowstorm at Cincinnati	68
1967 Dec. 8	Peruvian Faucett DC-4	Crashed near Huanuco, Peru	66
1968 Mar. 5	Air France Boeing 707	Crashed into mountain on Guadeloupe island	63
1968 Mar. 24	Irish International Viscount	Crashed into Irish Sea	61
1968 Apr. 20	S. African Airways Boeing 707	Crashed on takeoff, Windhoek, S. Africa	122
1968 May 3	Braniff International Electra	Crashed in storm near Dawson, Tex.	85
1968 Sept. 11	Air France Caravelle	Caught fire, crashed off Nice, France	95
1968 Dec. 12	Pan American Boeing 707	Crashed into Caribbean off Caracas, Venezuela	51
1969 Jan. 18	United Boeing 727	Exploded, fell in ocean off Los Angeles	38

Date	Aircraft	Site of Accident	Deaths
1969 Mar. 16	Venezuelan DC-9	Crashed after takeoff from Maracaibo, Venez.	155[10]
1969 Mar. 20	United Arab Ilyushin-18	Crashed at Aswan airport	87
1969 Apr. 2	Polish AN-24	Crashed near Cracow	51
1969 June 4	Mexican Boeing 727	Rammed into mountain near Monterrey	79
1969 Sept. 9	Allegheny DC-9	Collided with student pilot's plan, Shelbyville, Ind.	83
1969 Nov. 20	Nigerian VC-10	Crashed near Iju, Nigeria	87
1969 Dec. 3	French Boeing 707	Fell into Caribbean off LaGuaira, Venezuela	62

(1.) Including those on the ground and in buildings. (2.) First fatal crash of commercial jet plane. (3.) Caused by bomb planted by John G. Graham in insurance plot to kill his mother, a passenger. (4.) Worst disaster involving single plane. (5.) First crash of commercial helicopter. (6.) Dead included all 84 aboard jet, all 44 aboard other plane and 6 on ground. (7.) Including 34 English schoolboys. (8.) Including 74 army recruits. (9.) Tape recording indicated pilot was shot (10.) Worst airline disaster: killed all 84 on plane, 71 on ground.

occurred since 1937 in the United States and in other parts of the world.

Man-made Emergencies

In addition to the foregoing, there are certain man-made situations which may approach disaster proportions and require police action on a scale comparable to that taken in the event of a hurricane, tornado or earthquake. They include disorderly crowds, industrial disorders, mob situations, riot emergencies, prison outbreaks, criminal emergencies, traffic emergencies and jail emergencies.*

Riot and Mob Situations

These represent a direct assault upon the social order; in their threat to civil authority, they present a serious challenge to the ability and striking power of police forces. Riots, mob situations and other forms of acute social unrest are unpredictable in advance so far as the hour and the scale of disorder are concerned. On one recent occasion, a sailor became involved in a quarrel with a naval patrol officer on the streets of one American city and a civilian came to his rescue. A crowd gathered, and before order could be restored, a monumental riot was in progress.

The transformation of a crowd into a mob is an amazing sociological and psychological phenomenon. A normal crowd will be found obeying the law, with a respect for law and order; it is simply an assemblage of people. A disorderly crowd is an assemblage of people willing to be led into lawlessness but lacking courage and unity of purpose. It is unorganized as a rule — hesitant, uncertain and vacillating. Within such assemblages, there are usually three well-defined groups — a few determined leaders, many active participants and a large majority of spectators who are perfectly harmless in the beginning. They are drawn to the scene of the disorders desiring excitement and hoping for a chance to witness a fight. Curiosity is the basic motivation. During the

---

*Criminal, traffic and jail emergencies are reserved for treatment in Chapter V, *The Reserve Force Concept.*

crowd stage, there may be much commotion and noise. If the police are present, they may be subjected to verbal abuse and other minor annoyances or harassment.

Under the stimulus of intense excitement and swayed by the efforts of agitators, a crowd may be rapidly transformed into a mob. The subtle change from confusion to unity, from the vacillating crowd to the determined mob, may take only a few minutes. A single, successful act of violence on the part of a member of the crowd or an unfortunate act by an untrained officer may ignite the emotions and whet the appetite for disorder and destruction. One of the primary responsibilities of the police is to insure that such a transformation does not take place, that crowds are dispersed while they still remain crowds. Once the transformation has taken place, the members of a mob can only be brought to their senses by an overwhelming demonstration of force or by the actual use of that force.*

The amount of force necessary to overcome resistance in a specific situation depends somewhat on community respect for authority in general and on the amount and character of training that the officers have received. The Northwest Mounted Police were so respected that one officer could accomplish what would, in some other police forces, require several to do. Similarly, the traditional performance of the Texas Rangers captured widespread attention. It is reported that during the oil boom in west Texas a number of years ago, the mayor of a community in that area telephoned to the headquarters of the Texas Rangers in Austin that disorder and riot prompted by a shooting brawl had developed on such a scale that local authorities were powerless to cope with the situation and requested that a company of Rangers be sent in immediately.

An hour later, one lone Ranger appeared in response to the mayor's desperate call for assistance. The latter official stormed ₐbout his office and berated the stupidity of headquarters for sending only one officer. The Ranger smiled and said, "There's only one riot, isn't there?" Only one Ranger was needed to restore order on that Saturday evening in a west Texas town. Ruffian,

*Leonard, V. A.: *Police Organization and Management.* Mineola, Foundation Press, Inc., 1971, p. 374.

murderer and thug had a wholesome respect, not for the personal strength of this lone officer, but for what he symbolized. They knew that disobedience of his orders would bring down upon them the determination and striking power of a force that never turned back from an assignment until the job was done.*

Within every large or small community, there are potentialities for riot and mob situations. No police official charged with the responsibility for the administration of police affairs would be facing up to that responsibility if he failed to prepare in advance well-laid plans for this form of emergency. Supplementing these plans, provisions must be made for training in the strategy and tactics of riot control for every member of the organization, since a riot or mob situation may involve the total striking power of the department. The services of commanding officers in the United States Army and in the National Guard, who are usually available in nearby military installations, should be engaged as instructors in such a training program. Their training and their experience will prove indispensable to the success of police plans and operations in this phase of the departmental program. Ample provisions must also be made at all times for appropriate riot control equipment.

Equally important as the plan of operation in this type of emergency is *planned prevention*. A professional attitude and professional know-how on the part of the police and their commanding officers are fundamental. A good department staffed with officers who are professionals in their field will not allow conditions to develop which may lead to riot, mob situations and other forms of acute social disorder, moving in to handle racial and other social tensions in their early stages. It should be determined that the same kind of law enforcement is administered in minority group districts as among the majority groups. If the department's lines of information are functioning properly, emerging situations will be uncovered at a time when the most effective work can be done. A properly-organized police

---

*The famous Texas Rangers became an integral part of the Texas State Department of Public Safety in 1936, and in that organization the tradition of high level performance has been perpetuated. Under the leadership of the late Colonel Homer Garrison, the Texas State Police System represents one of the nation's most outstanding police organizations today.

department is in a strategic position to become aware of tensions long before they become a matter of general knowledge in the community. Contact with disorder in its early stages is the best strategy.

Conferences with minority group leaders and organizations are helpful in gaining their confidence and in overcoming any unfavorable attitude toward the police. The police can make suggestions to minority group leaders for the education and guidance of their respective groups and can receive, in turn, suggestions for the improvement of law enforcement work among the minority groups.

Inflammatory movements or actions on the part of irresponsible members of a minority group become susceptible to control through cooperation with responsible leaders in the group. Confronted with an emerging situation, consultation with the press can lead to a constructive policy in the publication of news dealing with social tensions and promote cooperation with the police department. Similar contacts can also be made to good advantage with representatives of the minority press where there are such papers. A definite and constructive public relations policy and program is indispensable. A police department which is capable of developing a sound preventive effort will be in the best possible position to handle a riot or mob situation should its preventive efforts fail.*

Nuclear Attack

During the present century, the development of nuclear technology on a scale that almost completely overshadows scientific advances in any other area of human endeavor has created another threat to the safety and security of populations the world over. Today, nuclear energy is being harnessed for useful and constructive purposes. The number of nuclear reactors and other radio-active forces at work in industry and research is

---

*See *Prevention and Control of Mobs and Riots,* Washington, D. C., Federal Bureau of Investigation, 1967; *Civil Disturbances and Disasters,* Department of the Army Field Manual FM 19-15, Washington, D. C., Department of the Army, 1968; Momboisse, Raymond M.: *Store Planning for Riot Survival,* Sacramento, MSM Enterprises, 1968.

increasing month after month. But it is in the arsenals of the world where a potentially-useful force of great magnitude is being prostituted to destruction that mankind finds its major cause for concern. Stockpiles of nuclear weapons now in the possession of the major powers of the world present a tenuous situation in which nations and their peoples realize that they must be prepared for the contingencies of nuclear attack.

In the United States, a nuclear attack would take a high toll of lives. But the losses would be much less if people were prepared to meet the emergency, knew what actions to take and took them.* A nation-wide Civil Defense system has been developed in this country under the leadership and supervision of the Department of Defense, and it is being constantly enlarged and improved. The heart of the system is fallout shelters to protect people from the radio-active fallout that would result from a nuclear attack. The system also includes warning and communication networks, preparations to measure fallout radiation, control centers to direct lifesaving and recovery operations, emergency broadcasting facilities, local governments organized for emergency operations, large numbers of citizens trained in emergency skills and U. S. military forces available to assist civil authorities and the public in a time of emergency.

When a nuclear bomb or missile explodes, the main effects produced are intense light (flash), heat, blast and radiation, which all occur immediately. How strong these effects are, depends on the size and type of the weapon, how far away the explosion is, the weather conditions (sunny or rainy, windy or still), the terrain (whether the ground is flat or hilly) and the height of the explosion (high in the air or near the ground).

Explosions that are on or close to the ground create great quantities of large, dangerous radio-active fallout particles, most of which would fall to earth during the first 24 hours. Explosions high in the air create smaller radio-active particles, which would not have any real effect on humans until many months or years

---

*See *In Time of Emergency: A Citizen's Handbook on Nuclear Attack and Natural Disasters,* No. H-14. Prepared by the U. S. Office of Civil Defense with the cooperation of other governmental agencies. March, 1968. *This publication should be in the home of every American.*

later, if at all. These smaller particles would drift to earth slowly, losing much of their radio-activity before they reached the ground, and would be spread by the upper winds over vast areas of the world.

If the United States should be attacked, the people who happened to be close to a nuclear explosion — in the area of heavy destruction — probably would be killed or seriously injured by the blast or by the heat of the nuclear fireball. People a few miles away — in the *fringe area* of the explosion — would be endangered by the blast and heat and by fires that the explosion might start. However, it is likely that most of the people in the fringe area would survive these hazards.

People who were *outside* the fringe area would not be affected by the blast, heat or fire. Department of Defense studies show that in any nuclear attack an enemy might launch against the United States, tens of millions of Americans would be outside the fringe areas. To them — and to people in the fringe areas who survived the blast, heat and fire — radio-active fallout would be the main danger. Protective measures against this danger can be obtained by taking refuge in designated shelters.

When a nuclear weapon explodes near the ground, great quantities of pulverized earth and other debris are sucked up into the nuclear cloud where the radio-active gases produced by the explosion condense on and into this debris, producing radio-active fallout particles. Within a short time, these particles fall back to earth — the larger ones first, the smaller ones later. On the way down, and after they reach the ground, the radio-active particles give off invisible gamma rays — like X-rays — which can kill or injure people. These particles give off most of their radiation; therefore, the first few hours or days after an attack would be the most dangerous period.

In dangerously-affected areas, the particles themselves would look like grains or salt or sand, but the *rays* they would give off could not be seen, tasted, smelled or felt. Special instruments would be required to detect the rays and measure their intensity.

The distribution of fallout particles after a nuclear attack would depend on wind currents, weather conditions and other factors. There is no way of predicting in advance what areas of the country would be affected by fallout or how soon the particles would fall back to earth at a particular location. Some communities might get a heavy accumulation of fallout, while others — even in the same general area — might get little or none. No area in the United States could be sure of not getting fallout, and it is probable that some fallout particles would be deposited on most of the country.

Areas close to a nuclear explosion might receive fallout within 15 to 30 minutes, while it might take 5 to 10 hours or more for the particles to drift down on a community 100 or 200 miles away. Generally, the first 24 hours after the fallout began to settle would be the most dangerous period to a community's residents. The heavier particles falling during that time would still be highly radio-active and give off strong rays. The lighter particles falling later would have lost much of their radiation high in the atmosphere.

The invisible gamma rays given off by fallout particles can cause radiation sickness — that is, illness caused by physical and chemical changes in the cells of the body. If a person receives a large dose of radiation, he will die. But if he receives only a small or medium dose, his body will repair itself, and he will get well. The same dose received over a short period of time is more damaging than if it is received over a longer period. Usually, the effects of a given dose of radiation are more severe in very young and very old persons and those in poor health.

No special clothing can protect people against gamma radiation, and no special drugs or chemicals can prevent large doses of radiation from causing damage to the cells of the body. However, antibiotics and other medicines are helpful in treating infections that may follow excessive exposure to radiation, which weakens the body's ability to fight infection. Almost all of the radiation that people would absorb from fallout particles would come from particles *outside* their own bodies. Only simple precautions would be necessary to avoid swallowing the particles and because of their size (like grains of sand), it would be practically impossible to inhale them.

People can protect themselves against fallout radiation and have a good chance of surviving it by staying inside a fallout shelter. In most cases, the fallout radiation level outside the shelter would decrease rapidly enough to permit people to leave the shelter within a few days. But even in communities that received heavy accumulation of fallout particles, people might soon be able to leave the shelter for a few minutes or a few hours at a time.*

Other forms of disaster that may confront man include such things as a building collapse, a highway accident, a nuclear reactor accident, a ship disaster, an epidemic, an avalanche, a dam collapse and a panic.

This chapter has brought the implications and responsibilities of police service under disaster conditions into bold relief. It is just at such times — times of disaster or catastrophe — that the police function assumes its greatest importance. Provisions must be made for the general police duties of maintaining order, protecting life and property, directing traffic and caring for the lost and found. The police are also expected to aid other officials and cooperate with the U. S. Army and National Guard, if these agencies are called upon, and with the Red Cross and the Director of Civil Defense.

All of these regular police duties assume unusual and difficult proportions under disaster conditions. Traffic control may become especially difficult because of the large number of people who seek to escape from the ruined area and the large number who seek to enter it, either from anxiety for the welfare of friends and relatives or out of mere curiosity.

The protection of property from looting and the guarding of banks and other places where funds and valuables are kept are duties which the police may be called upon immediately to assume. In disasters of major proportions, such as earthquakes or hurricanes, telephone systems and electric power supply sources may be paralyzed at a time when they are most needed. Provisions should be made in advance for an independent auxiliary power supply for the police radio transmitter at headquarters. Advance inventories should also be made of medical services (including hospitals, nurses, doctors and ambulances), emergency communication facilities possessed by other organizations and other

*In Time of Emergency: A Citizen's Handbook on Nuclear Attack and Natural Disasters, No. H-14. Prepared by the U. S. Office of Civil Defense with the cooperation of other governmental agencies. March, 1968.

facilities, including reserve man-power which may be called upon by the police in such major emergencies.

It is now relevant to consider in detail the blueprints for police preparation in advance of the disaster, so that when it strikes, the police function will be discharged with a high degree of efficiency.

CHAPTER II

WHEN DISASTER STRIKES

T *HERE is no time to plan – then!*

Camille . . . the incredible

"The greatest storm of any kind that has ever affected this nation by any yardstick you want to measure with" – in those words, the National Hurricane Center in Miami described hurricane Camille for the history books. Weather experts could hardly believe reports of 210 miles per hour winds from a hurricane-hunter plane limping towards Houston after flying through Camille's center. Many Gulf Coast residents died because they found the forecasts of 20-foot storm tides unbelievable.

Incredible was the word for Camille. Striking first in Louisiana, she pushed up 4 1/2 feet of water into the hurricane-proof Weather Bureau station high on stilts at Boothville and sent the Gulf of Mexico surging up the mouth of the Mississippi River to burst the levees in lower Plaquemines Parish. Camille saved her worst on that day and evening of August 17, 1969, for the stretch of the Mississippi Gulf Coast that runs from Bay St. Louis to Pascagoula.

The phenomenal winds, spawning many storm-hidden tornadoes and monster tides, left more than fifty-five miles of coastal damage that in many areas could only be described as a complete wipe-out. Gulfport, Pass Christian, Biloxi, Waveland, Long Beach, Burns and Boothville became tragic names on a hurricane-swept map of death and human misery. The storm left thousands of front steps leading to wreckage or just nothing at all.

The carnage stretched from the Florida panhandle to Louisiana. The Mississippi coast and Plaquemines and St. Tammany Parishes in Louisiana were hardest hit. Here, some 43,000 homes and almost 1,300 mobile homes were destroyed or damaged, along with hundreds of small businesses, farm buildings and boats. Leaving in its wake destroyed communications, impassable roads and other earmarks of destruction, Camille moved inland. Hurricane-force winds struck as far north as Hattiesburg and Jackson in Mississippi.

Turning sharply eastward, Camille veered through Virginia and West Virginia, accompanied by torrential rains in the mountain areas which raised the James River and flooded a large area around Richmond the next day. Another 2,400 destroyed or damaged homes, along with over 1,400 mobile homes, were added to Camille's record of death and destruction through the Virginias.

Camille's official score on that fateful day — August 17, 1969 — is indicated on Table XIV.

Her Name was Celia

On Monday, August 3, 1970, Celia changed the face of Corpus Christi and the Coastal Bend of Texas. The weather was deceptive; it was just an ordinary August day. The heavy rains, gusty winds and total breathless calm which presage a storm were missing. Nevertheless, Celia came, and for four destructive hours, she moved on her way across the Coastal Bend — the worst disaster the area had known in half a century.

Corpus Christi and the surrounding areas thought they were ready, and as will be seen presently, they were. However, advance weather reports indicated hurricane Celia was just a small storm with winds of only 90 miles per hour.

But as Celia neared land, her wind speed increased to more than 100 miles per hour. Telephone poles in downtown Corpus Christi began to fall, and there was a breakdown in all communication within the area. Just before the full force of the storm struck the coast at 4:00 P. M., the windows and walls on the upper stories of Spohn Hospital began falling and the Coastal Bend knew that it was becoming the victim of one of the worst storms ever to strike the Texas coast.

Celia's winds were clocked at 161 miles per hour as she moved through Port Aransas, Aransas Pass, Sinton, Odem, Edroy, Mathis, Ingleside, Rockport, Portland and Hobstown — small towns on her

TABLE XIV

THE STATISTICS OF A HURRICANE'S FURY*

	The Gulf Coast	The Virginias
Dead	128	73
Missing	76	100
Injured	4,509	113
Homes destroyed	5,519	416
Homes, major damage	12,491	481
Homes, minor damage	25,090	1,524
Mobile homes destroyed	913	196
Mobile homes, major damage	474	54
Small businesses destroyed and major damage	726	
Families affected	66,200	3,809
Number of persons sheltered and fed	100,000	27,550
Number of meals served	352,387	

(All statistics as of August 31, 1969, 14 days after the strike)

*The American Red Cross: *Hurricane Camille.* August 17, 1969.

destructive path through the Corpus Christi area. Gusts were reported as high as 180 miles per hour. The toll was severe damage to property and the loss of 30 lives. At the height of the emergency, food, housing, first aid and other assistance were given to more than 120,000 victims of the hurricane.

Planning — Vital, Indispensable

The dimensions of death, human misery and destruction that lie in the wake of disaster demand that the police and the people of every community do no less than plan in advance for their containment. In no other way can the needless sacrifice of life be prevented, and suffering and distress, together with property damage, be reduced to a minimum. Far too many police departments and far too many communities have not yet learned the lesson. In fact, it must be said, with no small degree of concern, that a plan is the exception in the overwhelming majority of cases and not the rule.

The Lubbock Tornado

Planning in advance means preparedness and capability to meet the crisis when the threat appears and the impact is already in the offing. On May 11, 1970, when a tornado struck Lubbock, Texas, cutting a mile-wide path of death and destruction through the heart of the city, they had a plan. The tornado triggered a massive operation involving federal, state, local and non-govermental organizations to save lives and to start the city on the road to recovery.

Lubbock's Emergency Operating Center (EOC) in the basement of the City Hall was the hub of emergency operations. It was the nerve center where city officials and department heads worked as a team in coordinating life-saving and recovery operations. For example, plumbers volunteered their services and as a result of prior planning, cut off gas and water lines to eliminate hazards.

The EOC was equipped with emergency power and was linked to Radio Station KFYO, which also had emergency power furnished by the Office of Civil Defense under the Broadcast Station Protection Program. This enabled local officials to transmit emergency instructions and information to people in the community. The EOC was designed for an emergency staff of 43, most of whom were in the EOC when the tornado struck. They remained in the EOC after the disaster to carry out the functions of government during the recovery phase.

The EOC normally houses the Civil Defense Office, the standby radio communications center for the police and fire departments, the land-line switchboard, the mail room and a cafeteria. The EOC was the operating center of all city and county functions for the duration of the emergency and after the tornado had passed. Advance emergency planning was credited with saving many lives.

In Corpus Christi when hurricane Celia, with her awesome destructive power, was still some distance out in the Gulf but too close for comfort, they had a plan.* Weyland Pilcher, Director of Public Safety and responsible for Civil Defense in the city, started emergency preparedness actions Sunday morning, August 2. He met with Mayor Jack Blackmon, City Manager Marvin Townsend, city councilmen and the heads of city departments. *Condition 4* (department heads were to stay in touch) was declared at a time when Celia was expected to hit land in the Galveston area, nearly 200 miles northeast of Corpus Christi. A few months before in May, two Civil Defense hurricane-planning conferences had been held in Corpus Christi, as the hurricane season was approaching.

On Monday, August 3, Celia became a definite threat to the Corpus Christi community of 250,000 people. At 5:00 A. M., Pilcher declared *Condition 3* (batten down). He also ordered the floodtide gates closed in the Corpus Christi seawall. At 10:00 A. M., another Civil Defense meeting was held, and emergency crews were called in. *Condition 2* (prepare to execute emergency plans, including the evacuation of low-lying areas) was declared; instructions were broadcast ordering the evacuation.

City police cars with loudspeakers cruised the area to spread the warning. Some 3,000 people were moved in city buses to fourteen schools with hurricane shelters two miles from the coast. Red Cross personnel operated the shelters in accordance with the local hurricane plan. Meanwhile, Civil Defense evacuations were under way in other coast areas, including movement of people from Cameron Parish, Louisiana, north to Lake Arthur.

The first blast of hurricane Celia's winds, which were to reach gusts of 180 miles per hour, pounded into Corpus Christi at about 3:15 P. M. *Condition 1* (hurricane has arrived) was declared. The sledge-hammer winds knocked out electric power and communications throughout the 100 square mile area of Corpus Christi and nearby communities. A priority task was to restore power and

---

*See Appendix A – *The Corpus Christi Hurricane and Emergency Plan.*

communications. Within hours, 24 Civil Defense emergency generators, owned by the Office of Civil Defense, were dispatched from Bastrop, Texas, more than 200 miles away, to the stricken communities of Taft, Portland, Sinton, Aransas Pass, Gregory, Rockport, Port Aransas, Odem, Gallallen, Ingleside and Corpus Christi. The generators were used in a variety of ways, including emergency lighting, pumping water and lifting sewage. In Rockport, one was used to power the time lock on a bank vault.

Less than one week after Celia struck, United Press International from Aransas Pass carried this assessment by a professional hurricane expert:

"I have never seen so much damage and so few casualties as there have been in this area," said Dr. Robert H. Simpson, Director of the National Hurricane Center. "This is a tribute of virtually unparalleled proportions to the disaster prevention and preparedness measures that were drafted in advance of the emergency."

Each department and unit of local government must prepare an emergency plan covering its role and the use of its personnel and facilities in a disaster situation. But in addition, provisions must be made for an over-all advisory or control group, which may be designated the Disaster or Emergency Council, to insure coordination and the most effective use of the total resources of the community. The council's function is limited to planning and its membership should include the following persons: the mayor, city manager, Civil Defense director, chief of police, fire chief, city health officer, heads of other municipal departments, sheriff, the press and representatives from the Red Cross, the state police, the power company, the public school system and the communications systems — telephone, radio and television. The mayor would be the presiding officer, with meetings scheduled at periodical intervals to insure readiness for the emergency.

The IACP General Emergency Plan

The International Association of Chiefs of Police (IACP) has developed a model General Emergency Plan for the police departments. This plan, which is presented at the end of this chapter, offers a solid basis for police pre-disaster planning. Every police department, including the smaller departments with a personnel strength from one to seventy-five officers, should study this blueprint carefully in order to measure its readiness for emergency and to immediately take whatever steps are necessary to bring the organization in line with the requirements of a disaster situation.

The IACP maintains that police departments must be prepared to meet a wide range of emergency situations that call for responses beyond the capability of the day-to-day organizational posture. To deal with these unusual events, police departments should develop general and specific emergency plans. Although these plans may be lengthy and complex, the individual officer must know and understand what is expected of him under any contingency plan. This includes, but is not limited to, such information as:

What code words or signals are involved?

Who can implement the plan and under what circumstances?

If the individual patrol officer can implement the plan, how should this be accomplished?

What does the officer do upon implementation of a plan? What if he is off duty at the time?

Who will be in charge of the operations?

UNIT 4A11 Supplement I

General Emergency Plan

21:1 PURPOSE

21:1.1 Object of Plan. The General Emergency Plan has been developed to expedite the handling of an unusual emergency, a situation which requires the services of a large complement of police personnel. The Department in addition to its day-to-day responsibilities must be prepared to manage such unusual emergencies as:

(1) Flood

(2) Hurricane

(3) Earthquake

(4) Jail Break

(5) Riot

(6) Plane Crash

(7) Train Wreck

(8) Strike

(9) Tornado

(10) Fire (three alarms or more)

(11) Explosion (extensive nature)

(12) Enemy Bomb Attack or Invasion

(13) Group Disorder

This plan is designed to bring sufficient aid and equipment to any unusual emergency scene, so that the condition can be brought under control in the shortest possible time.

21:1.2 Need for the Plan. In recent years strikes, demonstrations and group disorders have presented problems of major proportions for the police. Where adequate plans had not been developed to meet these emergencies, the authorities were less able to prevent extensive property damage, personal injury and loss of life. However, in cities where plans had been developed to cope with anticipated emergencies, such control was effective and little or no injury or damage to person or property resulted.

21:2 IMPORTANCE OF PROPER POLICE ACTION

The importance of proper police action in the first few minutes of a major disorder or disaster cannot be too strongly stressed. Indecision on the part of the first officer to arrive on the scene, or on the part of a superior officer at the scene, or any improper, inefficient, or disinterested conduct on the part of any police officer, can result in a very serious situation. Experience has demonstrated conclusively that immediate mobilization and use of all units of the Police

Department in a *SHOW OF FORCE*, insured efficient dispersal of a threatening mob; whereas, delay, indecision and inaction at the first sign of trouble, inevitably required the *USE OF FORCE*, to disperse the threatening mob, and such action invariably resulted in property damage and personal injury, in addition to poor public relations for the Police Department.

21:3 RESPONSIBILITY

21:3.1 Responsibility for Instruction. All commanding officers are charged with the responsibility of instructing all police officers and civilian employees under their supervision in the details of the General Emergency Plan, and the Commanding Officer of the Police Academy shall include in all training programs, adequate instruction for recruits regarding this plan.

21:3.2 Copy of Plan to Be Available. A copy of the General Emergency Plan shall be kept in the Offices of the Police Director, the Chief of Police, each divisional commanding officer, each unit commanding officer and at each desk point supervised by a superior officer.

21:4 CONSTRUCTION OF THE FOUR PHASES OF THE PLAN

21:4.1 Four Phases of the General Emergency Plan. The General Emergency Plan is divided into four phases as follows:

PLAN #1	PLAN #3
PLAN #2	PLAN #4

21:4.2 Personnel and Equipment to Be Dispatched. The quota of personnel and general equipment which shall respond for each plan, upon being dispatched, is listed in the General Emergency Plan Chart.

MINIMUM AVAILABLE POLICE DEPARTMENT PERSONNEL AND EQUIPMENT THAT WILL RESPOND AT THE HOURS INDICATED

	PLAN #1			PLAN #2			PLAN #3			PLAN #4		
	9-5	5-1	1-9	9-5	5-1	1-9	9-5	5-1	1-9	9-5	5-1	1-9
POLICE DIRECTOR												
CHIEF OF POLICE				1			1	1	1	1	1	1
NIGHT SUPERVISORS		1	1		1	1		2	2		2	2
PATROL DIVISION												
Commanding Officer				1	1		1	1	1	1	1	1
Precinct Captains	1			1	1	1	2	2	2	3	3	3
Lieutenants							2	2	2	2	2	2
Sergeants	1	1	1	2	2	2	4	4	4	4	4	4
Patrolmen	6	6	6	10	10	10	18	18	18	26	26	26
Horses												
Patrol Cars	3	3	3	6	6	6	13	13	13	16	16	16
Patrol Wagons or Squadrols	1	1	1	1	1	1	2	2	2	3	3	3
EMERGENCY BUREAU												
Commanding Officer	1	1		1	1		1	1	1	1	1	1
Superior Officers	1	1	1	1	1	1	1	1	1	1	1	1
Patrolmen	3	3	3	3	3	3	6	6	6	6	6	6
Trucks	1	1	1	1	1	1	2	2	2	2	2	2
TRAFFIC DIVISION												
Commanding Officer				1	1		1	1	1	1	1	1
Superior Officers	3	2		4	4		4	4	4	4	4	4
Patrolmen	6	4		12	8		21	21	21	21	21	21
Traffic Cars	3	3		4	2		4	4	4	4	4	4
Speaker Cars	1	1		1	1		2	2	2	2	2	2
Motorcycles	3	2		8	8		8	8	8	8	8	8
DETECTIVE DIVISION												
Commanding Officer				1	1		1	1	1	1	1	1
Superior Officers	1			3	2	2	3	2	2	3	2	2
Detectives	2	2	2	4	3	3	6	4	4	6	4	4
Squad Cars	1	1	1	3	2	2	4	3	3	4	3	3
INVESTIGATION DIVISION												
Commanding Officer				1	1		1	1	1	1	1	1
Superior Officers				1	1		2	2	2	2	2	2
Detectives	2	2		2	2		3	3	3	13	13	13
Squad Cars				1	1		2	2	2	3	3	3
ADMINISTRATIVE DIVISION												
Commanding Officer				1	1		1	1	1	1	1	1
Superior Officers				1	1		1	1	1	1	1	1
Photographer				1	1	1	1	1	1	1	1	1
Identification Officer				1	1	1	1	1	1	1	1	1
Mobile Identification Unit				1	1	1	1	1	1	1	1	1
MINIMUM AVAILABLE PERSONNEL TO RESPOND	27	23	14	53	47	25	82	81	81	101	100	100

NOTE: The term Commanding Officer as used refers to the Officer in charge at the time of the emergency. Additional Precinct Captains obtained from adjoining Precincts.

21:4.4 Superior Officers to Institute Plan Although Sufficient Personnel Are at the Scene. At any unusual emergency scene, where the number of personnel present is equal to the quota of personnel specified in the plan, and no plan has been ordered into effect, the superior officer in charge at the scene shall immediately order the appropriate plan into operation.

21:4.4-1 Minimum Available Equipment from other Departments That Will Respond at the Hour Indicated.

	PLAN #1			PLAN #2			PLAN #3			PLAN #4		
	8-4	4-M	M-8	8-4	4-M	M-8	8-4	4-M	M-8	8-4	4-M	M-8
FIRE DEPARTMENT FIRE ENGINES				1	1	1	2	2	2	2	2	2
CITY HOSPITAL AMBULANCES				1	1	1	2	2	2	2	2	2
BUREAU OF TRAFFIC AND SIGNALS												
ENGINEERING TRUCKS				1	1		2	2	2	2	2	2

21:4.5 Specialized Equipment to Be Dispatched with the Designated Units. The following specialized equipment shall be dispatched with the designated units:

21:4.5-1 Emergency Bureau.

(1) All available nightsticks and helmets

(2) Walkie-talkie and loud speaking equipment

(3) Weapons, ammunition, tear gas, first aid kit. floodlights, generator and geiger counter, if necessary.

(4) Any other pertinent equipment needed for the emergency situation.

21:4.5-2 Bureau of Traffic and Signals.

(1) Sufficient "no parking" signs and street barricades

(2) Sufficient lanterns and flares, if necessary.

21:4.5-3 Fire Department. Request the Fire Department to assign sufficient firemen to guard fire alarm boxes in the vicinity of the emergency to prevent tampering or false alarms.

21:5 TO PLACE A PLAN INTO OPERATION

21:5.1 Good Judgment to Be Exercised. All police officers and civilian employees of the Police Department shall exercise good judgment when arriving at an emergency scene. If one additional patrol car can bring the situation under control, that is all that should be summoned. However, if in the opinion of the officer an immediate *SHOW OF FORCE* is necessary to disperse a gathering crowd or mob, to bring the situation under control, he shall immediately call for a General Emergency Plan.

21:5.2 When First Police Officer at the Scene Is a Patrolman. If the first police officer to arrive at an emergency scene is a patrolman, and he determines that an emergency plan is necessary to cope with the condition, he shall place into operation Plan #1 or Plan #2 whichever, in his judgment, is needed.

21:5.3 When First Police Officer at the Scene Is a Superior Officer. If the first police officer to arrive at an emergency scene is a superior officer, and he determines that an emergency plan is necessary to cope with the condition, he shall place into operation any one of the four plans which, in his judgment, is needed.

21:5.4 Placing An Emergency Plan into Operation. To place an emergency plan into operation:

21:5.4-1 From Radio Equipped Vehicles. Patrolmen, detectives and plainclothesmen in a radio equipped car, shall give the car number, the location, and the number of the plan requested. Example: "Car 32, South and Pacific Streets, Place Plan #1 (or Plan #2) into operation.

21:5.4-2 By Way of Telephone. Patrolmen, detectives and plainclothesmen on foot, shall telephone the dispatcher, giving the location and number of the plan requested.

Example: "Patrolman Jones, Esso Service Station, South and Pacific Streets, phone MA 3-9089, place Plan #1 (or Plan #2) into operation.

21:5.4-3 By Off Duty Police Officers. The procedure for police officers who are off duty when requesting an emergency plan, shall be for them to telephone the dispatcher, giving the location and the plan requested.

21:5.4-4 By Superior Officers. The procedure for superior officers shall be the same as for patrolmen, except that the superior officer shall have the authority to place any one of the four plans into operation.

21:6 GENERAL RESPONSIBILITIES AND DUTIES OF FIRST POLICE OFFICER OF THE FORCE TO ARRIVE AT AN EMERGENCY SCENE

21:6.1 Assume Command. Assume command until the arrival of an officer of higher rank or until the arrival of a superior officer who shall be in charge, according to the plan in operation.

21:6.2 Inform Dispatcher. Inform the dispatcher if assistance is needed as detailed in 21:5.

21:6.3 Prevent Formation of Crowds. Use all efforts to prevent a crowd or mob from forming.

21:6.4 Disperse Crowds. If a crowd or mob has gathered, use all efforts for dispersing it until assistance arrives. Prevent its re-forming.

21:6.5 Prevent Loitering. Permit no one to loiter in the immediate vicinity—once the crowd has been dispersed.

21:6.6 Arrest Offenders. Arrest those who refuse to disperse, or who are committing or have committed any other violation of the law.

21:6.7 Remove Cause of Emergency. If the cause of the emergency can be removed to the precinct station, or to some other precinct station, and thus lessen or eliminate tension in the area, such action shall be taken immediately.

21:7 GENERAL RESPONSIBILITIES OF ALL SUPERIOR OFFICERS

21:7.1 Become Thoroughly Familiar with the Emergency Plan. The successful policing of a major emergency depends upon the instruction and supervision of subordinates by superior officers in the execution of the General Emergency Plan. Therefore, all superior officers shall familiarize themselves with every phase and detail of the plan.

21:7.2 Command the Execution of Police Tasks. Superior officers shall command, direct, and supervise the execution of police tasks at all times. They shall guide and instruct subordinates in the special duties but, shall not perform the subordinate's work.

21:7.3 Not Knowingly Countermand Orders. A superior officer shall not knowingly countermand orders given by another superior officer, unless the reason no longer exists for that order, and the situation requires a change of orders.

21:7.4 Maintain Communication with the Dispatcher. Superior officers in immediate command of their units shall maintain constant contact with the dispatcher, to keep him informed and to receive further instructions.

21:7.5 Return Police Officers Not Needed to Regular Assignments. Superior officers in charge at the emergency scene shall be responsible for directing the return of all police officers, whose services are no longer required, to their regular assignments.

21:7.6 Cancellation of Emergency Plan. The ranking superior officer at the emergency scene may cancel the operating plan if the situation is under control. He shall immediately notify the Communications Bureau to inform all units that the plan has been cancelled.

21:7.7 Establish a Recall Index File. All commanding officers shall establish at all desk points under their supervision, an emergency recall index file, listing the name, rank, badge number, street address, floor or apartment number, emergency telephone number and normal days and hours off duty for all police officers and civilian employees of their command.

21:7.8 Establish Duplicate Recall Index File Cards at Communications Bureau. All commanding officers shall have made or cause to be made emergency recall cards in duplicate for all police officers and certain civilian employees of their commands. The original shall be kept in command, and the duplicate shall be sent to the Commanding Officer of the Communications Bureau. In cases where an individual police officer or a civilian employee cannot be reached by telephone, the Communications Bureau shall so advise so that a district patrol car can be sent to contact that police officer or civilian employee at his residence.

21:7.9 Commanding Officer at Communications Bureau to Maintain Recall Index File. The Commanding Officer of the Communications Bureau shall be responsible for maintaining the duplicate emergency recall index file. On each individual recall card, he shall have recorded the motor patrol district in which that police officer or civilian employee resides.

21:7.10 Dispatch Necessary Personnel. All superior officers when assigned to desk duty at any command, upon notification that a General Emergency Plan is in operation, shall immediately dispatch personnel and equipment specified for such plan. Whenever General Emergency Plan #3 or #4 is placed into operation, they shall immediately begin recalling all off-duty men assigned to their command. Wherever possible, use shall be made of coin operated telephones to make these calls, leaving the regular police lines open for police business. When available assign other officers to make the calls.

21:8 GENERAL RESPONSIBILITY OF ALL UNITS TO RESPOND

21:8.1 All Personnel Subject to Call. Whenever a General Emergency Plan is placed into operation all police officers and civilian employees of the Police Department, regardless of their regular assignment, are subject to call. Superior officers, patrolmen and detectives assigned to radio-equipped cars, regardless of regular assignment, shall, when informed that a General Emergency Plan has been placed into operation, remain on the air for instructions. They shall immediately respond to orders of the dispatcher, until such time as these orders are changed by the superior officer in charge at the emergency scene.

21:8.2 Contact Command When Apprised that Plan #3 or #4 Is in Effect. All police officers and civilian employees when apprised that Plan #3 or Plan #4 has been placed into operation, shall immediately contact their respective commands for instructions.

21:8.3 Communication Car at Emergency Scene. The first radio-equipped car to arrive at the scene shall be designated as the communications car. This car shall keep its red signal light in operation at all times to identify it as the communications car. Police officers operating all other police vehicles at the emergency scene will shut off their red signal lights.

21:8.4 Personnel Dispatched to Report to Communication Car Upon Arrival. All police officers and civilian employees dispatched to the emergency scene shall report to the communications car for instructions and assignment. Vehicles dispatched to the emergency scene shall be parked as near as possible to the scene, properly secured and locked, and the occupants shall proceed on foot to the communications car.

21:8.5 Responding Personnel to Report to Superior Officer of Their Command at the Scene. Police officers and civilian employees of all units responding shall report to the superior officers of their commands or to the officer in charge at the scene.

21:8.6 Restrict Use of Sirens. Police officers operating vehicles responding to an emergency scene under a General Emergency Plan, shall not use their sirens. Sirens attract additional persons to the scene, increasing the police problem of control.

21:9 ESTABLISHMENT OF MOBILIZATION POINTS

21:9.1 Determine by the Seriousness of the Emergency. The seriousness of the situation may require that Plans #3 and #4 be placed in operation and the additional men kept on a standby basis. This ready reserve shall be assembled close to the scene but at a sufficient distance to insure that its presence will not be detected by persons at the scene.

21:9.1-1 Primary Mobilization Point. The primary mobilization point shall be the precinct in the affected area.

21:9.1-2 Secondary Mobilization Points. The secondary mobilization points shall be the fire houses in the affected area.

21:9.2 Necessity for Using the Secondary Mobilization Points. The officer in charge at the emergency scene shall determine the necessity for using the secondary mobilization points and in such cases, shall assign an officer to make the necessary arrangements with the captain in charge of the firehouse and to take charge of all police operations at that mobilization center.

21:9.3 Action of Personnel at Mobilization Center. All police officers and civilian employees dispatched to a mobilization center shall remain indoors, out of the sight of the general public, until specifically assigned to some task by the superior officer in charge.

21:9.4 Temporary Log. The superior officer in charge at the mobilization center shall arrange for the keeping of a temporary log in which the following entries shall be recorded in chronological order:

(1) Identity of police officer assigned to maintain log.

(2) Concise but complete description of the emergency.

(3) Identity of police officers and civilian employees reporting to mobilization center.

(4) Notifications made.

(5) Requests made.

(6) Assignments of personnel and changes thereof.

(7) Orders given and actions taken.

If possible, a walkie-talkie radio should be utilized at this point to keep the superior officer at the emergency scene informed as to the number of personnel and type of equipment available at the mobilization point.

21:9.5 Mobilization Points Utilized as Temporary Detention Centers. The mobilization points shall also be used as temporary detention centers for persons arrested, if that is found to be necessary.

21:10 SPECIFIC RESPONSIBILITIES AND DUTIES OF THE OFFICE OF THE CHIEF OF POLICE

21:10.1 Responsibilities of the Chief of Police or the Command Post Supervisor in Charge. Whenever a General Emergency Plan is placed into operation, the Chief of Police, or the night supervisor in charge, shall be responsible for the following action:

(1) **Nighttime, Weekend and Holiday Emergency.** If Plans #1, #2, #3, or #4 are placed into operation during the nighttime, during the weekend and on holidays, the Command Post supervisor shall proceed immediately to the scene.

(2) **Chief of Police to Respond.** If Plans (see chart), #3 or #4 are placed into operation, the Chief of Police shall immediately proceed to the scene and assume personal charge.

(3) **Verification of Compliance.** Verify that the equipment and personnel specified by the plan in operation has been dispatched to the scene.

(4) **Information on Action Taken.** Keep informed of the action being taken to restore law and order.

(5) **Coordination of Efforts.** Coordinate the efforts of all units of the Police Department toward the immediate restoration of law and order.

(6) **Press and Public Relations.** Supervise all matters involving the press, and the public relations of the Police Department.

(7) **Plan # 4.** If it is decided to place Plan #4 into operation, immediately advise the Police Director, so that the proper steps may be taken to alert the agencies as follows:

(1) Civil Defense

(2) Sheriff

(3) State Police

(4) State Department of Defense

(5) United States Army

21:11 SPECIFIC RESPONSIBILITIES AND DUTIES OF THE PATROL DIVISION

21.11.1 Commanding Officer of the Patrol Division. Whenever a General Emergency Plan is placed into operation the Commanding Officer of the Patrol Division shall be responsible for the following action:

21:11.1-1 Respond Immediately. If Plans #2 (see chart), #3 or #4 are placed into operation, immediately proceed to the emergency scene, and take personal charge of all police activities until relieved by the Chief of Police.

21:11.1-2 Verify Compliance. Verify that the equipment and personnel of his command, specified in the plan placed into operation, have been dispatched to the emergency scene.

21:11.1-3 Keep Informed on Action Taken. Keep informed of the action being taken to restore or maintain law and order.

21:11.1-4 Advise Dispatcher of Headquarters Location. Establish headquarters at the communications car or at a nearby telephone, and advise the dispatcher of your location. If necessary and if possible, secure three telephones for use—one for in-coming calls, one for out-going calls and one to be used as an open line to Central Communications.

21:11.1-5 Arrange for Temporary Headquarters Log. Arrange for a temporary log in which shall be recorded in chronological order the following entries:

(1) Identity of police officer assigned to maintain log.

(2) Concise but complete description of occurrence.

(3) Notifications made.

(4) Requests made.

(5) Assignments of personnel and changes thereof.

(6) Identity of officials and public agencies represented at the scene.

(7) Orders given, action taken, procedure adopted and developments at the scene.

21:11.1-6 Call for a Higher Plan. If the equipment and personnel on hand are insufficient to control the situation, immediately order the dispatcher to place Plan #3 or #4 into operation.

21:11.1-7 Supervise All Activities. Verify that all superior officers and subordinates at the scene are complying with the requirements set forth in this plan, and proceed to supervise all further activities at the scene, until the situation is brought under control.

21:11.1-8 Call Other Agencies If Necessary. If the conditions at the scene require the services of the public utilities crews, or the emergency crews of the Water Department, advise the dispatcher to summon the crews needed.

21:11.1-9 Establish Information and Press Center. When necessary, establish an "Information and Press Center" for the convenience of the press, officials, relatives, and concerned persons. Communicate its location to all personnel and direct that all inquiries be referred to the center.

21:11.1-10 Comply with General Instructions. Comply with the general instructions for all superior officers, listed under 21:7.

21:11.2 Precinct Captains. All precinct captains shall cause to be made and kept current, listings of the following information:

21:11.2-1 Weapons and Ammunition. All places within the precinct boundaries where weapons and ammunition may be stored or kept for sale.

21:11.2-2 Narcotic Drugs. All places within the precinct boundaries where narcotic drugs may be stored or kept for sale.

21:11.2-3 Alcoholic Beverages. All places where alcoholic beverages are kept for sale.

21:11.2-4 Important Business Houses. All important business houses which may be looted or damaged in the event of an emergency.

21:11.2-5 Public Utility Installations. All public utility installations which may be damaged in the event of an emergency.

21:11.2-6 File of Prominent Persons Residing in Command. The names, addresses, business addresses, and telephone numbers of prominent persons in the precinct who, in the event of an emergency, will upon request, speak to the people in the area of disorder, over the radio and over the police loud-speaking system in a personal tour of the area. This information shall be compiled on separate lists, one for each type information, and copies of these lists shall be attached to the desk copy of the General Emergency Plan, and to any other copy of the plan maintained at the precinct. Copies of these lists shall also be kept at the following points, and any change in the status of these lists shall be forwarded immediately to:

(1) Police Director

(2) Chief of Police

(3) Divisional Commanding Officers

(4) Community Relations Bureau

21:11.2-7 Responsibilities During an Actual Emergency. Whenever a General Emergency Plan is placed into operation, the Captain in charge of the precinct where the emergency exists, shall be responsible for the following action:

(1) *Verify Compliance.* Verify that the equipment and personnel of his command, specified in the Plan placed into operation, has been dispatched to the emergency scene.

(2) *Call Other Agencies.* When Plans #3 and #4 are placed into operation, contact the Fire Department, and the City Hospital and request that all the equipment and personnel of their agencies, as designated in the Plan, be alerted for use.

(3) *Respond to Emergency Scene.* Assign a Lieutenant to take charge of the precinct, and proceed immediately to the scene, with available plainclothesmen, when the Plan placed into operation requires his presence, i.e. Plans #2, #3 or #4.

(4) *Advise Dispatcher of Headquarters Location.* Upon arrival at scene, establish headquarters at the communications car, or at a nearby telephone, advising the dispatcher of his location.

(5) *Assume Command.* Assume personal charge at the scene until relieved by a higher ranking officer, when the plan in operation calls for his presence at the emergency scene.

(6) *Call for a Higher Plan.* If the equipment and personnel on hand are insufficient to control the situation, immediately request the dispatcher to place a higher numbered Plan into operation.

(7) *Utilize Surplus Personnel and Equipment.* Direct persons in charge of any equipment or personnel not immediately required at the scene to report either to a mobilization center, or to a temporary standby point in the immediate vicinity.

(8) *Assign Personnel.* Assign available superior officers, or if no superior officers are present, assign senior police officers, to specific groups, and instruct them with regard to their duties and assignment. Assign and instruct additional police officers as they arrive at the scene.

(9) *Disperse Loiterers.* Direct the immediate dispersal of any group, and issue instructions that no group is to be allowed to re-form, and that no individual is to be allowed to loiter in the immediate vicinity of the scene.

(10) *Arrest or Removal.* Direct the arrest and removal of persons who have refused to disperse, or who have, or who are committing, a violation of the law.

(11) *Assign a Lieutenant to Mobilization Center.* If arrests are being made in large numbers, assign a lieutenant to the mobilization center to handle the processing of the persons arrested.

(12) *Provide Patrol Wagons and Squadrols with Writing Pads.* Verify that the patrol wagon and squadrol drivers have sufficient blank pads to record the names and brief descriptions of persons arrested, the name, rank, badge number, the assignment of the arresting officer, and the place of occurrence and charge.

(13) *Assign Personnel to Mobilization Center.* Assign sufficient personnel to assist the lieutenant and the identification officer at the mobilization center, in processing the prisoners, and to act as guards.

(14) *Direct Removal of Sick or Injured Persons.* Direct the removal of any person taken sick or injured and, if large numbers of casualties are being sent to a hospital, assign a patrolman to the hospital to obtain the necessary information for police reports.

(15) *Re-route All Traffic.* Assign available policemen to the nearby intersections, with specific instructions to re-route all traffic, including pedestrians except bona-fide residents who have properly identified themselves.

(16) *Assign Personnel to Designated Posts.* When the emergency has been brought under control, and sufficient manpower is available, establish adequate foot and mobile patrols in the area, and fixed posts where needed. These patrols shall be established as soon as possible to prevent looting, damage to property, and personal injury, and they shall be maintained until the danger to life and property has passed.

(17) *Remove Cause of Emergency.* Whenever possible to lessen or eliminate tension in the area, immediately remove the cause to another area.

(18) *Order Nightsticks and Helmets for Riot Duty.* In cases of riot or other necessary circumstances issue to all police officers helmets and nightsticks available on the emergency trucks.

(19) *Assign Personnel to Rooftops During Rioting.* If rioting has broken out, or the circumstances require such action, assign available personnel to nearby roof-tops to discourage the throwing of articles down on the police. If at nighttime, make sure that the men are equipped with flashlights in good working order.

(20) *Cooperate with Other Commander.* Render full assistance and cooperation to the captain of the adjoining precinct upon request.

(21) *Survey Emergency Area.* As soon as conditions permit, direct that an accurate and complete survey be made of the entire affected area, to determine the location of premises that were damaged, or from which property is missing. The survey shall include the names of each person sustaining damage or loss, their addresses, business names, if any, and the nature of and estimated damage or loss. A complete report of the survey shall be prepared and forwarded to the Chief of Police.

(22) *Prepare Report of Emergency.* Prepare and submit a complete report listing all Departmental personnel, units and equipment at the scene, the name of the police officer who instituted the plan and the name of the police officer who cancelled the plan.

(23) *Ascertain that All Subordinates Understand the Plan.* Instruct all police officers and civilian employees of his command regarding the details of this plan, and he shall direct that all patrolmen record in their memorandum books a brief outline of their duties under this plan.

(24) *Comply With General Instructions.* Comply with the general instructions for all superior officers listed under 21:7.

21:11.3 Superior Officers On Desk Duty. Whenever a General Emergency Plan is placed into operation all superior officers, assigned to desk duty in the precinct in which the emergency exists, shall be responsible for the following action:

21:11.3-1 Dispatch Necessary Personnel and Equipment. Immediately dispatch or cause to be dispatched the wagon or squadrol and personnel specified in the Plan placed into operation, to the emergency scene. If the wagon or squadrol is on an assignment, which because of its serious nature will not permit its recall, obtain a wagon or squadrol from the nearest precinct and dispatch it to the emergency scene.

21:11.3-2 Furnish Writing Pads to Drivers. Furnish all wagon and squadrol drivers with sufficient blank pads to record:

(1) The names and identification of persons arrested

(2) The charge and place of occurrence

(3) The name, rank, badge number and assignment of the officer who turned the prisoner over to them.

21:11.3-3 Notify Captain of Precinct. Immediately notify the captain or acting captain.

21:11.3-4 Assign Personnel As Needed. Whenever Plan #3 or #4 is placed into operation, instruct all patrolmen making duty calls to report to the precinct immediately. If they are not immediately needed at the emergency scene, hold them in reserve until orders are received to send them to the emergency scene, or to return them to their posts.

21:11.3-5 Cooperate with Other Superiors. If an additional superior officer is assigned to the precinct to process the prisoners, or to assign available reserves, furnish him with whatever assistance is required.

21:11.3-6 General Responsibilities. Comply with the general instructions for all superior officers, listed under Section 21:7.

21:11.4 Superior Officers in Charge of Details at the Scene. Whenever a General Emergency Plan is placed into operation, each superior officer assigned in charge of work details at the emergency scene shall be responsible for the following action:

21:11.4-1 Deploy Personnel. Immediately upon being assigned to a sector, he shall proceed to that point with the patrolmen assigned to him and deploy the men to greatest effect, giving special attention to vulnerable and strategic points within his sector.

21:11.4-2 Instruct Personnel. He shall instruct the patrolmen specifically regarding their duties in accordance with the details of this Plan, particularly stressing that their action and language, if not proper, will be the subject of much criticism that will reflect unfavorably on the police force, resulting in poor public relations.

21:11.4-3 Direct Activities. He shall direct the activities of the men under his supervision towards the following objectives:

(1) The prevention of crowds from gathering.

(2) Where crowds have gathered prior to his arrival, he shall order their immediate dispersal.

(3) The prevention of individuals from loitering in the immediate vicinity of the emergency scene, and the prevention of the re-forming of crowds at the emergency scene.

(4) The removal, if possible, of the cause of the emergency to some other location, or to the precinct if this will lessen or eliminate tension in the area.

(5) The establishment of adequate patrols of the area until the danger has subsided.

21:11.4-4 Secure Vehicle and Equipment. If it is necessary to use the operators of police vehicles, he shall instruct them to properly lock the vehicles, and to secure all equipment against tampering. He shall not leave the vehicles unattended and shall assign one patrolman to guard the vehicles and other equipment.

21:11.4-5 Inform Officer in Charge as to Condition. He shall keep the officer in charge constantly informed as to conditions in his sector, and request additional assistance, if needed. He shall not wait until the situation is out of control before summoning assistance.

21:11.4-6 Supervise Activities. He shall keep the detail intact, and supervise its actions to insure compliance with the instructions contained in this Plan.

21:11.4-7 Prepare Assignment Sheet. He shall prepare a duplicate assignment sheet, as soon as possible, listing all persons at the scene under his immediate supervision, and send one (1) copy to the officer in charge, and one (1) to the precinct commander.

21:11.4-8 Release Surplus Personnel and Equipment. When orders have been received that the situation is under control, and the men under his supervision are no longer required at the scene, he shall check off the name of each man on the assignment sheet to be sure that he is accounted for, and then return with them to the precinct or mobilization point to await further orders.

21:11.4-9 Submit Report. At the termination of assignment, he shall submit a detailed report of his activities and observations while at the emergency scene, to the precinct commander.

21:11.4-10 Comply with General Instructions. He shall comply with the general instructions for all superior officers listed under section 21:7.

21:11.4-11 Acting Captain. If assigned as acting captain, or if he is the ranking officer to respond from the precinct, he shall be responsible for taking such action as is required of the captain at an emergency scene, listed under 21:11.2.

21:11.5 Superior Officers Assigned to Patrol Cars. Whenever a General Emergency Plan is placed into operation, superior officers assigned to patrol cars shall be responsible for the following action:

21:11.5-1 First Superior Officer at the Scene. If they are the first superior officers at the scene, they shall carry out the instructions listed for the captain or lieutenant at the scene.

21:11.5-2 General Responsibilities. They shall comply with the general instructions listed for all superior officers under section 21:7.

21:11.5-3 Assign Personnel. They shall promptly instruct and assign all personnel as they arrive at the scene.

21:11.6 Patrolman. Whenever a General Emergency Plan is placed into operation, all patrolmen sent to the scene of the emergency shall be responsible for taking the following action:

21:11.6-1 Control Crowds. They shall prevent crowds from gathering.

21:11.6-2 Disperse Crowds. Where crowds have gathered prior to their arrival, they shall disperse them immediately.

21:11.6-3 Prevent Loitering. They shall prevent loitering of individuals in the immediate vicinity of the emergency scene and prevent crowds from re-forming.

21:11.6-4 Remove Cause of Emergency. They shall remove, if possible, the cause of the emergency to some other location or precinct if this will lessen or eliminate the tension in the area.

21:11.6-5 Patrol Area. They shall patrol the area until the danger has subsided and perform all police duty to the best of their ability, without fear or favor, and remain calm, cool and collected at all times.

21:11.6-6 Enforce All Laws. They shall enforce all laws, regardless of race, color, creed, national origin or ancestry. They shall prevent crime, violence and breach of the peace. They shall protect life and property and arrest violators of the law. They shall act firmly, but courteously, whenever police action is necessary.

21:11.6-7 Use Caution in Action and Language. They shall be extremely careful that their action and language is proper, and that such action and language, does not encourage or initiate unlawful action on the part of others, or that will subject the police force to undue criticism.

21:11.6-8 Guard Against Unnecessary Conversation. They shall not engage in unnecessary conversation, nor make any comments or give opinions concerning the cause of the emergency.

21:11.6-9 Safeguard Vehicles and Equipment. When assigned to a police vehicle, they shall make every effort to safeguard the vehicle and its equipment from damage or theft. If police action requires that the vehicle shall be left unattended, they shall securely lock it and turn off the transmitter.

21:11.6-10 Ask for Clarification. Upon receiving an order from a superior officer which is not clear, they shall immediately ask that superior officer to clarify the order.

21:11.6-11 Obey Superior Officer. They shall obey the orders of superior officers at an emergency scene, regardless of their regular assignment, until such order is countermanded by an officer of higher rank. However, conditions may require a superior officer to countermand an order given by one of equal rank. When this occurs the patrolman shall bring to the attention of said superior officer the previous order, and then be guided by the decision of the second superior officer.

21:11.6-12 Notify Superior Officer Before Leaving Assignment. They shall obtain permission from the superior officer in charge of their group before leaving their assignment. If this is impracticable, they shall advise this superior officer of their action immediately upon returning to their assignment.

21:11.6-13 Record Arrest in Memorandum Book. If possible, whenever an arrest is made, they shall record in their memorandum books an adequate description of their prisoner so that they will be able to identify him in court. Before the prisoner is arraigned in court, they shall obtain a copy of the prisoner's photograph, if available, so that it can be used to refresh their memory.

21:11.6-14 Provide Driver of Wagon or Squadrol with Identification. Whenever an arrest is made and prisoners are turned over to a wagon or squadrol driver, the officers shall furnish the driver with their name, rank, badge number, assignment, place of occurrence and charge.

21:11.6-15 Cooperate with All Personnel. They shall extend the fullest cooperation to all other police officers and civilian employees at the scene at all times.

21:11.7 Emergency Bureau Captain. Whenever a General Emergency Plan is placed into operation, the Captain in charge of the Emergency Bureau shall:

21:11.7-1 Verify Compliance. Verify that the equipment and personnel of his command, specified in the Plan placed into operation, have been dispatched to the emergency scene.

21:11.7-2 Keep Informed of Action Taken. Keep informed of the action being taken to restore law and order.

21:11.7-3 Respond to Emergency Scene. If Plans #2, (see chart), #3, or #4 are placed into operation, proceed immediately to the scene and take personal charge of the activities of all personnel under his command.

21:11.7-4 Advise Dispatcher of Headquarters Location. Establish headquarters at the emergency truck, or at a nearby telephone, and notify the dispatcher of his location.

21:11.7-5 Cooperate with Others at the Scene. Consult and cooperate with the commanding officers of other units at the scene to bring the situation under control.

21:11.7-6 Assign Personnel. Assign and instruct personnel under his command in the establishment of street barricades, police lines, and any other police emergency function required by the circumstances.

21:11.7-7 Assume Command If Ranking Officer. If a higher ranking officer is not at the scene, he is responsible for carrying out the instructions contained in this plan until relieved by a precinct commander or by an officer of higher rank.

21:11.7-8 General Responsibilities. Comply with the general instructions for all superior officers listed under 21:7.

21:11.8 Emergency—Superior Officers. Whenever a General Emergency Plan is placed into operation, superior officers assigned to the Emergency Bureau shall:

21:11.8-1 General Responsibilities. Comply with the general instructions for superior officers listed under 21:7.

21:11.8-2 Desk Lieutenant Duties. Comply with the instructions for desk lieutenants listed under 21:11.3 where applicable.

21:11.8-3 First Aid Station. Establish a first aid station, if necessary.

21:11.8-4 Assign Personnel. Assign, direct and instruct the patrolmen under their supervision in the establishment of street barricades, police lines, and any other police emergency function required by the circumstances.

21:11.8-5 Assume Command If Ranking Officer. If the ranking officer at the scene, assume command until relieved by the captain of the precinct, or by an officer of higher rank, and be responsible for carrying out the instructions contained in this Plan. for the officer in charge of the emergency scene.

21:11.9 Emergency — Patrolmen. Whenever a General Emergency Plan is placed into operation, patrolmen assigned to the Emergency Plan shall:

21:11.9-1 Comply with General Instructions. Comply with the general instructions for patrolmen contained in this plan, listed under 21:11.4-6.

21:11.9-2 Cooperate with Others at the Scene. Cooperate with all police personnel to bring the situation under control as quickly as possible.

21:11.9-3 Direct Efforts as Required by Circumstances. Direct efforts towards the establishing of street barricades, police lines, and any other police emergency function required by the circumstances.

21:11.10 Patrolmen Assigned to Patrol Cars. Whenever a General Emergency Plan is placed into operation, all patrolmen assigned to patrol cars shall be responsible for the following action:

21:11.10-1 Notifying Dispatcher of Availability. When performing any other police assignment the patrolman upon being informed that a General Emergency Plan is in operation, and receiving an assignment in connection therewith, shall:

(1) Refer the assignment to the precinct for police action, if he can do so, and proceed to the emergency assignment immediately.

(2) Advise the dispatcher, that his present assignment will not permit him to leave and request him to dispatch another car to the emergency scene.

(3) If the assignment can be handled by one police officer, the senior officer shall remain with the assignment, and the other officer shall proceed immediately to the emergency assignment and advise the dispatcher that he is alone in the car.

21:11.10-2 First Car at the Scene. The first car to arrive at the emergency scene shall be designated as the communications car. The senior officer in the car shall assume command, and shall:

(1) Be responsible for all proper police action until relieved by a superior officer.

(2) Remain close enough to the radio car so that contact can be maintained with the dispatcher, to keep him informed, and to receive instructions.

(3) Assign and instruct patrolmen in accordance with the details of this Plan, and furnish them all

assistance possible.

(4) Keep a list of all vehicles responding to the emergency scene.

(5) Be responsible for taking any action required of a superior officer or patrolman whenever necessary.

21:12 SPECIFIC RESPONSIBILITIES AND DUTIES OF THE TRAFFIC DIVISION

21:12.1 Commanding Officer of the Traffic Division. Whenever a General Emergency Plan is placed into operation, the Commanding Officer of the Traffic Division shall:

21:12.1-1 Verify Compliance. Verify that the equipment and personnel of his Command, specified in the Plan placed into operation, have been dispatched to the emergency scene.

21:12.1-2 Keep Informed of Action Taken. Keep informed of the action being taken to restore or maintain law and order.

21:12.1-3 Respond Immediately. If (see chart), Plan #3, or #4 is placed into operation, immediately proceed to the emergency scene, and take personal charge of the activities of the men of the Traffic Division.

21:12.1-4 Advise Dispatcher of Headquarters Location. Establish headquarters at a radio-equipped car of his Command, or at a nearby telephone and advise the dispatcher of his location.

21:12.1-5 Cooperate with Others. Consult and cooperate with other divisional commanding officers at the emergency scene, to bring the situation under control.

21:12.1-6 Comply with General Instructions. Comply with the general instructions for all superior officers listed under 21:7.

21:12.1-7 Assume Command If Ranking Officer. When he is the ranking officer at the scene, he shall assume command of overall operations, and shall relinquish this command only on order from a higher ranking superior officer of the Patrol Division or from the Chief of Police.

21:12.2 Traffic Division — Superior Officers. Whenever a General Emergency Plan is placed into operation, superior officers assigned to the Traffic

Division shall be responsible for the following action. They shall:

21:12.2-1 Comply With General Instructions. Comply with the general instructions for superior officers listed under 21:7.

21:12.2-2 Comply with Desk Lieutenant Instructions. Comply with the instructions for desk lieutenants listed under 21:11.3 where applicable.

21:12.2-3 Assign Personnel. Assign, direct and instruct the patrolmen under his supervision in the rerouting of traffic, control of traffic, and exclude unauthorized persons or vehicles from the emergency scene.

21:12.2-4 Assume Command If Ranking Officer. If the ranking officer at the emergency scene, assume command and be responsible for carrying out the instructions contained in the Plan, until relieved by the captain of the precinct, or by an officer of higher rank.

21:12.3 Traffic Division — Patrolmen. Whenever a General Emergency Plan is placed into operation, patrolmen assigned to the Traffic Division shall:

21:12.3-1 Comply with General Instructions. Comply with the general instructions for patrolmen contained in this Plan under 21:11.6.

21:12.3-2 Cooperate with Others. Cooperate with all personnel of the police force to bring the situation under control as quickly as possible.

21:12.3-3 Re-route Traffic. In addition to complying with the instructions for patrolmen listed under 21:11.6, direct his efforts towards the control and re-routing of traffic, and the exclusion of unauthorized persons and vehicles from the emergency scene, upon receiving such instructions from a superior officer.

21:13 BUREAU OF TRAFFIC AND SIGNALS

Whenever a General Emergency Plan is placed into operation, the Commanding Officer of the Traffic Division or the superior officer in charge at the scene shall cause the superior officer or supervisory official in charge of the Bureau of Traffic and Signals to be notified of the specific needs, when the Plan placed into operation calls for the presence of equipment from that unit, and request that the superior officer or supervisor official comply with the following:

21:13.1 Respond with Sufficient Equipment. Pro-

ceed to the scene with the specified number of trucks and sufficient "no parking" signs and street barricades.

21:13.2 Instruct Personnel to Report to Traffic Division Commanding Officer. Instruct the drivers and helpers on such trucks to report to the Commanding Officer of the Traffic Division or to the superior officer in charge at the scene and under his direction assist in erecting street barricades, and in the posting of "no parking" signs.

21:13.3 Instruct Personnel to Report to Officer In Charge of Emergency Scene. Instruct the drivers of such trucks to comply with any instructions given by the officer in charge at the emergency scene, with regard to the use of the trucks for obtaining additional supplies, or for the transportation of police officers.

21:14 SPECIFIC FUNCTIONS AND DUTIES OF THE DETECTIVE DIVISION

21:14.1 Commanding Officer of the Detective Division. Whenever a General Emergency Plan is placed into operation, the Commanding Officer of the Detective Division shall:

21:14.1-1 Verify Compliance. Verify that the equipment and personnel of his command specified in the Plan placed into operation have been dispatched to the emergency scene.

21:14.1-2 Keep Informed of Action Taken. Keep informed of the action being taken to restore or maintain law and order.

21:14.1-3 Respond Immediately to the Scene. If Plan (see chart), #3, or #4 is placed into operation, proceed immediately to the scene of the emergency and take personal charge of the activities of the detectives assigned to his command.

21:14.1-4 Consult with Other Commands. Consult and cooperate with the commanding officers of other units at the emergency scene to bring the situation under control.

21:14.1-5 Advise Dispatcher of Headquarters Location. Establish headquarters at a radio-equipped Detective Division car, or at a nearby telephone, and advise the dispatcher of his location.

21:14.1-6 Establish Temporary Morgue. If necessary, establish a temporary morgue with the assistance and advice of the Chief Medical Examiner or his assistant.

21:14.1-7 Identify Ringleader. Assign, direct and instruct all personnel of his command in the investigation of the cause of the emergency; to identify and apprehend the ringleaders; to ascertain plans for the continuation of the disorder; to investigate any criminal acts resulting from the emergency; and to direct such other investigative tasks as may be required by the existing conditions.

21:14.1-8 General Responsibilities. Comply with the general instructions for all superior officers, listed under 21:7.

21:14.2 Detective Division — Superior Officers. Whenever a General Emergency Plan is placed into operation, superior officers assigned to the Detective Division shall:

21:14.2-1 Comply with General Instructions. Comply with the general instructions for superior officers listed under 21:7 of this Plan.

21:14.2-2 Comply with Desk Lieutenant Instructions. Comply with the instructions for desk lieutenants listed under 21:11.3, where applicable.

21:14.2-3 Advise Commander of the Youth Aid Bureau to Return to the Scene. If Plan #3 or #4 is placed into operation advise the Commanding Officer in charge of the Youth Aid Bureau to respond to the scene with all available personnel to handle any arrests of juveniles, or any other assignment.

21:14.2-4 Assign and Direct Subordinates. Assign, direct and instruct all personnel of their command in the investigation of the cause of the emergency; to identify and apprehend the ringleaders; to ascertain plans for the continuation of the disorder; to investigate any criminal acts resulting from the emergency; and to direct such other investigative tasks as may be required by the existing conditions.

21:14.3 Detective Division — Detectives. Whenever a General Emergency Plan is placed into operation, detectives assigned to the Detective Division shall:

21:14.3-1 Determine Cause. Investigate to determine the cause of the emergency.

21:14.3-2 Identify Ringleader. Identify and apprehend the ringleader and any other person who has committed criminal acts, obtaining warrants where necessary.

21:14.3-3 Ascertain the Plans of Troublemakers. Ascertain plans, if any, for the continuation of the disorder causing the emergency.

21:14.3-4 Interrogate Prisoners. Interrogate prisoners thoroughly so that adequate evidence of their criminal acts may be presented to the court, and for the purpose of developing information regarding other persons involved in criminal acts.

21:14.3-5 Interview Victims and Witnesses. Interview victims, witnesses or any other person who may have valuable information, and thoroughly investigate any statements made by such persons.

21:14.3-6 Identify and Preserve Evidence. Obtain, identify and properly preserve all evidence necessary for the proper presentation of the case in court, keeping in mind that evidence consists of actions and words as well as physical evidence.

21:14.3-7 Investigate Complaints. Investigate all complaints of theft of property, making adequate notes describing the property in detail, and the identity of the owner. Obtain descriptions of all suspects where possible.

21:14.3-8 Search the Scene for Evidence. Conduct a thorough and adequate search at the scene of any theft for fingerprints or other evidence that will identify the perpetrator.

21:14.3-9 Advise Owners of Recovered Property. Advise owners of stolen property whenever such property is recovered by the police.

21:14.3-10 Report Serious Crimes or Unusual Occurrences. Report promptly to their superior officer, any pertinent information regarding serious crimes, unusual occurrences, or any changes in the conditions within the emergency area.

21:14.3-11 Cooperate with Others. Cooperate in every way with members of the Police Department and assist them in bringing the situation under control.

21:14.3-12 Submit Complete Reports. Submit complete and adequate reports of all investigations conducted in connected with the emergency.

21:15 SPECIFIC FUNCTIONS AND DUTIES OF THE INVESTIGATION DIVISION

21:15.1 Commanding Officer of the Investigation Division. Whenever a General Emergency Plan is placed into operation, the Commanding Officer of the Investigation Division shall be responsible for the following action. He shall:

21:15.1-1 Respond Immediately to the Scene. If Plans (see chart), #3 or #4 is placed into operation, proceed immediately to the emergency scene and take personal charge of the activities of the men of his command.

21:15.1-2 Verify Compliance. Verify that the equipment and personnel of his command specified in the Plan placed into operation have been dispatched to the emergency scene.

21:15.1-3 Keep Informed of Action Taken. Keep informed of the action being taken to restore or maintain law and order.

21:15.1-4 Advise Dispatcher of Headquarters Location. Establish headquarters at a radio-equipped car of the Investigation Division, or at a nearby telephone and notify the dispatcher of his location.

21:15.1-5 Consult and Cooperate with Others. Consult and cooperate with the commanding officers of other units at the emergency scene to bring the situation under control.

21:15.1-6 Assign Personnel. Assign, direct, and instruct all personnel of his command in the following action, when conditions at the emergency scene require that such action be taken, and when orders to that effect have been received from the officer in charge at the emergency scene.

(1) Close all taverns and liquor stores.

(2) Close all places where weapons and ammunition are stored or kept for sale, and insure that proper safeguards are taken to prevent entry, and looting of such places.

(3) Advise all business places where narcotic drugs are stored so that they secure their supplies of narcotics, and suggest that they suspend operations temporarily.

(4) Advise that other business places in the area suspend operations temporarily, until conditions return to normal.

(5) Apprehend all known drug addicts found in the area.

21:15.2 Investigation Division—Superior Officers. Whenever a General Emergency Plan is placed into operation, superior officers assigned to the Investigation Division shall:

21:15.2-1 Comply with General Instructions. Comply with the general instructions for superior officers listed under 21:7 of this Plan.

21:15.2-2 Desk Lieutenant Duties. Comply with the instructions for desk lieutenant listed under 21:11.3 of this Plan, where applicable.

21:15.2-3 Assignment of Personnel. Assign, direct and instruct all personnel of their command in the activities listed under the duties of the Commanding Officer of the Bureau of Investigation.

21:15.3 Investigation Division—Detectives. Whenever a General Emergency Plan is placed into operation, detectives assigned to the Investigation Division shall be responsible for the following action:

21:15.3-1 Respond Immediately to Emergency Scene. If Plan #3 or #4 is placed into operation, all men who are not at headquarters when the emergency is brought to their attention, shall immediately respond to the scene, reporting to the superior officer of their command, or the officer in charge in the absence of a superior officer of their command.

21:15.3-2 Close Designated Business Houses. Upon being furnished with a list of business houses that are to be closed, they shall immediately proceed to such places and advise the owners to close temporarily until the situation has been brought under control.

21:15.3-3 Safeguard Designated Business Houses. In places where weapons, ammunition, and narcotics are stored or kept for sale, insure that adequate safeguards have been established to prevent entry and looting.

21:15.3-4 Advise Officials in Charge of Public Utility Installations. Advise the official in charge of any public utility installation of the emergency and see that an adequate guard is established.

21:15.3-5 Watch Known Drug Addicts in the Area. Keep a close watch for all known drug addicts and if found in the emergency area, take them into custody.

21:15.3-6 Be Alert for Agitators. Keep a close watch for persons agitating or inciting persons to riot, and arrest all such persons.

21:15.3-7 Prevent Unlawful Use of Fire Alarm Boxes. Keep a close watch on fire alarm boxes, and arrest anyone tampering unlawfully with such boxes.

21:15.3-8 Prevent Loitering. Apprehend all persons loitering under the influence of liquor at the emergency scene.

21:15.3-9 Advise Business Houses When to Resume Business. When the emergency has been brought under control, advise all business houses that were requested to close, that business can be resumed.

21:15.3-10 Advise Commanding Officer of Noncompliance by Licensed Premises. If any business house licensed by the city refuses or fails to suspend business when so requested, advise their commanding officer, and submit a detailed report covering the circumstances.

21:16 SPECIFIC RESPONSIBILITIES OF ADMINISTRATIVE DIVISION

21:16.1 Commanding Officer of Administrative Division. Whenever a General Emergency Plan is placed into operation, the Commanding Officer of Administrative Division shall be responsible for the following action:

21:16.1-1 Respond to Emergency Scene. If Plan (see chart), #3 or #4, is placed into operation, immediately proceed to the scene and take personal charge of the activities of the men assigned to his command.

21:16.1-2 Verify Compliance. Verify that the equipment and personnel of his command, specified in the Plan placed into operation, have been dispatched to the emergency scene.

21:16.1-3 Keep Informed of Action Taken. Keep informed of the action being taken to restore and maintain law and order.

21:16.1-4 Advise Dispatcher of Headquarters Location. Establish headquarters at a radio-equipped car of his command, or at a nearby telephone and advise the dispatcher of his location.

21:16.1-5 Consult and Cooperate with Others. Consult and cooperate with other divisional commanding officers at the emergency scene, to bring the situation under control.

21:16.1-6 Assign Personnel. Assign, direct and instruct the personnel of his command, when conditions at the emergency scene require the services of photographers and identification officers.

21:16.1-7 General Instructions. Comply with the general instructions for superior officers listed under 21:7 of this Plan.

21:16.2 Dispatchers. Whenever a General Emergency Plan is placed into operation, the dispatcher shall:

21:16.2-1 Dispatch Designated Cars Immediately. Upon receipt of request for any one of the four (4) Emergency Plans, immediately dispatch the designated cars to the scene.

21:16.2-2 Advise Telephone Operator of Number of Emergency Plan in Operation. Inform the telephone operators of the number of the Emergency Plan placed into operation.

21:16.2-3 Keep Airways Clear. Instruct personnel assigned to all cars to remain off the air unless their message is urgent, and to stand by for emergency assignment.

21:16.2-4 Maintain Constant Contact with Communications Car. Maintain constant contact with the communications car at the emergency scene.

21:16.2-5 Advise All at Scene of Location of Communications Car. Advise personnel assigned to all cars dispatched to the scene of the exact location of the *communications car.*

21:16.3 Telephone Operators. Whenever a General Emergency Plan is placed into operation, the telephone operators shall:

21:16.3-1 Make Notifications. Upon receipt of signal from dispatcher that a General Emergency Plan is in operation, immediately notify the man in charge at the various bureaus or units of the Police Department, designated in the Plan placed into operation.

21:16.3-2 Maintain List of Notifications Required. Keep available at all times a list of the notifications required for each Plan.

21:16.3-3 Alert All Commands by Teletype. Alert all commands by teletype that an emergency plan is in operation.

21:16.4 Civil Defense and Auxiliary Police. All Civil Defense and Auxiliary Police responding to the emergency shall be directed to report to the command post at the communications car.

21:17 GENERAL INSTRUCTIONS FOR ALL POLICE OFFICERS AND CIVILIAN EMPLOYEES OF THE POLICE DEPARTMENT

21:17.1 Each Police Officer and Civilian Employee to Keep His Commanding Officer Duly Notified Regarding the Following Information:

(1) Name, rank, badge number, address, floor or apartment number.

(2) Telephone number at which he can be reached in an emergency.

(3) Report any change of address at least twelve (12) hours prior to such change.

(The foregoing are all in compliance with *Rule and Regulation* 7:18.2)

21:17.2 Off Duty Personnel. All police officers who who may be off duty shall report to the nearest precinct station whenever Plan #3, or Plan #4 is placed into operation.

21.17.2-1 Report to Command Post at Scene. All off-duty personnel responding to the emergency shall be directed to report to the command post at the communications car where their presence will be recorded in the log by the superior officer in charge.

21:17.2-2 Display Badge on Outermost Garment. All off-duty personnel shall display their badge on their outermost garment.

21:17.2-3 Assign Off-duty Personnel. Assignments of off-duty personnel shall be based on the requirements of the emergency and the experience and qualifications of the police officer.

21:17.3 Air Raid Alert. All police officers shall take the following action in the event of an actual air raid alert, or an actual enemy bomb attack in time of war:

21:17.3-1 Air Raid Alert—Off Duty.

(1) Display badge on outermost garment and proceed to the nearest public thoroughfare in the vicinity of his location.

(2) Direct all moving vehicles, except emergency vehicles, to park at the curb or in a place that will allow free movement of emergency vehicles.

(3) Direct the operators of such vehicles, and all other persons in the vicinity to seek shelter.

(4) Take shelter himself, as soon as all persons are safely in shelters.

(5) If no *actual attack* has taken place, upon the all clear signal being sounded, *and as soon as conditions in the immediate area have returned to normal,* report in person to the nearest precinct station.

21:17.3-2 Air Raid Alert—On Duty.

(1) Uniformed police officers same as (2), (3), and (4) above.

(2) Detectives same as (1), (2), (3), and (4) above.

(3) If no actual attack has taken place, *resume regular duty assignment,* as soon as conditions return to normal or on order of a superior officer.

21:17.3-3 Actual Bomb-Attack—On Duty.

(1) When no radiation is detected *five minutes after bomb attack, uniformed officers* shall resume their regular duty assignments, performing all necessary police duties to restore and maintain law and order, to prevent panic and looting, and to aid casuals.

(2) Five minutes after bomb attack, all detectives shall attempt to contact their offices for instructions. If this is not possible, they shall report to the nearest precinct station that it is possible to reach, and comply with any instructions issued by the officer in charge of the precinct station.

21:17.3-4 Actual Bomb Attack—Off Duty.

(1) When no radiation is detected *five minutes after bomb attack,* police officers shall place their badges on their outermost garment and perform all necessary police duties to restore and maintain law and order, to prevent panic and looting, and to aid casuals, in the immediate vicinity of their location.

(2) As soon as conditions will permit, police officers shall telephone their command for instructions. If telephone communication is impossible, they shall proceed to the nearest precinct station that it is possible to reach.

21:18 NEGLECT OF DUTY

A violation of any section of the General Emergency Plan shall be deemed neglect of duty, and shall be punishable as provided under 6:6 of the *Police Manual of Rules and Regulations.*

CHAPTER III

THE BURBANK UNUSUAL OCCURRENCE CONTROL PLAN

THE Police Department of Burbank, California, has developed in considerable depth a police emergency plan — *UNUSUAL OCCURRENCE CONTROL MANUAL*. It stood the test in 1971 when an earthquake struck Burbank and the surrounding area, resulting in severe damage to many parts of the city. Chief Loranger reports that loss by looting was held to a minimum and traffic continued to move almost without interruption even though electric power for traffic signal operation was not available for more than two hours. The *MANUAL* is, in effect, the Law Enforcement Annex to the Emergency Operations Plan for the City of Burbank, approved in 1970 by both state and federal Civil Defense agencies.

The *UNUSUAL OCCURRENCE CONTROL MANUAL,* presented at the end of this chapter, is an excellent example of the steps that can and should be taken by every police department in organizing its resources and procedures to meet the emergency or disaster situation. It presents in detail police department policy, department functions, command responsibilities and the tactical, operational and reporting procedures for unusual occurrence control. The plan became effective on May 1, 1965. It is adaptable to any size organization, including the smaller police departments with a personnel strength from one to seventy-five officers. It supplements the IACP *GENERAL EMERGENCY PLAN* with a detailed description of emergency organization, procedures and actions that must be taken at a time that calls for responses beyond the capability of the day-to-day organizational posture.

Presented in readable language, the *MANUAL* provides the answers to the following key questions that would confront any chief of police and his commanding officers as they undertake the preparation of a police emergency plan:

What are the first steps in the preparation of a police emergency or disaster plan? What are the guidelines?

What is an emergency?

What are the components of an organization chart for emergency operations? How does it differ from the organization chart for normal day-to-day police operations?

What are the specific objectives of a police emergency plan?

What is the chain of command in an emergency or disaster situation?

What is the *emergency control center?* How does it differ from the *field command post?*

What are the functions of the *emergency control center?*

Where is the *emergency control center* located? How is it staffed?

Who determines when the police emergency plan is to be activated?

What are the basic functions of a police department in an emergency or disaster situation?

Why does the emergency plan need to be flexible?

What are the circumstances that would indicate activation of the emergency plan?

Who is the field commander, and what are his duties?

In an emergency situation, what are the functions of the uniform division? The investigation division? The services division?

What are the functions of the traffic bureau?

What is *fanout procedure?* The *disaster file?*

What is the *perimeter of control?*

Where is the *medical post* located?

How is the *medical post* staffed, and what are its functions?

What are emergency or disaster communications requirements?

Where is the *missing person post* located; how is it staffed, and what are its functions?

Where is the *morgue post* located; how is it staffed, and what are its functions?

What is the formula for determining minimum personnel needs in the involved area?

What is the evacuation procedure? What are the duties of the *evacuation detail?*

What are the duties of personnel at *fixed posts?* At *mobile posts?*

What is the *mass care center,* and by whom is it activated?

What is the *animal shelter?*

What are the functions of Civil Defense?

What is the nature of emergency equipment that should be provided for, and who is in control?

What is the responsibility of the sheriff's department?

When is activation of the militia indicated, and how is this done?

What is the *posse comitatus,* and what is its duties?

What are the duties of the auxiliary police?

What is the procedure with an unlawful or riotous assembly?

What record and reporting forms should be provided for in advance of an emergency or disaster situation?

Burbank Police Department
GENERAL ORDER

PROPOSED G.O. No. 101
Eff: May 1, 1965

UNUSUAL OCCURRENCE CONTROL

I.   Unusual Occurrence, Defined
II. Policy
III. Facilities
IV. Procedure

I.   *Unsual Occurrence, Defined*

An unscheduled, physical event, involving actual or potential personal injury or property damage arising from fire, flood, storm, earthquake, landslide, or other natural or man-caused incident, requiring police action, but in the control of which the police are not the primary agent.

II. *Policy*

It is the policy of the Burbank Police Department to encourage organized preparedness by establishing guide lines for the control of unusual occurrences.

III. *Facilities*

A system of internal communication has been devised utilizing the following:

A. An Unusual Occurrence Manual (ready reference for all). The manual contains information concerning department functions, command responsibilities, and the tactical, operational, and reporting procedures for unusual occurrence control.

B. A Disaster File (available 24-hours in the Record Bureau). Contains an alphabetical listing of available equipment; the names of persons/ agencies through whom/which equipment may be obtained; names and assignments of all department personnel.

IV. *Procedure*

The Watch Commander, upon receipt of verified information that an unusual occurrence of such proportion the facilities available to one Watch are inadequate to establish control and which requires temporary modification of the department organization, shall activate the procedures outlined in the Unusual Occurrence Control Manual.

REX R. ANDREWS
Chief of Police

TABLE OF CONTENTS

INDEX

INTRODUCTION

ORGANIZATION CHART — UNUSUAL OCCURRENCE

UNUSUAL OCCURRENCE CONTROL

100 Definitions
110 Unusual Occurrence, defined
120 Emergency Control Center, defined
130 Area, defined
140 Key Personnel, defined
150 Mass Care Center, defined
160 Perimeter of Control, defined
170 Post, defined

180 Transportation Facility, defined
190 Transportation Zone, defined

200 Functions
210 Department
215 Department Commander
220 Administrative Staff
230 Emergency Control Center
240 Uniform Division
250 Investigation Division
260 Services Division
270 Communications Department

300 Organization and Command
310 Modification of Organization
315 Department Commander — Succession of Command
320 Organization — Minor Unusual Occurrence
330 Organization for Line Control — Serious or Major Unusual Occurrence
340 Emergency Control Center

400 Procedure
410 Tactical Procedure
420 Operational Procedure
430 Reporting Procedure
440 Directory
450 References

ANNEX

INDEX

	Page
INTRODUCTION	iii
ORGANIZATION CHART — UNUSUAL OCCURRENCE	iiii
DEFINITIONS	1

FUNCTIONS
1. Department   4
2. Department Commander
3. Administrative Staff
4. Emergency Control Center
5. Uniform Division

Page

    a. Field Commander   5
  6. Investigation Division
  7. Services Division
  8. Communications Department

ORGANIZATION AND COMMAND
  1. Modification of Organization   6
  2. Department Commander — Succession
     of Command
  3. Organization — Minor Unusual Occurrence
  4. Organization for Line Control — Serious
     or Major Unusual Occurrence
    a. Delegation   7
    b. Field Commander
    c. Command for Line Control
    d. Responsibility of Senior Officer
      to Assume Field Command
    e. Field Command Authority and
      Responsibility   8
    f. Field Command Priority
    g. Field Command Supervision of
      Requisitioned Personnel
    h. Functional Supervision of Involved
      Area
    i. Unity of Command
    j. Assumption of Command
    k. Assumption of Command by Officer of
      Equal or Junior Rank
    l. Appearance or Presence of Ranking
      Senior Officer   9
    m. Countermanding of Orders

  5. Emergency Control Center
    a. Location   9
    b. Commander
    c. Personnel

TACTICAL PROCEDURE
  1. Headquarters
    a. Patrol Bureau   10
      1) Desk Officer
      2) Watch Commander   11
    b. Traffic Bureau
    c. Record Bureau   12

Page

      1) Sworn Personnel
      2) Clerical Personnel
      3) Automotive Serviceman
    d. Training Bureau
    e. Detective Bureau
    f. Juvenile Bureau
    g. Vice Control Bureau
  2. Field
    a. Patrol Bureau   13
      1) First Officer
      2) Second Officer
      3) First Supervisor
      4) Field Commander
      5) Investigator   14
      6) Non-Assigned Personnel
    b. Traffic Bureau
    c. Record Bureau   15
      1) Sworn Personnel
      2) Clerical Personnel
    d. Detective Bureau
    e. Juvenile Bureau

OPERATIONAL PROCEDURE
  1. Fan-Out Procedure   16
    a. Disaster File
    b. Implementation
    c. Key Personnel
    d. Notification Schedule
  2. Command Post   20
  3. Medical Post   22
  4. Missing Person Post   25
  5. Morgue Post   27
  6. Evaluation of Extent of Involved Area   30
  7. Isolation of Unusual Occurrence   33
  8. Evacuation of Involved Area   39
  9. Special Notifications   42
    a. Communications
    b. Medical   43
    c. Supplies   44
    d. Coroner   45
    e. Animal Shelter
    f. Mass Care Center
    g. Transportation   46
    h. Public Works   47

Page

i. Utilities
j. Aircraft Incident   48
    1) Civilian
    2) Military
k. Earthquake
l. Explosion   49
m. Flood
n. Freeway
o. Landslide
p. Law Enforcement Agencies
    1) F.B.I.
    2) L.A.P.D.
    3) L.A.S.O.
q. Nuclear Incident   50
    1) Commercial Device
    2) Military Device
r. Train Accident

REPORTING PROCEDURE
  1. Headquarters   51
  2. Field   52

DIRECTORY   54

REFERENCES   57

REPORTS
   1. Unusual Occurrence Command Assignment   Annex 1
   2. Unusual Occurrence Detail Assignment   Annex 2
   3. Mobilization Roster   Annex 3
   4. Unusual Occurrence Hazard Report   Annex 4
   5. Special Notification Report   Annex 5
   6. Special Notification Reference   Annex 5A
   7. Citizen Contact Report   Annex 6
   8. Mass Care Center Report   Annex 7
   9. General Case Report (ML 673)   Annex 8
  10. Medical Assistance Report   Annex 9
  11. Medical Supply Inventory Control   Annex 10
  12. Missing Person Report (ML 218)   Annex 11
  13. Death Report Form (ML 49)   Annex 12
  14. Identification Tag Report   Annex 13
  15. Equipment Inventory Control   Annex 14
CHECK SHEET   Annex A
ACTIVITY DIAGRAM   Annex B

INTRODUCTION

This plan has been designed to serve as a guide in achieving control of unusual occurrences and in restoring such situations to normal as rapidly and efficiently as possible.

Public awareness of the police responsibility is especially accented by unscheduled emergency incidents, since other agencies, as a rule, cannot operate effectively until the police have successfully performed their emergency duties.

It should be understood that the most important function of the police at disaster type occurrences is to *assist and expedite* emergency operations of agencies whose prime duties lie in directly combating the cause or effect of the occurrence.

In this respect, the police responsibility and functions are little different from normal day-to-day handling of emergency situations of lesser scope. The control methodology is the same; the application, however, must be expanded in proportion to the magnitude and scope of the problem.

Embracing the theory that no two occurrences will be similar in nature, scope, and magnitude, it is necessary for such a plan to be basic, flexible in nature, and subject to modification as the need arises.

This plan encourages organized preparedness by establishing *command* responsibility, and the tactical, operational, and reporting procedures for unusual occurrence control.

DEFINITIONS   100

Unusual Occurrence   110
    An unscheduled physical event involving actual or potential personal injury or property damage arising from fire, flood, storm, earthquake, landslide, wreck, or other natural or man-caused incident requiring police action, but in the control of which the police are not the primary agent.

Minor Unusual Occurrence   110.05
    An unusual occurrence which could be handled by the facilities of one Watch with the assistance normally available from other bureaus.

Burbank Police Department

ORGANIZATION CHART - UNUSUAL OCCURRENCE

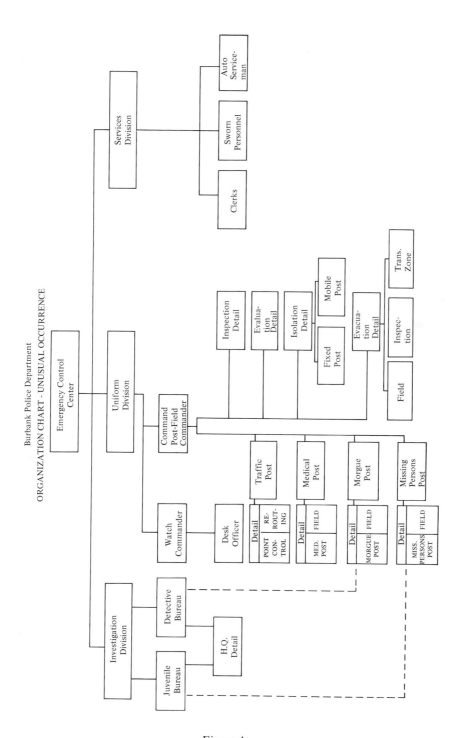

Figure 1.

Serious Unusual Occurrence   110.10

An unusual occurrence of such proportion that the facilities available to one Watch are inadequate to establish control and which requires temporary modification of the department organization.

Major Unusual Occurrence   110.15

An unusual occurrence which threatens the health and safety of the city to such an extent that, in the opinion of the Chief of Police or the officer acting in his stead, it is necessary to activate the entire department for control purpose.

Emergency Control Center   120

The department command post for serious or major unusual occurrence control.

Area   130

A physical location at which the unusual occurrence exists.

Closed Area   130.05

An area where ingress/egress to vehicular and/or pedestrian traffic is restricted on three or more sides.

Semi-Closed Area   130.10

An area where ingress/egress to vehicular and/or pedestrian traffic is restricted on parallel sides.

Semi-Open Area   130.15

An area where ingress/egress to vehicular and/or pedestrian traffic is restricted on one side or adjacent sides.

Open Area   130.20

An area where ingress/egress to vehicular and/or pedestrian traffic is unrestricted.

Involved Area   130.25

The area enclosing in one rectangle ALL unusual occurrence scenes.

Key Personnel   140

Department employees responsible for mobilizing other employees.

Mass Care Center   150
A facility which furnishes food, clothing, and shelter.

Perimeter of Control   160
The distance which will effectively protect the integrity of the scene and expedite emergency operations.

Post   170
A field location established to command, direct, and coordinate particular activity.

Command Post   170.05
A post established by the Field Commander to direct emergency operations at unusual occurrence scenes.

Fixed Post   170.10
A selected post location.

Medical Post   170.15
A post established by the Field Commander to direct emergency medical assistance and routing of injured/ dead.

Missing Person Post   170.20
A post established by the Juvenile Bureau to receive, record, and investigate reports of persons reported missing.

Mobile Post   170.25
A roving post assignment.

Morgue Post   170.30
A post established by the Detective Bureau to direct procedures involving deceased persons.

Transportation Facility   180
The agency furnishing vehicles for evacuation.

Transportation Zone   190
The location where evacuees assemble.

FUNCTIONS   200
Department   210

*Achieve control and restore the situation to normal as rapidly and effectively as possible.

*All officers and employees of the department whose regularly assigned duties are not essential to control the occurrence shall become a part of the personnel pool from which assignments shall be made for control purposes.

Department Commander   215
The Chief of Police, as the Department Commander, or the officer acting in his stead, is responsible for evaluating department needs and issuing appropriate instructions for the purpose of insuring coordinated and effective deployment of personnel and equipment to control the unusual occurrence and effectively police the remainder of the city.

Administrative Staff   220
The Administrative Staff shall coordinate department plans for control of major unusual occurrences and shall activate, staff, command, and deactivate the Emergency Control Center.

Emergency Control Center   230
The purpose of the Emergency Control Center is to maintain constant communication with the Field Command Post and the Communication Department; provide auxiliary personnel, services, equipment, and supplies when requested; collect and disseminate information to other divisions, news gatherings, Civil Defense, and other agencies; maintain a situation map; establish emergency ingress/egress traffic routes; approve all "Sigalert" broadcasts; prepare a final report of the unusual occurrence.

Uniform Division   240
Command, direct, and coordinate all police activity within the involved area and the remainder of the city; reassign and/or requisition personnel, auxiliary services, equipment and supplies; establish a Field Command Post (delegating any officer to act as Field Commander); provide a Traffic Control Plan.

Field Commander 240.05

Exercise line control in the involved area, maintaining communication with the Emergency Control Center. The Field Commander shall establish the periphery of the involved area providing ingress/ egress traffic routes facilitating operations of all authorized personnel and agencies; aid persons; protect property; requisition needed personnel, equipment, and supplies; maintain disaster log and prepare a final report.

Investigation Division 250

Investigate crime, apprehend and interrogate offenders; protect and recover property; assist coroner in identification of dead; coordinate activity relative to missing persons; provide personnel for radio cars as required; prepare department injury and/or death reports; assist at hospital or morgue posts; prepare, maintain, and disseminate, as necessary, lists of injured and/or dead.

Services Division 260

Maintain files of manpower comprising a personnel pool including, but not limited to, names and telephone numbers of authorized persons in other departments and agencies who might be called upon for assistance and/or equipment, making such notifications as required; provide and prepare vehicles for immediate and protracted use, establishing and staffing repair and/or service points; obtain and dispatch/transport all necessary equipment and/or supplies; provide time-keeping services; assign officers and provide personnel as required.

Communications Department 270

Provide personnel and equipment for installation, maintenance, and repair of fixed and mobile units for communication and/or power as required.

ORGANIZATION AND COMMAND 300

Modification of Organization 310

Police organization may be modified temporarily during a serious or major unusual occurrence. A Field

Command Post and the Emergency Control Center will be activated and commanded as outlined, the Chief of Police being the department commander.

Department Commander — Succession of Command   315
When the Chief of Police or his assistant is unavailable, the officer then in command of the Uniform Division, or the officer acting in his stead, shall assume interim command of the department. When he is relieved, unless a staff officer has been appointed department commander by the Chief of Police or his assistant, the succession shall be:

*On weekends, and holidays, the Administrative Duty Officer

*Captain, Commander, Uniform Division

*Captain, Commander, Investigation Division

*Captain, Commander, Services Division

*Lieutenants by seniority in rank

*Sergeants by seniority in rank

Command of more than one function may be the responsibility of one of the above officers.

Organization — Minor Unusual Occurrence   320
During the course of a minor unusual occurrence, departmental organization will remain unchanged. The Watch of occurrence shall be responsible for policing the situation.

Organization for Line Control — Serious or Major Unusual Occurrence   330
The Commander, Uniform Division, or person acting in his stead, shall be charged with the direct responsibility of protection of life and property and overall command of all police operations in the field incident to any threatened, imminent, or existing serious or major unusual occurrence.

Delegation of Command 330.05

The Uniform Division Commander may designate a Uniform Division Lieutenant or Sergeant to represent him. He shall be known as the Uniform Division Commander's representative, and may represent the Uniform Division Commander in the field or in the Emergency Control Center. The commander, Uniform Division, may delegate any officer of his command to direct tactical operations at the scene of a serious or major unusual occurrence. Such officer shall be known as the Field Commander.

Field Commander 330.10

In the absence of the Uniform Division Commander at the scene of a serious or major unusual occurrence, or when a specific designation as Field Commander has not been made, the succession of command shall be:

*Patrol Bureau watch commander

OR

*Senior lieutenant of the Uniform Division who is present

OR

*Senior sergeant of the Patrol Bureau who is present at the scene

OR

*Senior policeman of the Patrol Bureau who is present at the scene.

Command for Line Control 330.15
*Chief of Police or Department Commander

*Commander, Uniform Division

*Field Commander

*Supervisory personnel assigned or present at the scene.

Responsibility of Senior Officer to Assume Field Command 330.20
The senior officer of the Uniform Division at the scene shall assume and exercise the responsibilities of field command until relieved from such responsibilities by a superior officer, assigned Field Commander or by an ensuing watch.

Field Command Authority and Responsibility 330.25
The Field Commander, regardless of rank, shall have complete authority and responsibility for conducting the field operations during an unusual occurrence.

Field Command Priority 330.30
The Field Commander shall have priority access to the full resources of the department, and shall requisition from the Emergency Control Center, when activated, departmental personnel and equipment necessary to contain the occurrence and prevent injury, loss of life, destruction of property, and/or threat of any of these.

Field Command – Supervision of Requisitioned Personnel 330.35
All personnel within, assisting, or assigned to the involved area shall be subject to the direct command and supervision of the Field Commander.

Functional Supervision in Involved Area 330.40
Supervisors of employees assigned to the involved area as specialists shall exercise functional, but not line, supervision over such employees.

Unity of Command 330.45
All orders or commands shall originate from the Field Commander or from an officer acting in his stead.

Assumption of Command 330.50
An officer of staff rank or the ranking officer in the chain of command may assume field command at

any time during the duration of the unusual occurrence. The officer, then acting as Field Commander, must be specifically informed that he has been relieved of command.

*Assumption of Command by Officer of Equal or
Junior Rank*   330.55
Any officer of equal or junior rank may relieve the Field Commander from his command by identifying himself and informing the Field Commander of his intent. Such action shall be undertaken only when the Field Commander is physically or mentally unable to perform his duties OR when delegated the authority to assume command by the Uniform Division Commander.

Appearance or Presence of Ranking Senior Officer   360.60
The mere presence of a ranking senior officer at the scene of an unusual occurrence shall not indicate his assumption of command. Such ranking SENIOR officer shall remain in an advisory and/or evaluating capacity unless he specifically assumes command.

Countermanding of Orders   330.65
The Field Commander's orders or request may be countermanded only after such countermanding officer has specifically relieved the Field Commander of his command; unless the situation requires the change in instructions and time will not allow such assumption, in which case, the countermanding officer shall inform the officer issuing the order that it has been countermanded and the reason therefor.

Emergency Control Center (Re. 220 and 230)   340
The department command post for serious or major unusual occurrence control.

Emergency Control Center Location   340.05
The Emergency Control Center shall be located in the Civil Defense Headquarters, 111 N. Third St.

Emergency Control Center Commander   340.10
The Emergency Control Center shall be commanded by the department commander or the officer acting in his stead.

Emergency Control Center Personnel   340.15
The following personnel are assigned to the
Emergency Control Center:

*Administrative Staff

*Traffic Bureau lieutenant

*Training Bureau lieutenant

*Vice Bureau personnel

*Such other personnel as needed

PROCEDURE   400

Tactical Procedure   410
The general plan shall be to evaluate the extent of
the unusual occurrence to determine personnel and
equipment needs in order to:

*Isolate and/or evacuate the area.

*Locate, identify, and assist in the removal of
injured and/or dead.

*Provide emergency medical aid.

*Protect property.

*Notify and assist appropriate departments
and/or agencies.

*Expedite traffic flow.

*Prepare appropriate reports.

Headquarters Procedure   415
Each Bureau shall perform the duties outlined in
Sections 415.05 through 415.35 of the Manual on
Procedures.

Patrol Bureau   415.05
This Bureau shall assign units and special personnel to

the scene; initiate the FANOUT procedure; notify appropriate departments and/or agencies; prepare vehicles for protracted service; provide EMERGENCY called-for service.

Desk Officer   415.05-05
The desk officer shall perform the following duties:

*Dispatch unit(s) and a Sergeant to the scene.

*Advise Watch Commander of nature, magnitude, and scope of unusual occurrence.

*Notify Fire Department to dispatch RESCUE TRUCK (Station # 5) and RESCUE CREW (Station #4) to scene.

*Notify AMBULANCE service (Section 429.10-10) for additional ambulances.

*Dispatch INVESTIGATOR to scene.

*Notify HOSPITALS (Section 429.10-05).

*Make special notifications (Section 429).

*Receive and relay Field reports to Watch Commander and/or Emergency Control Center.

*Screen calls for EMERGENCY service only.

*Prepare appropriate reports (Section 435.15).

Watch Commander   415.05-10
The Watch Commander shall perform the following duties:

*Advise Division Captain and/or Administrative Duty Officer of nature, magnitude and scope of the unusual occurrence.

*Assign Jailer to prepare paddy wagon and station vehicles for protracted use.

*Initiate the FANOUT procedure (Section 421).

*Designate frequency (A or B) to be used by units at the scene of an unusual occurrence.

*Prepare mobilization WORK SCHEDULE based on twelve (12) hour shift.

*Receive and forward Field reports to Emergency Control Center.

*Verify performance of field duties.

*Verify notifications to appropriate departments and/or agencies.

*Prepare appropriate reports (Section 435.10).

Traffic Bureau 415.10
This Bureau shall establish PRIMARY traffic routes; assign personnel for traffic POINT CONTROL; assign messenger(s) as needed.

Record Bureau 415.15
This Bureau shall provide personnel for special assignments and establish vehicle service/repair posts.

Record Bureau Sworn Personnel 415.15-05
The Record Bureau Sergeant, identification officer, warrant officer and subpoena officer shall report to the MORGUE POST and assist in recovery, identification and removal of dead.

Clerical Personnel 415.15-10
Clerical personnel shall immediately, upon request of the Watch Commander, make the appropriate notifications pursuant to the FANOUT procedure (Section 421.50-07).

Automotive Serviceman 415.15-15
The Automotive serviceman shall establish vehicle service/repair posts and furnish necessary equipment therefor.

Training Bureau   415.20
    The Training officer shall perform the following
    duties:

    *Mobilize the AUXILIARY POLICE whenever
    ISOLATION and/or EVACUATION details are
    assigned.

    *Assign Auxiliary Police to report to the
    Sergeant-in-charge of Isolation/Evacuation de-
    tails.

    *Assign Auxiliary Police to report to super-
    visor-in-charge of other details as requested.

    *Assign Auxiliary Police detail to transport
    Jeep, generator and lights to scene of unusual
    occurrence.

Detective Bureau   415.25
    This Bureau shall assign MORGUE details to report
    to the scene, field, and/or hospital morgue posts;
    provide personnel on request from the Uniform
    Division for called-for services.

Juvenile Bureau   415.30
    This Bureau shall establish a MISSING PERSON
    detail; establish liaison with WELFARE agencies.

Vice Control Bureau   415.35
    This Bureau shall report to the Emergency Control
    Center and perform such duties as may be required.

Field Procedure   417
    Each Bureau shall perform the duties outlined in
    Sections 417.05 through 417.25.

Patrol Bureau   417.05
    This Bureau shall establish the Field Command and
    Medical posts; evaluate, isolate and/or evacuate the
    involved area; provide emergency medical aid; pro-
    tect property; assist concerned Bureaus, departments
    and/or agencies; prepare appropriate reports.

First Officer   417.05-05

The first officer arriving on the scene shall perform the following duties:

*Assume interim field command
(Section 330.20).

*Evaluate the extent of the involved area
(Section 426.05).

*Prepare appropriate reports
(Section 437.30-05).

Second Officer   417.05-10

The second officer arriving on the scene shall perform the following duties:

*Determine the periphery, scope and magnitude of unusual occurrence (Section 426.10).

*Assist the first officer.

*Perform such other duties as may be assigned.

*Prepare appropriate reports (Section 437.20).

First Supervisor   417.05-15

The first supervisor arriving on scene shall perform the duties of the Field Commander (Section 417.05-20) until relieved or reassigned.

Field Commander   417.05-20

The Field Commander shall perform the following duties:
*Establish Command post (Section 422).

*Establish Medical post (Section 423).

*Communicate location of Command and Medical posts to Headquarters.

*Advise ingress route for Ambulance traffic.

*Maintain chronological log.

*Assign isolation, medical, inspection and/or evacuation details.

*Communicate HAZARDS and personnel/ equipment needs to Headquarters.

*Isolate area (Section 427).

*Advise Headquarters of ingress/egress routes for Emergency traffic.

*Evacuate area, when necessary (Section 428).

*Maintain continuous communication with Headquarters.

*Maintain rosters of personnel assignments (Sections 437.05-10 and 437.05-15).

*Prepare final report.

Investigator   417.05-25
  The assigned investigator shall perform the following duties:

*Photograph the scene of the unusual occurrence.

*Assist injured until medical detail assigned.

*Assist in the location, identification and removal of dead (Section 425).

Non-assigned Personnel   417.05-30
  All non-assigned personnel (Patrol Bureau) shall report to the Command post.

Traffic Bureau   417-10
  This Bureau is responsible for the expeditious movement of traffic at the scene of an unusual occurrence and such other locations as necessary.

*Route traffic to PRIMARY routes.

*Institute traffic POINT CONTROL tactics.

*Obtain equipment to close arterial routes.

*Assign personnel to HOSPITAL posts for traffic control.

*Prepare appropriate reports (Section 437.45).

Record Bureau   417.15
This Bureau shall provide personnel to assist the Morgue detail and Field Commander.

Sworn Personnel   417.15-05
The Record Bureau Sergeant, identification officer, warrant officer, and subpoena officer shall report to the Command post for assignment as part of the Morgue detail.

Clerical Personnel   417.05-10
A civilian employee shall be assigned to assist the Field Commander:

  *Maintain chronological log.

  *Maintain rosters of personnel assignments.

Detective Bureau   417.20
This Bureau shall establish Morgue post(s) and assist in the location, identification and removal of dead (Section 425).

Juvenile Bureau   417.25
This Bureau shall establish a Missing Person post (Section 424).

Operational Procedure   420
The specific plans which will facilitate the implementation of tactical and reporting procedures.

Fanout Procedure   421
During a serious or major unusual occurrence, the WATCH COMMANDER shall mobilize personnel

utilizing the DISASTER FILE.

Disaster File   421.05
The Record Bureau shall maintain a master assign-
ment roster and a card file of all personnel in the
following manner:

 *Name, address, and telephone number.

 *Segregate personnel by DIVISION.

 *Segregate division personnel by BUREAU.

 *Segregate PATROL BUREAU personnel by
 WATCH.

 *Segregate Watch personnel by DAY-OFF.

The watch commander shall be responsible for
removing from the disaster file cards of personnel on
leave or vacation.

Implementation   421.10
The watch commander and Record Bureau clerk(s)
shall notify KEY PERSONNEL, or person acting in
their stead, according to the notification schedule
(Section 421.50), advising them of the nature of the
unusual occurrence.

 Note: In the event KEY PERSONNEL are
   unavailable, contact his immediate
   supervisor who shall make appropriate
   notifications.

Key Personnel   421.15
Immediately after being advised of an unusual
occurrence, the key personnel, or person acting in his
stead, shall report to headquarters and complete
notifications as outlined in the NOTIFICATION
SCHEDULE.

Notification Schedule   421.50

Watch Commander   421.50-05

*Captain, Uniform Division

*Administrative duty officer

*PBX operator

*Lieutenant, Patrol Bureau (on-coming Watch)

*Lieutenant, Traffic Bureau

*Lieutenant, Training Bureau

Record Bureau Clerk(s)   421.50-07
*Sergeants, Patrol Bureau (on coming Watch)

*Supervisor, Record Bureau

*Desk officer, (on-coming Watch)

*Dispatcher (on-coming Watch)

*Jailer (on-coming Watch)

*Patrolmen (off-duty from WATCH OF OCCURRENCE)

Chief of Police   421.50-10
*City Manager

Assistant Chief of Police   421.50-15
*Commander, Vice Bureau

Captain, Uniform Division   421.50-20
*Chief of Police

*Assistant Chief of Police

*Captain, Investigation Division

*Captain, Services Division

Captain, Investigation Division   421.50-25
*Lieutenant, Detective Bureau

*Lieutenant, Juvenile Bureau

Administrative Duty Officer   421.50-30
    *All members of the administrative staff

Lieutenant, Detective Bureau   421.50-35
    *Sergeant, Crimes against person

    *Sergeant, Crimes against property

Lieutenant, Juvenile Bureau   421.50-40
    *Two detectives/investigators

Lieutenant, Traffic Bureau   421.50-45
    *Sergeant, Traffic Bureau

    *Follow-up Investigator, Traffic Bureau

    *Clerk, Traffic Bureau

Lieutenant, Training Bureau   421.50-50
    *Rangemaster

    *Clerk, Training Bureau

Sergeant, Crimes Against Person   421.50-55
    *Detectives/Investigators to TOTAL 3

Sergeant, Crimes Against Property   421.50-60
    *Detectives/Investigators to TOTAL 3

Sergeants, Patrol Bureau (on-coming Watch)   421.50-65
    *Investigators (on-coming Watch) to TOTAL 4

    *Patrolmen (on-coming Watch) to TOTAL 26

Sergeant, Traffic Bureau   421.50-70
    *Motor officers to TOTAL 7

Commander, Vice Bureau   421.50-75
    *Investigator, Vice Bureau

Supervisor, Record Bureau   421.50-80
    *Identification officer

    *Senior Clerk, Record Bureau

*Automotive Serviceman

Senior Clerk   421.50-85
   *Typist Clerks to TOTAL 4

Clerk, Training Bureau   421.50-90
   *Auxiliary Police to TOTAL one-half strength

PBX Operator   421.50-95
   *Director and alternate, Civil Defense

   *Director and alternate, Communications De-
   partment

Command Post   422
   The field commander shall establish the command
   post on an ingress route for emergency vehicles.

Ingress Route   422.05
   Ingress route shall bisect the perimeter of control.

Perimeter of Control   422.10
   The perimeter of control shall be a minimum of one
   (1) block from the outer margin of an unusual
   occurrence scene.

Facilities   422.15
   The command post shall consist of a temporary or
   permanent facility.

Temporary Facility   422.20
   A marked police vehicle equipped with a COMMAND
   POST KIT.

Permanent Facility   422.25
   The COMMUNICATION TRUCK and/or a private or
   public building.

Command Post Kit   422.30
   The command post kit shall consist of the following:

   *Manual — Unusual Occurrence Control

   *Map — city of Burbank

*Pens — black and red

*Appropriate reports (Section 437.05)

*Legal tablet for chronological log

*Signs for MEDICAL and MORGUE POSTS

Special Equipment　　　　　　　　　　　　　422.35
Communications personnel shall install a direct line telephone and provide four (4) portable transceivers.

Considerations　　　　　　　　　　　　　　422.40
Where has ingress route for emergency vehicles been established?

What perimeter of control is necessary?

What building could be used?

Questions　　　　　　　　　　　　　　　　422.45
Has ingress route been established?

Has perimeter of control been established?

Has headquarters been advised of command post location?

Have communication facilities been ordered?

Medical Post　　　　　　　　　　　　　　　423
The field commander shall establish a medical post at an intersection adjacent to the perimeter of control.

Perimeter of Control　　　　　　　　　　　423.05
The perimeter of control shall be a minimum of one (1) block from the outer margin of the unusual occurrence scene.

Intersection　　　　　　　　　　　　　　　423.10
Medical treatment shall be administered within the intersection.

Intersecting Streets　　　　　　　　　　　423.15

Injured and/or dead shall be routed on the intersecting streets.

Routing   423.20
Routing shall be handled in accordance with Sections
423.25 through 423.40.

Removal of Injured/Dead from Scene   423.25
The intersecting street leading from the SCENE to
the MEDICAL POST shall be known as the IN-
GRESS route. All injured and/or dead shall be routed
through the medical post via the INGRESS route.

Injured Requiring Hospitalization   423.30
One intersecting street shall be designated the IN-
GRESS/EGRESS route for AMBULANCE traffic.

Dead   423.35
One intersecting street shall be designated as the
INGRESS/EGRESS route for CORONER traffic.

Treated   423.40
One intersecting street shall be designated as the
EGRESS route. This route shall be used by persons
who have been treated and released.

Personnel   423.45
The field commander shall assign a medical detail to
assist injured at the medical post and unusual
occurrence scene.

Personnel Assigned to Medical Post   423.45-05
The field commander shall assign at least two (2)
members of the medical detail to assist the physician
and/or nurse at the medical post. The officers
assigned shall perform the following duties:

   *Route injured and/or dead.

   *Record names and addresses of injured.

   *Advise command post of ambulance needs.

   *Advise command post of nature of injuries

requiring treatment at a hospital.

*Advise command post of supply needs.

*Complete appropriate reports
(Section 437.30).

Personnel Assigned to Unusual Occurrence Scene   423.45-10
The field commander shall assign sufficient personnel
to expeditiously assist the injured at the unusual
occurrence scene and perform the following duties:

*Locate and identify injured.

*Render emergency first aid using portable
FIRST AID KITS (obtain from MEDICAL
POST).

*Remove injured to MEDICAL POST.

*Prepare appropriate reports
(Section 437.30-05)

Supplies   423.50
The RESCUE TRUCK shall be used for emergency
medical supplies. Additional needs shall be obtained
from Civil Defense through COMMAND POST.

Special Equipment   423.55
The Communications Department shall install a
direct-line telephone at the MEDICAL POST.

Considerations   423.60
What intersection will best expedite medical
assistance?

What personnel are needed at the medical post?

What supplies are needed?

Questions   423.65
Have intersecting streets been designated for routing?

Have personnel been assigned?

Have assignments been recorded?

Has hospital been advised to dispatch physician and/or nurse?

Has rescue truck arrived?

Has telephone service been established?

Missing Person Post   424
The Juvenile Bureau shall establish a missing person post at the COMMAND post.

Personnel   424.05
The post shall be staffed by a missing person detail.

Function   424.10
The MISSING PERSON DETAIL shall receive information, prepare reports, and conduct FIELD investigations relating to persons reported missing.

Missing Person Information   424.15
All reports of missing persons shall be referred to the MISSING PERSON POST.

Missing Person Report Form   424.20
The departmental form (ML 218) shall be used to record all pertinent information.

Missing Person Investigation   424.25
Reports of missing persons shall be investigated by the MISSING PERSON DETAIL and/or headquarters.

Missing Person Detail Investigation   424.25-05
This detail shall conduct a field investigation as follows:

 *Determine if missing person has been processed at the MEDICAL POST.

 *Determine if missing person has been processed at the MORGUE POST.

 *Determine if missing person has been processed at a TRANSPORTATION ZONE.

*Determine if missing person has been processed at a MASS CARE CENTER.

*Determine if missing person has been processed at a HOSPITAL.

*Determine if missing person has been contacted by ISOLATION DETAIL.

*Advise persons reporting other(s) missing to notify Headquarters if subject is located.

*Refer reports requiring further investigation to Headquarters.

Headquarters Investigation   424.25-10
Reports requiring an investigation beyond inspection of rosters at various FIELD and HOSPITAL posts shall be handled by Headquarters personnel using established procedures.

Morgue Post   425
The Detective Bureau shall establish a morgue post on a street designated the INGRESS/EGRESS route for Coroner traffic, adjacent to the MEDICAL post.

Medical Post   425.05
The intersection selected by the Field Commander for routing and/or treatment of injured and/or dead, adjacent to the perimeter of control.

Perimeter of Control   425.10
The perimeter of control shall be a minimum of one (1) block from the outer margin of the unusual occurrence scene.

Function   425.15
The MORGUE post shall perform the following duties:

*Assist the coroner

*Locate and remove remains of deceased persons to the MORGUE post

*Determine the identity of deceased persons

*Permit removal of deceased persons from the MORGUE post to an authorized morgue by designated coroner vehicles

*Prepare appropriate reports (Section 437.40)

Personnel   425.20
The MORGUE post Commander shall assign a morgue detail to assist at the Morgue post and unusual occurrence scene.

Personnel Assigned to Morgue Post   425.20-05
Morgue post personnel shall perform the following duties:

*Assist the coroner's representative

*Segregate male/female bodies

*Take prints of deceased persons

*Inventory and protect personal property of deceased persons

*Prepare appropriate reports (Section 437.40-05)

Personnel Assigned to Unusual Occurrence Scene   425.20-10
The commander of the MORGUE POST shall assign sufficient personnel to perform the following duties:

*Assist coroner's representative.

*Locate deceased persons.

*Place identification stakes at location where bodies found.

*Attach numbered tag to bodies.

*Attach similarly numbered tag to identification stake.

*Locate severed members of bodies, placing identification stakes bearing similarly numbered tag at location where dismemberment found.

*Attach similarly numbered tag to severed members.

*Collect and tag personal property. (When appropriate, use tag number consistent with remains to which property belongs.)

*Obtain coroner's approval to remove body and/or dismembered parts.

*Remove body and/or dismemberments to the MORGUE POST.

*Prepare appropriate reports (Section 437.40-10).

Auxiliary Morgue Post   425.25
When appropriate, the morgue post commander shall establish field and/or hospital morgue posts.

Personnel Assigned to Auxiliary Morgue Post   425.25-05
Auxiliary morgue post personnel shall perform the duties outlined in Section 425.20-05.

Supplies   425.30
The morgue post commander shall transport the following supplies to the morgue post:

*Camera

*Fingerprint kit(s)

*Identification stakes

*Serially numbered identification tags

*Unnumbered identification tags

*Containers for personal property

*Blankets

*Appropriate report forms (Section 437.40)

Morgue Detail Supplies   425.30-05
Personnel assigned to the Morgue detail shall obtain
appropriate supplies from the MORGUE POST.

Releasing Identity of Deceased Persons   425.35
The Emergency Control Center may authorize the
release of information concerning the identity of
decreased persons to authorized persons.

Authorized Persons   425.35-05
Information concerning the identity of deceased
persons may be released to the following:

*Military agencies

*Next-of-kin

*News media

Notification   425.35-10
A member of the Morgue detail shall notify
authorized persons.

NOTE: The identity of military personnel shall
only be released to appropriate military agencies.

Evaluation of Extent of Involved Area   426

First Officer on Scene   426.05
Determine and communicate to headquarters the
TYPE and EXACT LOCATION(S) of the unusual
occurrence.   426.05-05

Render emergency medical assistance
(Section 423.45-10).   426.05-10

Assign the SECOND OFFICER to determine
RANGE of the unusual occurrence.   426.05-15

Give a verbal report to the FIRST SUPERVISIOR
and/or headquarters.   426.05-20

Second Officer on Scene   426.10
The second officer on the scene of an unusual
occurrence shall perform the following duties:

Determine and communicate to the command
post and/or headquarters the periphery
(RANGE) of the unusual occurrence.   426.10-05

Determine and communicate to the command
post and/or headquarters the TYPE and LO-
CATION of hazards.   426.10-10

*Public utility

**Power lines down

**Water mains broken

**Escaping vapors

*Blocked or damaged streets

*Fires

*Explosions

*Cave-ins

*Slides

*Falling, flying, or floating debris

*Structural damage

*Crowds

*Panic

*Traffic congestion

*Polluted water

Determine and communicate to the command post
and/or headquarters the SCOPE and MANGITUDE
of the unusual occurrence.   426.10-15

  *Extent of damage

  *Approximate number injured and/or dead

Assist the first officer at the scene.   426.10-20

Prepare appropriate reports (Section 437.20).   426.10-25

First Supervisor on Scene   426.15
The first supervisior on the scene of an unusual
occurrence shall perform the following duties:

  *Assume interim command (Section 417.13).   426.15-05

  *Perform the duties of the SECOND OFFICER
  (Section 424.10) until/unless someone assigned.   426.15-10

  *Assign inspection detail to assist second
  officer.   426.15-15

  *Establish a command post (Section 422).   426.15-20

  *Advise headquarters of personnel and/or
  equipment needs.   426.15-25

  *Prepare appropriate reports (Sec. 437.10).   426.15-30

Considerations   426.20
What immediate action will minimize hazards?

How many men will be needed to rapidly gather
needed information?

  *Hazards?

  *Range?

  *Injured/dead?

What hazards must be eliminated to permit emergency operations?

What specialist(s) (is) (are) needed?

What equipment is needed?

Questions   426.25
Has TYPE of disaster been determined?

Has EXACT LOCATION(S) been determined?

Has RANGE been determined?

Has medical assistance been initiated?

Has command post been established?

Has headquarters been kept informed?

Have hazards been identified? located? reported?

Have available manpower been assigned?

Have equipment requisitions been made?

Have personnel needs been reported?

Have assignments been recorded?

Isolation of Unusual Occurrence   427
Personnel and/or equipment shall be deployed by the
field commander to control ingress/egress routes at
unusual occurrence scenes.

Ingress/Egress Routes   427.05
All streets which permit access to/from the involved
area.

Involved Area   427.10
The area enclosing in one rectangle *ALL* unusual
occurrence scenes.

Types of Areas   427.15
An unusual occurrence may occur in one of four
areas defined in Section 130, consisting of the
following:

*Closed area

*Semi-closed area

*Semi-open area

*Open area

Determining Ingress/Egress Routes   427.20
The perimeter of control will establish the number
and location of ingress/egress routes.

Perimeter of Control – Closed Area   427.25
The perimeter of control is fixed by the natural
boundaries surrounding the involved area.

Perimeter of Control – Semi-closed Area   427.30
The perimeter of control is fixed on two sides and
need only be extended on open sides to permit safety
(minimum of one (1) block).

Perimeter of Control – Open or Semi-open Area   427.35
The perimeter of control shall be a minimum of one
(1) block from the outer margins (fixed by encircling
the involved area).

Encircling the Involved Area   427.40
The field commander shall use the map from the
command post kit and encircle the involved area as
follows:

  *Mark "X" in each block where unusual occur-
  rence scene reported.

  *Extend, until they bisect, horizontal and
  vertical lines externally abutting streets adjacent to the most outlying unusual occurrence
  scenes.

  *The resultant rectangle is the encircled in-
  volved area (Section 427.10).

Personnel Requirements   427.45
The actual number of personnel needed to effectively

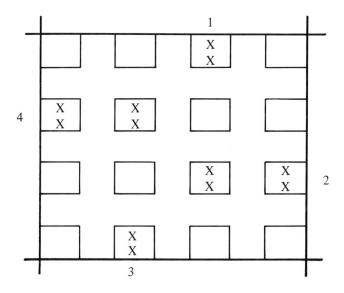

Figure 2: Numbers 1, 2, 3 and 4: Most outlying scenes. Heavy Line: Bisecting of horizontal and vertical lines.

isolate the unusual occurrence depends on the perimeter of control and range.

Range of Closed or Semi-closed Area   427.50
The range of a closed or semi-closed area is fixed by natural boundaries.

Range of Open or Semi-open Area   427.55
The total number of blocks which abut two adjacent sides of the rectangle encircling the involved area.

Formula for Personnel Needs in Open Area   427.60
The total number of blocks abutting two adjacent sides of the rectangle encircling the involved area (RANGE) is reduced by one (1). This number is multiplied by two (2), and a fixed factor (eight [8] times perimeter of control [in blocks]) is added.

Example: Range = 7 - 1 = 6 x 2 = 12 + 8 = *20*

The resultant number is the minimum personnel

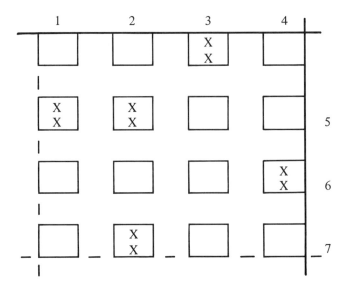

Figure 3: Solid line is two adjacent sides. Range = 7.

needed to isolate the involved area at a perimeter of
control of one (1) block.

> Note: If number of blocks affected multiplied
> by eight (8) is a number less than
> formula computes, isolate each scene
> independently.

Formula for Personnel Needs in Semi-Open Area   427.65
The minimum personnel needed to isolate a semi-
open area using a minimum perimeter of control is
one-half (1/2) the number of an open area.

Formula for Personnel Needs in Semi-Closed Area   427.70
The minimum personnel needed to isolate a semi-
closed area is determined by number of ingress/egress
routes entering the involved area.

Formula for Personnel Needs in Closed Area   427.75
The minimum personnel needed to isolate a closed
area is the sum of ingress/egress streets, and a fixed
factor (two [2] times perimeter of control [in
blocks]).

Example: Ingress/egress streets = 4 + 2 = 6.

The resultant number is minimum personnel with a perimeter of control of one (1) block.

Personnel Assignments   427.80
The field commander shall assign an isolation detail to mobile and fixed posts.

Personnel Assigned to Fixed Post   427.80-05
Personnel of the ISOLATION DETAIL assigned to fixed posts shall perform the following duties:

*Restrict ingress/egress to authorized persons or vehicles.

*Record name and address of all unauthorized persons leaving the involved area and forward to supervisor (Section 437.25-10).

*Record description and license number of all vehicles leaving the involved area and forward to supervisor (Section 437.25-10).

*Refer persons requesting information to the appropriate post.

Personnel Assigned to Mobile Posts   427.80-10
Personnel of the isolation detail assigned to mobile posts shall perform the following duties:

*Patrol involved area, reporting hazards.

*Patrol involved area to prevent looting.

*Obtain name and address of unauthorized persons within involved area (Section 437.25-10).

*Perform other duties as directed.

Isolation Detail Supervisor   427.80-15
The supervisory officers assigned to the isolation detail shall perform the following duties:

*Assign personnel to posts.

*Record assignments (Section 437.10).

*Make frequent inspections of posts to obtain information and provide relief.

*Insure the effective isolation of the involved area.

*Make appropriate notifications to the command post.

Ingress/Egress Routes   427.85
The field commander shall establish ingress/egress routes for emergency vehicles.

Considerations   427.90
What natural boundaries would reduce personnel needs?

What routes could best be utilized by emergency vehicles?

Could ingress/egress routes for emergency vehicles be separated?

What instructions have been issued to men on posts?

What assignments could Auxiliary Police handle?

Where can barricades, ropes, or vehicles be used?

Questions   427.95
Has TYPE of area been determined?

Has perimeter of control been determined?

Has RANGE been determined?

Has access to area been restricted to authorized persons?

Have all natural boundaries been utilized?

Have emergency ingress/egress routes been established?

Have post men been instructed?

Have Auxiliary Police been assigned?

Have assignments been recorded?

Have supervisors and/or command post been advised of assignments?

Have arrangements been made for relief?

Have barricades been effectively utilized?

Have unauthorized persons been effectively restricted?

Evacuation of Involved Area   428
    The field commander, upon approval of the emergency control center, shall assign an evacuation detail to order unauthorized persons from the involved area whenever imminent or impending danger to health and safety exists.

Transportation Zone   428.05
    The field commander shall establish the transportation zones(s) for assembling and dispersing evacuees to a mass care center.

Mass Care Center   426.10
    Civil Defense shall select and activate the mass care center to provide food, clothing, and lodging.

Evacuation Detail   428.15
    The supervisor of the evacuation detail shall assign personnel to field, inspection, and transportation zone squads.

Field Squad   428.15-05
    Personnel assigned to a field squad shall perform the following duties:

*Start evacuation from most hazardous area outward in a circular manner.

*Advise all persons contacted that the scene has been declared a disaster area.

*Advise all persons, not authorized to remain, to leave the area (409.5PC).

*Advise all persons, not authorized to remain, the location of transportation zone(s).

*Advise all persons, not authorized to remain, they may report to the transportation zone for removal to a mass care center.

*Determine if persons have pets.

*Obtain address where pets located and forward to supervisor.

Inspection Squad   428.15-10
Personnel assigned to the inspection squad shall perform the following duties:

*Circulate through involved area in vehicles, using P.A. to advise scene is declared a disaster area.

*Advise persons to report to transportation zone (give location).

*Re-check residences and/or buildings to insure occupants have left.

*Request tow trucks to remove hazardous abandoned vehicles.

*Protect abandoned valuables and forward to supervisor (Section 437.15-15).

Transportation Zone Squad   428.15-15
Personnel assigned to the transportation zone squad shall perform the following duties:

*Assemble evacuees.

*Obtain name and address of evacuees.

*Prepare appropriate reports (Section 437.15).

Special Notifications   428.20
When the evacuation order is approved, the field
commander shall request headquarters to notify the
Animal Shelter and transportation facilities.

Animal Shelter   428.20-05
Animal Shelter personnel shall report to the com-
mand post and be furnished with addresses where
pets are located.

Transportation Facility   428.20-10
Headquarters shall advise the transportation facility
the location of the transportation zone(s) and mass
care center.

Considerations   428.25
How extensive is area requiring evacuation?

What area or building could be used to assemble
evacuees?

Where is mass care center?

How many persons are needed to make notifications?

What facilities are necessary to remove evacuees?

What hazards must be removed?

Questions   428.30
Has mass care center been activated?

Has transportation been requested?

Has area been declared a disaster?

Has Animal Shelter been notified?

Have personnel started evacuation nearest the most hazardous scene?

Have buildings been re-inspected?

Have names of evacuees been recorded?

Have all unauthorized persons been removed?

Have transportation facilities removed evacuees to mass care center?

Special Notifications   429

Headquarters personnel shall initiate appropriate notifications to implement post operation, expedite emergency procedures, and control specific unusual occurrences.

Special Notification Procedure   429.01

Headquarters personnel shall inform persons notified of the following:

  *Type of unusual occurrence

  *Location(s) where assistance needed

  *Ingress/egress route (when appropriate)

  *Anticipated needs.

Command Post   429.05

Equipment necessary to facilitate command post operations can be obtained as outlined in Sections 429.05-05 and 429.05-10.

Telephone Company   429.05-05

Mobil and/or direct-line telephones.

  *Emergency Supervisor   783-0610
                    OR
  *Chief, Special Agent   623-2221

Communication Department   429.05-10

Portable transceivers and/or temporary direct-line telephones.

*Communications Department	846-2141	
8AM-5PM, Monday-Friday	Ext. 261	

OR

*Robert Brookings   845-4860
1713 Scott, Apt. 6

OR

*Bill Norvell   848-2083
251 N. Buena Vista

OR

*Sheldon Light   842-9781
2141 N. Pass

Medical Post   429.10

Medical facilities, equipment, supplies, and special equipment can be obtained as outlined in Sections 429.10-05 through 429.10-25.

Hospitals   429.10-05

The hospital nearest the unusual occurrence scene shall be requested to send a physician and/or nurse to the medical post.

*Burbank Hospital   846-3135
466 E. Olive Avenue

Present capacity:	80 beds
Expanded capacity:	100 beds
Emergency:	100 patients

*St. Joseph Hospital   848-5531
501 S. Buena Vista

Present capacity:	500 beds
Expanded capacity:	650 beds
Emergency:	100-1000 patients

*Sun Valley Hospital   767-3310
9449 San Fernando

Present capacity:	100 beds
Expanded capacity:	125 beds
Emergency:	40 patients

*L.A. Co. General Hospital   225-3115
1200 State Street

OVERFLOW

Ambulances   429.10-10
    *Burbank Ambulance Service   842-4833
    1830 Burbank Blvd.

        Two vehicles
        Capacity: 3 up; 4 down ea.
        Total: 14

    *L.A. Fire Department   785-2151
    Captain on duty

        Seven vehicles
        Capacity: 1 up; 2 down ea.
        Total: 21

    *Miller Ambulance Co.   245-3349
                                        243-2146
        Five vehicles
        Capacity: 4 up; 3 down each
        Total: 35

    *Los Angeles Sheriff   626-9511
    Dispatcher   Ext. 82550

Physicians' Exchange   429.10-15
    *Burbank   848-4414
                                        781-1030
                                        788-1813

    *Glendale   241-5152

Supplies   429.10-20
    *Burbank Fire Department   845-2411 OR
    1420 W. Verdugo   Ext. 311
    Station #5

        RESCUE TRUCK (1)

    *Civil Defense Director   846-2141
    Mr. Ben Watson   Ext. 247
    9AM-5PM, Monday-Friday

Other   846-9755

*Lockheed Aircraft Company   847-2632
Captain-Plant Protection

First Aid Station #582
(Same supplies as rescue
truck)

West end of Empire near
Bldg. 341 inside Gate 100

Telephone Company   429.10-25
   Direct-line telephone. (See Section 429.05-05)

Morgue Post   429-15
   The coroner shall assign personnel and vehicles. He
   may authorize local mortuaries to assist.

Coroner   429.15-05

Deputy Coroners   429.15-10
   LOCAL MORTUARIES
     Staff: 6
     Vehicles: 5

Evacuation of Involved Area   429.20
   Equipment, personnel, and facilities to expedite an
   evacuation can be obtained as outlined in Sections
   429.20-05 through 429.20-15.

Animal Shelter   429.20-05
   Animal Shelter

     OR

Poundman

Mass Care Center   429.20-10
   The Civil Defense Director or the person acting in his
   stead shall activate and advise the location(s) of the
   mass care center.

Transportation   429.20-15
The Civil Defense Director or the person acting in his stead shall provide transportation vehicles. Emergency transportation may be obtained from the following:

Public Works

Other:

AND/OR

Bus Lines

Other:

Vehicles: 5
Capacity: 265

Evaluation of Involved Area   429.25
Personnel and/or equipment necessary to expedite an evaluation of the involved area are outlined in Sections 429.25-05 through 429-25.20.

Fire Equipment   429.25-05
Burbank Fire Department

OR

L. A. County Fire Dept.

Medical Supplies   429.25-10
Refer to Section 429.10-20.

Public Works   429.25-15
Heavy equipment and/or supplies.

Public Works

Other:

Utilities   429.25-20
Public Service Department

AND/OR

Gas Company

Other:

AND/OR

Emergency Supervisor

Chief Special Agent

Isolation of Involved Area   429.30
Special equipment necessary to isolate the area
(barricades, ropes, etc.) may be obtained from Public
Works, Street Department, as outlined in Section
429.25-15.

Aircraft Accident   429.35
Headquarters shall be advised if incident involves
Civilian or *Military* aircraft. The appropriate agencies
shall be notified as outlined in Sections 429.35-05
and 429.35-10.

Civilian Aircraft Accident   429.35-05
Sheriff's Aero Detail

Central Radio Dispatcher

AND

F.A.A. Accident Duty Officer

AND

C.A.B.

AND

County Coroner

Military Aircraft Accident   429.35-10
Sheriff's Aero Detail

AND

F.A.A. Accident Duty Officer

AND

A.P.C.D. Dispatcher

Earthquakes   429-40
Notify Civil Defense Director or person acting in his
stead. Additional assistance for *locating* victims may
be obtained from the following:

Burbank Fire Department

OR

L. A. County Fire Dept.

Explosion   429.45
Sheriff's Bomb Squad

A.P.C.D. Dispatcher
(nuclear device)

Flood   429.50
County Flood Control Dist.

Other:

OR

State Div. Water Resources

OR

U.S. Army, Corps of Engineers

Other:

Freeways   429.55
Division of Highways

Other:

Landslides   429.60
U.S. Army Corps of Engineers

Other:

Law Enforcement Agencies   429.65
     F.B.I. Duty Agent

     L.A.P.D. Duty Officer,
     Business Office

     L.A.S.O. Duty Officer,
     Communications

Nuclear Incident   429.70
     Headquarters shall be advised if incident involves a
     Commercial or *Military* nuclear device.

Commercial Device   429.70-05
     A.P.C.D. Dispatcher
(Air Pollution Control District: personnel and instruments for surveying area)

          AND/OR

     U.S. Atomic Energy Commission

Military Device   429.70-10
     A.P.C.D. Dispatcher

          AND

     Fort McArthur

          OR

     Long Beach Naval Station

          OR

     Norton Air Force Base

Train Accident   429.75
     Headquarters shall be advised of the appropriate
     railroad carrier.

     Santa Fe Railroad,
     (Trainmaster on duty)

          OR

Southern Pacific Railroad, Superintendent
Los Angeles Division

OR

Union Pacific Railroad, Superintendent,
Los Angeles Division

Reporting Procedure   430
Headquarters and Field personnel shall prepare
appropriate reports to expedite and coordinate the
control of unusual occurrences.

Headquarters Procedure   435
Appropriate Headquarters personnel shall prepare
reports outlined in Sections 435.05 through 435.15.

Emergency Control Center   435.05
The Emergency Control Center shall prepare the
following reports:

  *Unusual Occurrence Command assignments
  (Annex 1)   435.05-05

  *Unusual Occurrence Hazard reports
  (Annex 4)   435.05-10

Watch Commander   435.10
The Watch Commander shall prepare the following
reports:

  *Mobilization roster (Annex 3)   435.10-05

Desk Officer   435.15
The Desk Officer shall prepare the following reports:

  *Desk report   435.15-05

  *Special notification report (Annex 5)   435.15-10

Field Procedure   437
Appropriate Field personnel shall prepare reports
outlined in Sections 437.05 through 437.45

Field Commander   437.05

The Field Commander shall prepare the following reports:

    *Chronological log   437.05-05

    *Unusual Occurrence Command assignments
    (Annex 1)   437.05-10

    *Unusual Occurrence Detail assignments
    (Annex 2)   437.05-15

    *Unusual Occurrence Hazard reports
    (Annex 4)   437.05-20

Detail Supervisor   437.10
All Detail Supervisors shall prepare the following report:

    *Unusual Occurrence Detail assignments
    (Annex 2)   437.10-05

Evacuation Detail   437.15
Personnel assigned to the Evacuation Detail may prepare the following reports:

    *Citizen Contact report (Annex 6)   437.15-05

    *Mass Care Center report (Annex 7)   437.15-10

    *Property report (Annex 8)   437.15-15

Inspection Detail   437.20
Personnel assigned to the Inspection Detail may prepare the following reports:

    *Unusual Occurrence Hazard report (Annex 4)   437.20-05

    *Citizen Contact report (Annex 6)   437.20-10

Isolation Detail   437.25
Personnel assigned to the Isolation Detail may prepare the following reports:

    *Unusual Occurrence Hazard report (Annex 4)   437.25-05

*Citizen Contact report (Annex 6)	437.25-10

Medical Detail   437.30
Personnel assigned to the Medical Detail may prepare
the following reports:

    *Medical Assistance report (Annex 9)   327.30-05

    *Medical Supply Inventory Control report
    (Annex 10)   437.30-10

Missing Person Detail   437.35
Personnel assigned to the Missing Person Detail shall
prepare the following report:

    *Missing Person report (Annex 11)   437.35-05

Morgue Detail   437.40
Personnel assigned to the Morgue Detail may prepare
the following reports:

    *Dead Body report (Annex 12)   437.40-05

    *Identification Tag reports (Annex 13)   437.40-10

Traffic Bureau   437.45
The Supervisor, Traffic Detail, shall prepare the
following reports:

    *Unusual Occurrence Detail assignments
    (Annex 2)   437.45-05

    *Equipment Inventory Control (Annex 14)   437.45-10

Directory   440
A local resource list of emergency equipment and
through whom they may be obtained.

Multiple Sources   440.05
Civil Defense contact is recommended when listed as
ONE of several sources. Inadequate or depleted
supplies may then be more readily replenished.

Location/Ownership   440.10

Items available at various locations through Civil Defense are owned and controlled by them.

ITEM	LOCATION	CONTACT
Air Compressors	City Yard Parks & Rec.	City Yard Parks & Rec. Department
Bags, Sand	City Yard	Public Works Department

Blankets	Starlight
	  Theatre
	Olive Rec.
	  Grandstand
	Civil Defense
	  Center
	Red Cross
	  Headquarters
		Civil Defense

Canvas	Purchasing
	  Department
	  Warehouse
		Civil Defense

Communications
  (Radios,
  Field Phones
	Communications
	  Shop
		Communications
		  Engineer

Cots	Starlight
	  Threatre
	Olive Recreation
	  Grandstand
	Civil Defense
	  Center
	Red Cross Head-
	  quarters
		Civil Defense

Hospital, Field
  (200 bed)
	St. Joseph
	  Hospital
		Civil Defense

Housing & Care
  Centers
	Park & Rec.
	  Department
	Red Cross
		Civil Defense

ITEM	LOCATION	CONTACT
Jacks and Heavy Tools	C.D. Rescue Trk. City Yard	Fire Department City Yard
Kitchen Units (Mobile, gasoline)	Fire Department	Civil Defense
Oxygen, Medical	St. Joseph Hospital	Civil Defense
Pumping Units	City Yard Public Service Park & Recreation Department	City Yard Public Service Civil Defense
Radiological Instruments and Assistance	Fire Department High Schools Hospitals Atomic Energy Commission	Civil Defense
Stretchers	Civil Defense Center Olive Recreation Grandstand Burbank Community Hospital St. Joseph Hospital Starlight Theatre	Civil Defense
Torches, Acetylene	C.D. Rescue Trk. City Yard Park & Rec. Public Service	Fire Department City Yard Park & Rec. Public Service
Trucks, Emergency Transportation	Park & Rec. Red Cross Volunteers	Civil Defense Red Cross Civil Defense
Drugs and Medicines	Burbank Community Hospital	Civil Defense

ITEM	*LOCATION*	*CONTACT*
	St. Joseph Hospital Starlight Theatre Lockheed Airport Area	
Feeding	Civil Defense Mass Feeding Unit Red Cross	Civil Defense
First Aid (Personnel & Equipment	Burbank Community Hospital St. Joseph Hospital Starlight Theatre Lockheed Airport Area Red Cross Headquarters	Civil Defense Red Cross
First Aid Stations	Burbank Community Hospital St. Joseph Hospital Starlight Theatre Lockheed Airport Area Red Cross Headquarters	Civil Defense
Flood Lights	City Yard Public Service City Yard	Auxiliary Police Public Service Civil Defense
Generators	City Yard Public Service Starlight Theatre	City Yard Public Service Civil Defense

ITEM	*LOCATION*	*CONTACT*
Hardware	Purchasing Dept. Warehouse	Civil Defense
	C.D. Rescue Truck	Fire Department

References   450
> Appropriate sections of California codes which are most likely to apply in emergency situations.

Administrative Code   451
> Disaster plans for hospitals and schools.

Section 17.1, Civil Defense Drill   451.05
> The governing board of any school district shall adopt a written civil defense plan which shall be reviewed by the governing board not less frequently than annually. By regulation, the board may provide for a civil defense drill on any day when school classes are maintained. Such plan and/or regulation may provide that such a drill may be conducted in any of the following ways:
>
> (a) Requiring pupils to walk from school to their residences or other place of safety designated by the principal, parents, or guardian.
>
> (b) Requiring pupils to go to a shelter area on the school grounds.
>
> (c) Loading pupils on school vehicles and volunteer vehicles at customary loading areas for pupils, and moving them not more than one mile from the school ground.
>
> A record shall be kept on the principal's office of the date and hour of each civil defense drill and the time consumed for a drill conducted under subsection (b) or (c).

Section 277, Disaster and Mass Casualty Program   451.10
> (a) All institutions subject to these requirements shall adopt a written disaster and mass casualty program.

(b) Evidence of a written disaster and mass casualty program shall be available on the premises of the licensed institution.

(c) The disaster and mass casualty program shall provide plans for disasters occurring within the facility, local disasters occurring in the community, and widespread disasters.

(d) The written program shall include at least the following:

(1) Administrative procedures, including designated authority, personnel duty assignments, continuation of services, stockpiling (hospitals only), traffic control, and collection and dissemination of information.

(2) Plans for evacuation of patients when necessary, including means of egress, methods of handling and transporting patients, and disposition and care of patients after removal.

(e) The plan shall be brought up to date annually and all personnel be instructed in its duties.

Education Code   452
The emergency use of school property.

Section 16555.5, Use of School Property and
Equipment   452.05
The governing board of any school district may grant the use of school buildings, grounds, and equipment to public agencies, including the American Red Cross, for mass care and welfare shelters during disasters or other emergencies affecting the public health and welfare, and may cooperate with such agencies in furnishing and maintaining such services as the governing board may deem necessary to meet the needs of the community.

Government Code   453
Emergency powers, responsibilities, and duties.

Section 25369.5, Rescue and First Aid   453.05
In any county having a department under the
management and control of a county forester and
fire warden, the board may authorize rescue or first
aid service, or both, as a function of that department,
and may appoint agents and employees and acquire
needed property and equipment for such purposes.

Section 25458, Emergency Work by Counties   453.10
In cases of great emergency, including, but not
limited to, states of disaster defined in Section 1505
of the Military and Veterans Code, when repair or
replacements are necessary to permit the continued
conduct of county operations or services, or to avoid
danger to life or property, the board of supervisors,
by majority consent, may proceed at once to replace
or repair any and all structures without adopting the
plans, specifications, strain sheets, or working details
or giving notice for bids to let contract.

The work may be done by day labor under the
direction of the board, by contract, or by a combination of the two. If the work is done wholly or in part
by contract, the contractor shall be paid the actual
cost of the use of machinery and tools and of
material, and labor and compensation insurance
expended by him in doing the work, plus not more
than 15 per cent to cover all profits and administration. No more than the lowest current market prices
shall be paid for materials whenever possible.

Section 26600, Responsibility of Sheriff   453.15
The sheriff shall preserve peace, and to accomplish
this object, may sponsor, supervise, or participate in
any project of crime prevention, rehabilitation of
persons convicted of crime, or the suppression of
delinquency.

Section 26602, Responsibility of Sheriff   453.15-05
The sheriff shall prevent and suppress any affrays,
breaches of the peace, and insurrections which come
to his knowledge, and investigate public offenses
which have been committed.

Section 26604, Responsibility of Sheriff 453.15-10
The sheriff shall command the aid of as many male
inhabitants of his county as he thinks necessary in
the execution of his duties.

Section 27491, Responsibility of Coroner 453.20
It shall be the duty of the coroner to inquire into and
determine the circumstances, manner, and cause of
all violent, sudden, or unusual deaths; . . ., deaths
known or suspected as resulting in whole or in part
from or related to accident or injury either old or
recent; . . . .

Section 27491.2, Responsibility of Coroner 453.20-05
The coroner or his appointed deputy, on being
informed of a death and finding it to fall into the
classification of deaths requiring his inquiry, may
immediately proceed to where the body lies, examine
the body, make identification, make inquiry into the
circumstances, manner, and means of death, and, as
circumstances warrant, either order its removal for
further investigation or disposition, or release the
body, to the next of kin. For purposes of inquiry,
the body of one who is known to be dead under any
of the circumstances enumerated in Section 27491,
shall not be disturbed or moved from the position or
place of death without permission of the coroner or
his appointed deputy.

Section 27491.3, Responsibility of Coroner 453.20-10
Authority of coroner to take charge of personal
effects, etc., of deceased at scene of death. Locking
or sealing premises: Costs as legal charge against
estate . . .: Prohibition against willful disturbance of
body or related evidence. In any death into which
the coroner is to inquire, he may take charge of any
and all personal effects, valuables, and property of
the deceased at the scene of death and hold or
safeguard them until lawful disposition thereof can
be made . . . .

Section 38791, Powers of Municipal Corporations 453.25
By ordinance the legislative body of a city may

provide for a chief executive who, during periods of great public calamity such as extraordinary fire, flood, storm, epidemic, earthquake, sabotage, or enemy attack, shall have complete authority over the city and the right to exercise all police power vested in the city by the Constitution and general laws.

Section 53019, Emergency Powers of Local Agencies   453.30
It is hereby declared to be the public policy of the State of California that the control of fires and dangerous conditions caused by great public calamities is a matter of statewide concern and interest to all inhabitants and citizens.

Section 53021, Emergency Powers of Local Agencies   453.30-05
Services performed or expenditures made by a local agency within or without its territorial limits are conclusively deemed for the direct protection and benefit of its inhabitants and property if made or performed for:

(a) A national or local emergency created by military attack or sabotage.

(b) Providing adequate national or local defense.

(c) Local peril consisting of the existence of conditions, within the territorial limits of a local agency, in the absence of a duly proclaimed state of extreme emergency or state of disaster, which conditions are a result of an emergency created by great public calamity such as extraordinary fire, flood, storm, epidemic, earthquake, or other disaster which is, or is likely to be, beyond the control of the services, personnel, equipment, and facilities of that agency and require the combined forces of other local agencies to combat.

(d) Before one local agency may respond to a request for material fire protection or aid pursuant to this article, the requesting agency must have primary fire protection by an organized fire department pursuant to law, and the request for

aid must come from the chief or other authorized agent of such requesting agency.

Notwithstanding budget limitations and restrictions
imposed by law, except limitations imposed by the
Constitution, all such services performed or expenditures made are payable from any funds of the public
agency rendering the services or making the expenditure upon the adoption of a resolution by the
governing body of that agency determining that the
services were performed or the expenditures were in
connection with such an emergency and designating
the fund or funds from which the obligation is to be
paid.

Section 53022, Emergency Powers of Local Agencies   453.30-10
If such services are performed outside the local
agency's limits, they shall be ordered by the chief
administrative officer of the office or department
performing them unless otherwise provided by the
legislative body of the local agency.

Section 53023, Emergency Powers of Local Agencies   453.30-15
Notwithstanding any other provisions of law or any
local ordinance all the privileges and immunities from
liability, exemptions from laws and rules, all pension,
relief, disability, workmen's compensation, and other
benefits which apply to officers, agents, or employees of the local agency when performing functions within the local agency's limits apply to them
to the same extent while performing functions
extraterritorially pursuant to this article.

Health and Safety Code   454
Fire protection.

Section 13050, Exchange of Fire Protection Assistance   454.05
The apparatus, equipment, and fire fighting force of
any city, or city and county, or of any county fire
protection district may be used for the purpose of
extinguishing any fire which occurs:

(a) In any city, or city and county, or in any county
    fire protection district, which is of such

proportion that it cannot be adequately handled
by the fire department of the city, city and
county, or any fire protection district.

(b) Outside the limits of any city, or city and
county, or any county fire protection district.

Section 13051, Exchange of Fire Protection Assistance   454.05-05
The reasonable value of the use of, and repairs and
depreciation on, apparatus and equipment, and other
expenses reasonably incurred in furnishing fire
fighting services, constitutes a charge against the city,
city and county, or the county fire protection
district in which the fire occurs, or if the fire occurs
outside the boundaries of any city, city and county,
or any county fire protection district, a charge
against the county in which it occurs.

Section 13052, Exchange of Fire Protection Assistance   454.05-10
The entity rendering the service shall present a claim
to the entity liable therefor, in accordance with
predetermined schedules of payments agreed upon
by the respective entities. If the claim is approved by
the head of the fire department, if any in the entity
to which presented, and by its governing body, it
shall be paid in the same manner as other charges,
and if not paid, an action may be brought for its
collection.

Section 13052.5, Exchange of Fire Protection Assistance   454.05-15
.... All the privileges and immunities which
surround the activities of any city fire fighting force
or department when performing its functions within
the territorial limits of the city shall apply to the city
fire fighting force or department while furnishing fire
protection outside the city under any contract with a
county fire protection district pursuant to this
section 14406. Whenever a fire occurs within the
limits of any district and is of such proportions that
it cannot be adequately handled by the fire department of the district, or whenever a fire occurs in any
unincorporated territory not included within a
district, or whenever a fire occurs in a city and upon
request of the fire chief or authorized authority of

said city, the apparatus, equipment, and fire fighting force of any district within the county may be used for the purpose of extinguishing the fire.

Section 14406, Exchange of Aid in Fighting Fires   454.05-20

Whenever a fire occurs within the limits of any district and is of such proportions that it cannot be adequately handled by the fire department of the district, or whenever a fire occurs in any unincorporated territory of a county not included in the district, or whenever a fire occurs in a city and upon request of the fire chief or authorized authority of said city, the apparatus, equipment, and fire fighting force of any district within the county may be used for the purpose of extinguishing the fire.

Military and Veterans Code   455

Employment of militia.

Section 146, Activation of Militia   455.05

The Governor may call into active service such portion of the active militia as may be necessary and if the number available be insufficient, he may call into active service such portion of the unorganized militia as may be necessary, in any of the following events:

(a) In case of war, insurrection, rebellion, invasion, tumult, riot, public calamity, or catastrophe, or other emergency or imminent danger thereof, or resistance to the laws of this State or the United States.

(b) . . . .

(c) . . . .

(d) Upon call of the chief executive officer of any city or city and county, or any Justice of the Supreme Court, or of any Judge of the Superior Court, or of any sheriff, setting forth that there is an unlawful or riotous assembly with intent to commit a felony, or to offer violence to person or property, or to resist the laws of the State or

the United States, or that there has occurred a
public calamity or catastrophe for which aid to
the civil authorities is required.

(e) Upon call of the sheriff setting forth that the
civil power of the county is not sufficient to
enable him to execute process delivered to him.

Section 365, Activation of Militia   455.05-05

When an armed force is called out for the purpose of
suppressing an unlawful or riotous assembly, or
arresting the offenders, and is placed under the
temporary direction of any civil officer, it shall obey
the orders of such civil officer which extend only to
the direction of the general or specific object to be
accomplished. The tactical direction of the troops,
the kind and extent of force to be used, and the
particular means to be employed to accomplish the
object specified by the civil officer of the active
militia on duty.

Section 433.5, Use of Armories   455.10

All state armories may be used for civil defense
purposes on such terms and conditions as shall be
mutually agreeable to the Military Department and
the California Disaster Office.

Section 1509.95, Removal of Prisoners   455.15

In any case in which fire, flood, enemy attack, or
other disaster endangering the lives of inmates of a
state, county, or city penal or correctional institution
has occurred or is imminent, the person in charge of
the institution may remove the inmates from the
institution. He shall, if possible, remove them to a
safe and convenient place and there confine them as
long as may be necessary to avoid the danger, or if
that is not possible, may release them. Such person
shall not be held liable, civilly or criminally, for acts
performed pursuant to this section.

Penal Code   456
Restrictions, powers, and duties during disaster.

Section 150, Posse Comitatus   456.05

Every male person above 18 years of age who neglects or refuses to join the posse comitatus of the county, by neglecting or refusing to aid and assist in taking or arresting any person against whom there may be issued any process, or by neglecting to aid and assist in retaking any person who, after being arrested or confined, may have escaped from such arrest or imprisonment, or by neglecting or refusing to aid and assist in preventing any breach of the peace, or the commission of any criminal offense, being thereto lawfully required by any sheriff, deputy sheriff, coroner, constable, judge, or other officer concerned in the administration of justice, is punishable by fine of not less than fifty dollars ($50) nor more than one thousand dollars ($1,000).

Section 402, Sightseeing at Scene of Disaster   456.10

Every person who goes to the scene of a disaster or stops at the scene of a disaster for the purpose of viewing the scene or the activities of policemen, firemen, other emergency personnel, or military personnel coping with the disaster in the course of their duties during the time it is necessary for emergency vehicles or such personnel to be at the scene of the disaster or to be moving to or from the scene of the disaster for the purpose of protecting lives or property, unless it is part of the duties of such person's employment to view such scene or activities, and thereby impedes such policemen, firemen, emergency personnel or military personnel in the performance of their duties in coping with the disaster, is guilty of a misdemeanor.

For the purposes of this section, a disaster includes a fire, explosion, an airplane crash, flooding, windstorm damage, a railroad accident, or a traffic accident.

Section 404, Riot, Defined   456.15

Any use of force or violence, disturbing the public peace, or any threat to use such force or violence, if accompanied by immediate power of execution, by two or more persons acting together, and without authority of law, is a riot.

Section 409.5, Powers of Peace Officers in Emergency   456.20
Whenever a menace to the public health or safety is
created by a calamity such as flood, storm, fire,
earthquake, explosion, accident, or other disaster,
officers of the California Highway Patrol, police
departments, or sheriff's office may close the area
where the menace exists for the duration thereof by
means of ropes, markers, or guards to any and all
persons not authorized by such officer to enter or
remain within the closed area. Any person not
authorized willfully entering the area or willfully
remaining within the area after notice to evacuate
shall be guilty of a misdemeanor.

Nothing in this section shall prevent a duly authorized representative of any news service, newspaper,
or radio or television station or network from
entering the area closed pursuant to this section.

Section 410, Duty of Peace Officers in Emergency   456.25
If a magistrate or officer having notice of an unlawful
or riotous assembly, mentioned in this chapter,
neglects to proceed to the place of assembly, or as
near thereto as he can with safety, and to exercise
the authority with which he is invested for suppressing the same and arresting the offenders, he is guilty
of a misdemeanor.

Section 726   456.25-05
Where any number of persons, whether armed or not,
are unlawfully or riotously assembled, the sheriff of
the county and his deputies, the officials governing
the town or city, or the judges of the justice courts
and constables thereof, or any of them, must go
among the persons assembled, or as near them as
possible, and command them in the name of the
people of the state immediately to disperse.

Section 727   456.25-10
TO ARREST RIOTERS IF THEY DO NOT DIS-
PERSE: If the persons assembled do not immediately
disperse, such magistrates and officers must arrest
them, and to that end may command the aid of all
persons present or within the county.

Vehicle Code   457
    Authorized emergency vehicles and responsibility
    during disaster.

Section 30, Authorized Emergency Vehicles   457.05
    It is declared as a matter of legislative policy that red
    lights and sirens on vehicles should be restricted to
    authorized emergency vehicles engaged in police, fire,
    and lifesaving services; and that other types of
    vehicles which are engaged in activities which create
    special hazards upon the highways should be
    equipped with flashing amber warning lamps.

Section 165   457.05-05
    An authorized emergency vehicle is:

    (a) ....

    (b) ....

    (c) ....

    (d) Any state-owned vehicle used in responding to
        emergency fire, rescue, or communications calls
        and operated either by the California Disaster
        Office or by any public agency or industrial fire
        department to which the California Disaster
        Office has assigned such vehicle ....

Section 40830, Negligence Defense   457.10
    In either of the following circumstances, a violation
    of any provision of this code does not establish
    negligence as a matter of law, but in any civil action
    under either of the circumstances, negligence must be
    proved as a fact without regard to the violation. The
    circumstances under which this section applies are
    either:

    (a) Where violation of the provision was required by
        a law of the Federal Government or by any rule,
        regulation, directive, or order of any agency of
        the Federal Government, the violation of which
        is subject to penalty under an act of Congress or
        by any valid order of military authority.

(b) Where violation of the provision was required in order to comply with any regulation, directive, or order of the Governor promulgated under the California Disaster Act.

Section 41401   457.10-05

No person shall be prosecuted for a violation of any provision of this code if the violation was required by a law of the Federal Government, by a regulation of the Interstate Commerce Commission promulgated pursuant to law, by any rule, regulation, directive or order of any agency of the Federal Government, the violation of which is subject to penalty under an act of Congress, or by any valid order of military authority.

Section 41402   457.10-10

No person shall be prosecuted for a violation of any provision of this code when violation of such provision is required in order to comply with any regulation, directive, or order of the Governor promulgated under the California Disaster Act.

Burbank Police Department

UNUSUAL OCCURRENCE COMMAND ASSIGNMENT

Date:_____
Time:_____ (AM) (PM)

Department Commander:_____

Division Commander:_____

Duty Watch Commander:_ _____ Watch I II III

Field Commander:_____

Command Post: _____ _____ _____
                    (Location)   (Unit)   (Phone Number)

POST/DETAIL	LOCATION	SUPERVISOR	UNIT	TIME Assign Relief
Evacuation	_____	_____	___	_____
Inspection	_____	_____	___	_____
Isolation	_____	_____	___	_____
Medical	_____	_____	___	_____
Missing Person	_____	_____	___	_____
Morgue	_____	_____	___	_____
Other:				
_____	_____	_____	___	_____
_____	_____	_____	___	_____
_____	_____	_____	___	_____

Annex 1

Burbank Police Department

UNUSUAL OCCURRENCE DETAIL ASSIGNMENT

Supervisor: _____

Detail: _____ Date: _____

NAME/UNIT #	ASSIGNMENT	LOCATION	TIME Assign Relieve
1.			
2.			
3.			
4.			
5.			
6.			
7.			
8.			
9.			
10.			
11.			
12.			
13.			
14.			
15.			
16.			
17.			
18.			
19.			
20.			
21.			
22.			
23.			
24.			

Annex 2

Burbank Police Department
MOBILIZATION ROSTER

Duty Watch Commander:_____Watch I II III

Date:_____Time Start:_____ (AM)(PM)   Time Complete:_____ (AM)(PM)

DIVISION/BUREAU	WATCH	NUMBER	YES	NO

Administrative Staff

Chief of Police
Assistant Chief
 of Police*
Captain   1 2 3

Uniform Division

Captain*
Lieutenant, Patrol   I II III   1 2 3 4
Lieutenant, Traffic*
Sergeant, Patrol*   I II III   1 2 3 4 5 6 7 8
Sergeant, Traffic*   1 2
Investigator, Patrol   I II III   1 2 3 4 5 6 7
Patrolman, Desk   I II III   1 2 3
Patrolman, Followup
Patrolman, Jail   I II III   1 2 3
Patrolman, Patrol   I II III   1 2 3 4 5 6 7 8 9 10
                                       11 12 13 14 15 16
                                       17 18 19 20 21 22
                                       23 24 25 26 27 28
                                       29 30
Patrolman, Traffic   1 2 3 4 5 6 7 8 9 10
                                       11 12 13 14 15
Clerks   1 2

Investigation Division

Captain*
Lieutenant, Detective*
Lieutenant, Juvenile*
Sergeant, Detective*   1 2 3 4
Detective/Investigator   1 2 3 4 5 6 7 8 9 10
                                       11 12 13 14 15
Clerks   1 2 3

Services Division

Captain
Supv., Record Bureau*
Lieutenant, Training*
Identification Officer
Rangemaster
Clerks*   1 2 3 4 5 6 7 8 9 10
                                       11 12
Automotive Serviceman
Auxiliary Police

Vice Bureau

Supervisor*
Investigator

*Key Personnel

Burbank Police Department

UNUSUAL OCCURRENCE HAZARD REPORT

Reporting Officer: _____ Date: _____

Detail Assigned: _____ Time: _____(AM) (PM)

Street: _____ Condition: _____
      (100 block)

Buildings:

Fire   Yes ☐   No ☐   _____

                                          (street address)

Structural Damage   Yes ☐   No ☐   _____

                                          (street address)

Utility Damage   Yes ☐   No ☐   _____

                                          (street address)

If YES, explain: _____

_____

_____

_____

Utilities:

Gas   Yes ☐   No ☐

Power   Yes ☐   No ☐

Telephone   Yes ☐   No ☐

Water   Yes ☐   No ☐

If YES, explain: _____

_____

_____

_____

Vehicles:

Description and license number: _____

_____

_____

Other:

Explain: _____

Annex 4

Burbank Police Department

SPECIAL NOTIFICATION REPORT

Reporting Officer:_____ Date:_____

Agency/Person	Who Notified	By Whom	Time
1._____	_____	_____	_____
2._____	_____	_____	_____
3._____	_____	_____	_____
4._____	_____	_____	_____
5._____	_____	_____	_____
6._____	_____	_____	_____
7._____	_____	_____	_____
8._____	_____	_____	_____
9._____	_____	_____	_____
10._____	_____	_____	_____
11._____	_____	_____	_____
12._____	_____	_____	_____
13._____	_____	_____	_____
14._____	_____	_____	_____
15._____	_____	_____	_____
16._____	_____	_____	_____
17._____	_____	_____	_____
18._____	_____	_____	_____
19._____	_____	_____	_____
20._____	_____	_____	_____

Annex 5

Burbank Police Department

SPECIAL NOTIFICATION REFERENCE

1. Aero Detail,
   Los Angeles Sheriff's Office   626-9511

2. Ambulance, Burbank   842-4833

3. Ambulance,
   Los Angeles Fire Department   785-2151

4. Ambulance,
   Los Angeles Sheriff's Office   626-9511   Ext. 82550

5. Ambulance, Miller's   245-3349

6. Animal Shelter   846-3487   OR Ext. 266

7. A.P.C.D.   629-4711   Ext. 66075

8. Army Corps of Engineers   623-1311   OR 623-5323

9. Atomic Energy Commission   341-1120

10. Bomb Squad,
    Los Angeles Sheriff's Office   626-9511

11. C.A.B.   776-0117

12. Civil Defense   846-2141   OR Ext. 247

13. Communications Department   846-2141   OR Ext. 261

14. Coroner   629-2451   Ext. 82486

15. Deputy Coroner Eckerman   848-2131

16. Deputy Coroner Fillbach   846-1151

17. Deputy Coroner Kubasak   845-3766

18. F.A.A.   678-5259

19. F.B.I.   483-3551

20. Fire Department, Burbank   845-2411   OR Ext. 311

21. Fire Department,
    Los Angeles County   262-2111

SPECIAL NOTIFICATION REFERENCE

22. Flood Control, Los Angeles County	223-2111	
23. Gas Company of Southern Calif.	243-1158	
24. Highways, State Division of	662-8135	
25. Hospital, Burbank	846-3135	
26. Hospital, St. Joseph	848-5531	
27. Hospital, Sun Valley	767-3310	
28. Hospital, Los Angeles County General	225-3115	
29. Los Angeles Police Department	624-5211	Ext. 3261
30. Los Angeles Sheriff's Office	626-9511	Ext. 82551
31. Lockheed Aircraft Company	847-2632	
32. Physicians' Exchange	848-4414	
33. Physicians' Exchange	781-1030	
34. Physicians' Exchange	788-1813	
35. Public Service Department	846-2141	OR Ext. 291
36. Public Works, Street Department	846-2141	OR Ext. 267
37. Railroad, Santa Fe	628-0111	
38. Railroad, Southern Pacific	624-6161	
39. Railroad, Union Pacific	685-4350	
40. Telephone Company	783-0610	
41. Transportation, Private	846-3087	
42. Transportation, Public	846-2141	OR Ext. 267
43. Water Resources, State Division	620-4107	

Annex 5A

Burbank Police Department

CITIZEN CONTACT REPORT

Burbank Police Department
FIELD INTERROGATION REPORT

Last Name First (Print)					Div. of Occur.	
Address					Phone	
Location				Date		Time
Age	Hgt.	Wgt.	Build	Complexion		Race
Eyes	Hair	Date of Birth		Operators No.		
Dress						
Make of Car		License No.		Type		Color

Reason for Interrogation

_____

_____

_____

_____

Disposition

OFFICER _____
                  Name   Serial No.

OFFICER _____
                  Name   Serial No.

_____
                  Division   Detail

Burbank Police Department

MASS CARE CENTER REPORT

Reporting Officer: _____ Date:_____

Detail Assigned: _____ Time:_____ (AM) (PM)

Location:_____ Destination:_____

	NAME	ADDRESS	SEX	AGE	NO. IN FAMILY
1.					
2.					
3.					
4.					
5.					
6.					
7.					
8.					
9.					
10.					
11.					
12.					
13.					
14.					
15.					
16.					
17.					
18.					
19.					
20.					
21.					
22.					

Annex 7

BURBANK POLICE
GENERAL CASE REPORT

(1) CASE CLASSIFICATION

(2) DR

(3) BEAT   (4) AREA   (5) DAY   (6) DATE AND TIME OCCURRED   (7) DATE AND TIME REPORTED

Name of Victim, Loser or Finder

(8) LAST NAME   (9) FIRST   (10) INITIAL   (11) SEX   (12) AGE   (13) LOCATION OF OCCURRENCE

(14) RESIDENCE ADDRESS   (15) BUSINESS ADDRESS   (16) RES. PHONE   (17) BUS. PHONE

(18) PERSON REPORTING CASE   (19) RESIDENCE ADDRESS   (20) RES. PHONE   (21) BUS. PHONE

(22) (1) SUSPECT OR PERSONS ARRESTED, NAME   (23) ADDRESS   (24) RES. PHONE   (25) I.B. NO.   (26) A. NO.

(27) SEX   (28) RACE   (29) AGE   (30) HEIGHT   (31) WEIGHT   (32) HAIR   (33) EYES   (34) MARKS, SCARS, CLOTHING

(35) (2) SUSPECT OR PERSONS ARRESTED, NAME   (36) ADDRESS   (37) RES. PHONE   (38) I.B. NO.   (39) A. NO.

(40) SEX   (41) RACE   (42) AGE   (43) HEIGHT   (44) WEIGHT   (45) HAIR   (46) EYES   (47) MARKS, SCARS, CLOTHING

DETAILED REPORT: LIST ADDITIONAL SUSPECTS, PERSONS ARRESTED AND DESCRIPTIONS, PERSONS INTERVIEWED. IS VICTIM INSURED? WILLING TO PROSECUTE?

ACCOUNT FOR PRISONER'S PROPERTY ON ARREST REPORT. ITEMIZE AND DESCRIBE ALL OTHER PROPERTY INVOLVED, INCLUDE SERIAL NUMBER AND VALUE. SHOW DISPOSITION OF ALL PROPERTY AND EVIDENCE. | (48) TYPE OF PROPERTY:

(49) CROSS REFERENCE ALL NUMBERS	(50) PHOTOS TAKEN	(51) NUMBER	(52) BY WHOM	(53) TOTAL LOSS	(54) TOTAL RECOVERY
	YES ☐ NO ☐			$	$.
(55) REPORT SUBMITTED BY	(56) DATE	(57) TIME	(58) APPROVED BY	(59) EVIDENCE TAG NUMBER	

USE THIS FORM ONLY TO REPORT THOSE INCIDENTS SPECIFICALLY PERMITTED   TT SENT

CHIEF _____ UNIF. CAPT. _____ INV. CAPT. _____ DET. _____ JUV. _____ COURT _____ REPORTERS _____ YES ☐ NO ☐

Annex 8

Burbank Police Department

MEDICAL ASSISTANCE REPORT

Detail:_____ Supervisor:_____

Reporting Officer:_____ Date: _____

Victim:

| (last name) | (first) | (middle) | (sex) | (age) |

_(street address)   (city)   (state)

Injury:

_____   Code for Injury
(type code)

K - Dead before report made
A - Bleeding wound, distorted member, etc.
B - Other visible injury (bruises, swelling, etc.)
C - No visible injury, unconscious, or pain

(Location-time of injury)   (Location found)

Disposition:

Check One
☐   Treated and released   Time:_____(AM) (PM)
☐   Sent to:_____
                    (Hospital)
☐   Dead on Arrival   Time:_____(AM) (PM)

Attending Physician/Nurse:

_____
                    (Name)

How Injury Occurred:

_____
_____
_____
_____
_____
_____

Annex 9

Burbank Police Department

MEDICAL SUPPLY INVENTORY CONTROL

Detail:_____ Supervisor:_____ Date:_____

QUANTITY	ITEM	LOCATION
1. _____	Bandage, gauze dressing	_____
2. _____	Bandage, triangular	_____
3. _____	Blankets, paper	_____
4. _____	Blankets, wool	_____
5. _____	Compress, burn dress. lg.	_____
6. _____	Compress, burn dress. sm.	_____
7. _____	Cotton	_____
8. _____	Dressing, large	_____
9. _____	Dressing, medium	_____
10. _____	Dressing, small	_____
11. _____	Litter cot	_____
12. _____	Portable kit, first-aid	_____
13. _____	Splint, arm	_____
14. _____	Splint, leg	_____
15. _____	Tourniquet	_____
16. _____	Truck, first aid	_____

	OFFICER	UNIT #	LOCATION	ITEM	QUANTITY
1.					
2.					
3.					
4.					
5.					
6.					
7.					
8.					
9.					
10.					
11.					
12.					
13.					
14.					
15.					
16.					

Annex 10

BURBANK POLICE
MISSING PERSON REPORT

BEAT	AREA	DAY	DATE & TIME REPORTED	DR

NAME _____ ADULT ( ) JUV. ( ) MALE ( ) FEMALE ( )

ADDRESS _____ PHONE _____ BUS. PHONE _____

OCCUPATION _____ EMPLOYED BY _____

AGE _____ DATE OF BIRTH _____ HEIGHT _____ WEIGHT _____ HAIR _____ EYES _____

LAST SEEN AT _____ DATE LAST SEEN _____ TIME _____

LAST SEEN BY _____ ADDRESS _____ PHONE _____

PROBABLE DESTINATION _____ PHOTO REC'D _____ PUBLICITY DESIRED _____

CAUSE OF ABSENCE _____ MENTAL CONDITION _____

KNOWN ASSOCIATES _____

RACE _____ MARRIED _____ SINGLE _____ DIVORCED _____ SPOUSE DEAD _____

NOSE _____ CHIN _____ COMPLEXION _____

MARKS - SCARS - AMPUTATIONS AND TATTOO MARKS _____

NAME OF DENTIST _____ ADDRESS _____

KNOWN DENTAL WORK _____

AUTO DESC. _____ LICENSE # _____

EVER ARRESTED? _____ WHERE? _____ CHARGE _____

LAUNDRY MARKS _____ CLOTHES MADE BY _____

JEWELRY WORN _____ MONEY CARRIED _____

HAT _____ SUIT _____ CAPRIS _____

COAT _____ TROUSERS _____ SHOES _____

JACKET _____ BLOUSE _____ STOCKINGS _____

SWEATER _____ SKIRT _____ NECKTIE _____

SHIRT _____ DRESS _____ GLOVES _____

REPORTED BY _____ ADDRESS _____ PHONE _____

RELATIONSHIP _____ REPORTED TO _____

FATHER'S NAME _____ ADDRESS _____ PHONE _____

MOTHER'S NAME _____ ADDRESS _____ PHONE _____

REMARKS:

CHIEF _____ UNIF. CAPT. _____ DET. _____ JUV. _____ REPORTERS _____ OFFICER: _____ TT SENT: _____ YES ☐ NO ☐

BURBANK POLICE DEPARTMENT

☐ HOMICIDE   DR _____

☐ SUICIDE

☐ DEAD BODY FOUND   Date of This Report _____

ML
_____

Name_____Date Occurred _____ Time_____
     Last Name   First Name   Middle Name
Res. Address_____ Phone_____
Bus. Address_____ Phone_____
_____

Where Committed _____   Reported by_____
_____   Address _____
How Committed _____   Phone_____
Description of Means Used _____   Date Reported_____Time_____
_____   Reported to _____
_____   Act Discovered by_____
Description of Victim _____   Address_____
Race_____ D.O.B. _____   Phone_____
Age_____ Sex_____   Reported to Coroner by _____
Height_____ Build_____   _____
Weight_____ Birthplace_____   Victim Removed to_____
Hair_____ Occupation_____   _____
Marks _____   By Order of_____
_____   Relatives:_____
Clothing _____   Name_____ Phone_____
_____   Address_____
_____   Relationship _____
Witnesses:_____   Name_____ Phone _____
_____   Address _____
_____   Relationship_____
Suspect _____
_____

Details

_____   _____   _____
Approved By   **Reporting Officer**   **Investigating Officers**

Annex 12

Burbank Police Department

IDENTIFICATION TAG REPORT

NAME:_____ SEX:_____

ADDRESS:_____ AGE:_____

LOCATION OF RECOVERY:_____

DATE:_____TIME:_____ (AM) (PM)

NO:**123**

_____
Reporting Officer

Instructions (reverse)

1. Fill out with all available information.

2. If severed member found, insert PART in NAME blank.

3. Tie tag to extremity (do NOT attach to clothing).

4. Place property in container and use blank card with same number as attached to body.

5. Use *same* number for all severed members belonging to particular body (if known).

Burbank Police Department

EQUIPMENT INVENTORY CONTROL

Detail: _____ Supervisor: _____

Date: _____

QUANTITY	ITEM	LOCATION
1. _____	Batteries	_____
2. _____	Barricades	_____
3. _____	Blankets	_____
4. _____	First Aid Kits	_____
5. _____	Flares	_____
6. _____	Flashlights	_____
7. _____	Floodlights	_____
8. _____	Generator, Aux.	_____
9. _____	Jeep	_____
10. _____	Lanterns	_____
11. _____	Maps	_____
12. _____	Megaphones	_____
13. _____	Radio, Portable	_____
14. _____	Rope	_____

	OFFICER	UNIT #	LOCATION	ITEM	QUANTITY
1.	_____	_____	_____	_____	_____
2.	_____	_____	_____	_____	_____
3.	_____	_____	_____	_____	_____
4.	_____	_____	_____	_____	_____
5.	_____	_____	_____	_____	_____
6.	_____	_____	_____	_____	_____
7.	_____	_____	_____	_____	_____
8.	_____	_____	_____	_____	_____
9.	_____	_____	_____	_____	_____
10.	_____	_____	_____	_____	_____
11.	_____	_____	_____	_____	_____
12.	_____	_____	_____	_____	_____
13.	_____	_____	_____	_____	_____
14.	_____	_____	_____	_____	_____
15.	_____	_____	_____	_____	_____

Annex 14

Burbank Police Department

UNUSUAL OCCURRENCE CONTROL

HEADQUARTERS

Desk Officer:

1. Unit(s) assigned? Yes ☐ No ☐
2. Supervisor assigned? Yes ☐ No ☐
3. Ambulance dispatched? Yes ☐ No ☐
4. Hospital(s) notified? Yes ☐ No ☐

Watch Commander:

1. Fanout procedure initiated? Yes ☐ No ☐
2. E.C.C. briefed? Yes ☐ No ☐
3. Mobilization roster complete? Yes ☐ No ☐
4. Command Post established? Yes ☐ No ☐

FIELD

Field Commander:

1. Posts established? Yes ☐ No ☐
    (a) Command? Yes ☐ No ☐
    (b) Medical? Yes ☐ No ☐
    (c) Missing Person? Yes ☐ No ☐
    (d) Morgue? Yes ☐ No ☐
2. Details assigned? Yes ☐ No ☐
    (a) Evacuation? Yes ☐ No ☐
    (b) Evaluation Yes ☐ No ☐
    (c) Inspection? Yes ☐ No ☐
    (d) Isolation? Yes ☐ No ☐
    (e) Medical? Yes ☐ No ☐
    (f) Missing Person? Yes ☐ No ☐
    (g) Morgue? Yes ☐ No ☐
3. Procedures initiated? Yes ☐ No ☐
    (a) Evacuation of involved area? Yes ☐ No ☐
    (b) Evaluation of involved area? Yes ☐ No ☐
    (c) Hazards identified? Yes ☐ No ☐
    (d) Hazards reported? Yes ☐ No ☐
    (e) Hazards removed? Yes ☐ No ☐
    (f) Isolation of involved area? Yes ☐ No ☐
    (g) Injured located? Yes ☐ No ☐
    (h) Injured treated? Yes ☐ No ☐
    (i) Inspection of involved area? Yes ☐ No ☐

Detail Supervisor:

1. Personnel assigned? Yes ☐ No ☐
2. Assignments recorded? Yes ☐ No ☐
3. Personnel instructed? Yes ☐ No ☐
4. Supplies distributed? Yes ☐ No ☐
5. Reports received? Yes ☐ No ☐
6. Reports forwarded? Yes ☐ No ☐
7. Equipment needs identified? Yes ☐ No ☐
8. Appropriate agencies requested? Yes ☐ No ☐

Annex A

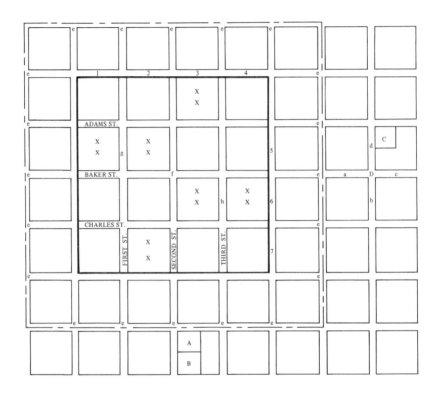

Figure 4: ACTIVITY DIAGRAM FOR UNUSUAL OCCURRENCE SCENE: A = Command Post; B = Missing Persons Post; C = Morgue Post; D = Medical Post; a = Egress Route to Medical Post; b = Egress Route for Treated Persons; c = Ingress/Egress Route for Ambulance; d = Ingress/Egress Route for Coroner Traffic; e = Isolation Detail − Fixed Post; f = Isolation Detail − Mobile Unit; g = Evaluation Detail; h = Inspection Detail or Evacuation Detail
= Perimeter of Control
= Encircled Involved Area

See Appendix A for another excellent example of a disaster plan worked out in advance.   *ANNEX B*

CHAPTER IV

THE CONTAINMENT OF
CIVIL DISORDER

 T HE social phenomena of civil disorder were given preliminary attention in Chapter I, *The Anatomy of Disaster.* Under man-made emergencies, civil disorder includes mass demonstrations, mob situations, riot emergencies, industrial disorders, prison outbreaks and others.

As indicated earlier, the foregoing emergencies may on occasion approach disaster proportions and require police action on a scale equal to that taken in the event of a hurricane, tornado or earthquake. In most cities and communities, there are potentialities for mob and riot situations.

Recent years have witnessed a sharp increase in social disturbances across the nation. Chiefs of police and their command personnel in measuring up to their responsibility in this area of police operations must prepare well-laid plans in advance for coping with this form of emergency.* Emphasizing the key importance of police pre-disaster preparation, the International Association of Chiefs of Police has made available a tool publication, *Guidelines for Civil Disorder and Mobilization Planning.* It was developed by Dean Smith, Director of the IACP Research, Development and Planning Division and Richard W. Kobetz, consultant for the President's Advisory Commission on Civil Disorders, and prepared under a contract from the Office of the Attorney General, U. S. Department of Justice. Advisors were Deputy Chief Daryl F. Gates of Los Angeles, Major Adam Klimkowski, Director of Training for the Miami Police Department and Mr. Arnold Sagalyn, Associate Director of Public Safety for the President's Advisory Commission on Civil Disorders.

---

*See Lund, Donald A.: Confrontation Management. *Police.* March, 1972. Captain Lund draws a useful distinction between spontaneous outbreaks of violence and deliberately planned confrontations which openly solicit a dramatic police response and the national attention accompanying that response.

Guidelines for Civil Disorder and Mobilization Planning is a professional blueprint for police action and planning in the approach to the control of civil disturbances and for the convenience of police personnel, it is presented here in its entirety through the courtesy of the International Association of Chiefs of Police as the basic content of this chapter.

GUIDELINES FOR CIVIL DISORDER AND MOBILIZATION PLANNING

I. PURPOSE

In developing a model police plan of any type, it is impossible to assure that the plan will automatically fit the needs of all departments, large, medium or small. At best, the plan should be capable of scaling up or down and should contain the basic elements necessary to function regardless of the size of the organization. Any police department can select these basic elements and tailor from them a plan that will meet its specifications and requirements and enable it to respond quickly and effectively to any emergency.

These guidelines are geared to a medium-sized operation so that they will be suitable for the greatest number of police agencies. As a plan is built to a department's individual specifications, all phases must be field tested to insure that it works.

The nature of civil disorders involving large numbers of people requires planning, training and operations which will allow the police to function as a disciplined, military-type team with effective command and control. Any attempt to undertake an immediate total departmental training program would result either in insufficient application or serious interference with everyday police responsibilities. Success, therefore, depends primarily on a small staff to control and direct a police task force in dealing quickly and effectively with the emergency.

This staff will have the primary control and command responsibilities during an unusual occurrence and should be trained and tested on a continuing basis. The majority of personnel selected for the cadre will be experienced in the specialized duties to which they will be assigned. However, not all the personnel will possess this experience. In a major emergency, some routine police functions will be discontinued and personnel normally assigned to them will become available for some form of riot duty. These individuals will require considerably more training than those officers whose duties will be changed little by the emergency. Unless such training is provided, however, the police agency will not obtain the maximum benefit from these individuals or from the basic cadre.

The mayor, as the chief elected official, must take ultimate responsibility for all governmental action in times of disorder. To do so, he must become fully involved in disorder planning and operations so that he may understand the nature of the problems posed by the disorder. Similarly, police chiefs should understand this responsibility and involve the mayor in their planning activities and operations.

II. POLICE POLICY

It is the responsibility of the chief of police to insure that sound policies are formulated to serve as guidelines to members of his department in their contacts with the public. An even greater responsibility is to articulate the policy throughout his entire organization and insure that his personnel are certain that support is intended and expected for their actions within such policy.

A. *Administrative Policy*

1. *Administrative Policy* involves a stated position on the issues of police-community relations, human relations and civil disturbances. This position would recognize the right of lawful demonstration and at the same time point out the responsibilities of those who demonstrate. It should contain a pledge of fair and impartial enforcement for all members of the community.

An example of such a policy position follows:

a. *Demonstrations*

The department has a responsibility to protect lawful demonstrators. In some instances, lawful demonstrations can serve to reduce community tensions. However, any serious unlawful incident that threatens public safety must be dealt with quickly and decisively by utilizing every necessary department resource to protect the rights and property of all citizens.

b. *Civil Disturbance*

The control of a civil disturbance is to be distinguished from the control of a crowd, such as those at parades, special events, large meetings and peaceful demonstrations. Civil disturbances have a lawless element intent on damage of property, injury of persons and interference with normal business and traffic operations, usually resulting in other crimes related to acts of violence. When a civil disturbance develops on any scale, the restoration of law and order becomes the primary objective of all department operations.

c. *Force*

In maintaining law and order the department should use only that force which is lawful, necessary and reasonable. *Minimum* rather than *maximum* force should be this rule in application.

2. Policy statements should be prepared in written form.

3. Concurrence of chief executive and appropriate city officials should be obtained.

4. Appropriate dissemination of policy should be provided through:

   a. News media.

   b. Departmental orders.

   c. Staff meetings.

   (releases to the public would consist of a clear explanation of the general principles upon which the policy is based and a full discussion of its importance to the public. Material distributed to the department would be specific and detailed.)

5. Without inspections for positive implementation, policy may become nothing more than an archive. Inspections should produce an affirmative answer to each of the following questions:

   a. Are they following policy?

   b. Does everyone really understand it?

c. Are the supervisors supporting it?

If the answer to any of these questions is negative, there is an apparent need for a reassessment of the policy statement. Policy which is generated from above without regard to its impact on or suitability in the field should be carefully examined with the aim of making it both appropriate and workable. Lack of understanding tends to point up the need for training, while disagreement reveals the more serious problem of failing to involve all levels of personnel in the development of policy.

B. *Organizational Policy*

While it is true that community relations is a responsibility shared equally by all police personnel, some means of measuring the attitude of the community must be established. The chief of police needs communications with all facets of the community in order to obtain information concerning possible problem areas.

1. The size of the department and the magnitude of the problem will determine whether the channeling of community relations information will be an assignment for one individual as a full-time responsibility or that of a special unit.

2. The individual or unit should operate in a staff capacity and should report directly to the chief.

3. Information should be reviewed and analyzed for possible community tensions, and derived intelligence should be brought to the attention of the department head on a regular and special basis.

C. *Operational Policy*

1. Specific guidelines for disturbances will be discussed in later sections.

2. Special attention must be given to firearms because of the adverse effect which their employment may generate. The use of firearms for the protection of the officer, of other officers and of innocent citizens is not questioned. However, when other alternatives such as tear gas are available, use of firearms against riot participants should be avoided. Before employing firearms, the following must be considered:

a. In looting and rioting, the application of deadly force against women and children cannot be justified in the absence of overt acts which *immediately* endanger the lives of others.

b. Once an establishment has been broken into, looting is a continuous action. The act of removing from such premises an article, regardless of its value, does not justify the use of deadly force. (Consider the discharge of chemical agents into the building to prevent further looting.) (See Appendix 2.)

c. The selection of shoulder weapons for applying fatal force should be considered. Automatic weapons would be undesirable where their indiscriminate fire patterns would endanger the lives of innocent persons.

d. The possibility that use of fatal force will *worsen* rather than *lessen* the disorder must be considered. When necessary to protect life, fatal force should be *used discriminately;* but whenever possible, such force should be *avoided.*

III. PLANNING

A police administrator cannot predict the exact time, place or persons that will be involved in any single incident. However, the nature of probable occurrences can be predicted and planned for.

A. *Planning Concepts*

1. Basic considerations:

    a. Recognize the need for certain plans. (define the problem)

    b. Establish objectives of the plans.

    c. Gather and analyze relevant data.

    d. Develop the plans.

    e. Obtain concurrence within and outside the department.

    f. Take steps to implement the plans in an orderly manner.

    g. Provide for inspection to assure proper implementation.

2. Types of plans:

    a. *Goal Plans:* Outline ways to realize the end objectives.

    b. *Standing Plans:* Furnish standard operating procedures wherein the same problems are generally handled the same way each time.

    c. *Short Term or Single-Use Plans:* Deal with foreseeable problems of a special nature (e.g. beach riots, campus disturbances, special parades or demonstrations, etc.)

3. Classification of plans:

    a. *Management Plans:* Relate to equipping, staffing, and preparing the department to do the job.

    b. *Operational Plans:* The work programs of the line divisions.

    c. *Procedural Plans:* Cover the standard action to be taken by all members of the department under specified circumstances.

    d. *Tactical Plans:* Cover the specific action to be taken at given locations under specific situations.

    e. *Extra-Departmental Plans:* Those that require action or assistance from persons and agencies outside the police department.

B. *Training Plans*

1. Department-wide training plans should include:

    a. Programs dealing with community relations.

    b. Means for coping with lawful demonstrations.

    c. Means for coping with civil disturbances.

    d. Regular evaluation and critique of operations.

2. Special-purpose units should receive in-depth specialized training. This training applies particularly to:

    a. Community relations units.

    b. Crowd control units.

    c. Riot squads.

Also, training in community relations should be more detailed and sophisticated for special-purpose units than for the other police department personnel.

3. Supervisory and command personnel require additional training and exercises in:

    a. Objectives of the disorder control plan.

    b. That portion of the plan which they are responsible for.

    c. Strategy and tactics to be employed.

    d. Controlling and directing subordinates under stress conditions.

4. Auxiliary police and civil defense personnel should be included in the departmental training program, since they will frequently work with, or in support of, regular officers in the field.

5. Certain other city employees assigned to support tasks need, as a minimum, training in the following areas:

    a. Courses familiarizing them with police duties and responsibilities during emergencies.

    b. Training in traffic direction and other routine tasks. Such training would enable them to act as a manpower supplement and temporarily replace regular officers in places outside the disturbance areas.

6. Fire employees could train policemen regarding incendiary devices and arson, emergency rescue, securing utilities, etc.

7. Regional training and coordination with military, state and neighboring police agencies should be planned.

C. *Mobilization Plans*

Meeting the demands for every-day police services understandably becomes a matter of habit. When an unusual occurrence develops, it is difficult to shift suddenly from accustomed responsibilities to meet the needs of the new situation. Nevertheless, normal police activities must be looked at in a different light, and the designated field commander must be provided immediately with the necessary manpower to fulfill the new police responsibilities.

Recent experience indicates that effective control during an unusual occurrence depends upon immediate activation of a police department's manpower resources. Time is critical. Rapid, substantial mobilization is particularly important in civil disturbances where immediate, organized redistribution of personnel is necessary to protect life and property and prevent escalation.

1. A *tactical alert* is a means of alerting all personnel that an unusual occurrence is either anticipated or already going on. The *tactical alert* can be divided into three phases:

   a. *Blue Alert: A minor unusual occurrence* which will be handled by the on-duty patrol division with the assistance normally available from other divisions. Those units not assigned to the involved area should continue with their normal functions but should maintain radio contact in the event of escalation. Off-duty personnel would not be affected. The decision to declare a Blue Alert is that of the ranking on-duty officer. Key staff personnel, local and state officials should also be alerted.

   b. *White Alert: A serious, unusual occurrence* of such proportion that the normal on-duty structure is insufficient to establish control. The rapid mobilization of a sufficient number of men is the paramount need here. The longer the wait for help, the greater the possibility of further escalation of the disturbance. It is imperative that the maximum effort be made to overwhelm the rioters as rapidly as possible to prevent escalation. The organization should discontinue normal non-emergency functions. The on-coming shift should be called up early to augment on-duty forces. All other personnel should be placed on a 24-hour standby. The decision to declare a White Alert must be that of the chief of police or his designated representative. Local and state officials should be informed immediately.

The call-up of off-duty forces is a relatively slow process which is aggravated by the long distances that in coming personnel must travel. A rehearsal may establish valuable data on estimation of manpower available and reaction time. The most expeditious means of assembling needed manpower quickly is to secure the assistance of the on-duty personnel in neighboring police agencies. Such a plan assumes that Mutual Aid programs have been agreed upon some time earlier.

c. *Red Alert: A major disorder* which threatens the safety of the jurisdiction of an indefinite period of time and which necessitates a completely restructured police organization. The primary function of the entire organization is to subdue the riot. The responsibilities require that the reorganization of the department be accompanied by:

(1) Immediate extension of the work day to twelve-hour watches. Reporting times may change, once the initial major violence has subsided, and it is likely that the larger percentage of men will be placed on duty during hours of darkness when new outbreaks are most likely to occur.

(2) Deferment of days off, vacations, etc.

(3) Requests for major assistance from other police departments, National Guard and other governmental agencies.

The decision to declare a Red Alert must be that of the chief executive of the department. Likewise, it is his decision from this point on, as the riot situation de-escalates, to declare a White Alert, then a Blue Alert and finally, the discontinuance of the Alert.

2. Total mobilization is a difficult and time-consuming task. In some cities partial mobilization has disclosed that the number of men available for riot duty was far less than the original estimates.

If mobilization plans are to be realistic, they must be developed with the following key points always at the forefront:

a. Identification of the normal police functions to be curtailed or modified at each stage of mobilization.

b. Determination of the manpower available for riot duty at each stage of mobilization.

Decisions must be made in advance as to the functions which can or must be modified during serious and major emergencies. Some police agencies are normally responsible for the issuance of certain licenses or for vehicle inspection. It is obvious that during emergencies these activities and such services as investigation of bad check complaints, landlord tenant disputes, minor accidents and so forth can be dispensed with. However, alternative reporting methods should be devised for post-disturbance follow-up.

3. The cancellation of certain functions does not insure that the manpower made available is prepared or able to perform specific riot duties. The individual's previous training, physical ability and special qualifications and the specific emergency needs of the department must be considered. Personnel in such categories should be advised in advance as to where and how they will be employed in the event of an emergency. Such personnel must receive the training necessary to perform their emergency assignments.

It is an exercise in futility for riot orders to call for tasks to be performed if personnel are not available for the tasks. Plans should be tested during the various shifts on various days of the week to gain the most accurate assessment of probable manpower availability at any given time. It is only after testing that mobilization plans turn from pretentious theories into useful realities.

4. Call-up of Off-Duty Personnel

a. Each unit is responsible for setting up a recall system. A decentralized plan is essential. Several methods are suggested, including the *fan-out* or *pyramid,* the direct call-up by a special team or special arrangements with the telephone company.

b. The person calling should properly identify himself and inform the officer as to which location he should report.

c. In addition to direct telephone or personal contact, personnel can be notified via radio and TV spot announcements.

    d. An accurate status report of officers notified, accounted for or not located should be maintained.

5. An alert system for those responsible for necessary logistical support — equipment, transportation, facilities and communications — should be provided. Such an alert should have considerable lead time over a general alert.

6. It is most important that the mobilization plan be coordinated with Mutual Aid plans such as supplementary aid from surrounding departments and military and state police as authorized by state law.

    a. Will they be integrated with the police department?

    b. Will they be combined into one unit?

    c. Will they remain as intact separate units?

    d. Will they only be employed for sector control or as guards?

7. Activation: An initial and follow-through reaction to any incident *could* occur in this manner (See Appendix 3.):

    a. Officer on scene calls in what appears to be the start of a disturbance.

    b. After estimating the situation he summons assistance, establishes an assembly area and constantly keeps the communication center advised on the status of the situation.

    c. Supervisors and requested manpower proceed to scene.

    d. Watch Commander, detectives and intelligence personnel respond.

    e. Officers are assigned to direct pedestrian and vehicle traffic away from scene.

    f. Sufficient force of manpower is assembled to enter disturbance area.

    g. Other police units within department respond only to emergency calls and remain on standby for assignment.

    h. Personnel responsible for mass transportation, arrest procedures, logistics and security are alerted.

D. *Operational Planning*

  1. Strategy and tactics should be devised for the following:

    a. Riots.

    b. Political rallies, parades and demonstrations.

    c. Minority group protests and demonstrations.

    d. Campus disturbances and demonstrations.

    e. Counterdemonstrations.

    f. Labor disputes.

    g. Resort area problems.

    h. Public events.

    i. Disasters (man-made and natural).

    j. Weather emergencies.

  2. In Operational Planning the following factors should be considered:

    a. Nature and purpose of the event.

    b. Where event is to occur including legal jurisdiction.

    c. Time and duration; schedule.

    d. Estimate of attendance and number of vehicles.

    e. Character and temperament of the participants.

    f. Sponsoring organization and names of leaders, monitors, coordinators, etc.

    g. Identity, strength and tactics of potential counterdemonstrators.

h. Physical features of the area.

i. Traffic problems.

j. Number of personnel and equipment required.

k. Need for Mutual Aid.

l. Communications required.

m. Need for a command post — mobile or fixed.

n. Duty assignments and responsibilities.

o. Effect upon or hazard to public utilities.

p. First-aid centers and hospitals available.

q. Ambulance and tow car needs.

r. Obtainment and utilization of helicopters.

s. Arrest policy and disposition of arrestees.

t. Recovery from the event.

    (1) Preventive patrol.

    (2) Resuming normal public and police functions.

    (3) Establishing new and re-establishing old, lines of communications with the community.

E. *Legal Considerations*

It would be advisable to review existing laws and ordinances relating to civil disorder control operations for consideration of permanent or emergency legislation which could be enacted relative to:

1. Mutual aid between local, county, state police and National Guard.

2. Restrictions upon sales of gasoline, liquor and weapons.

3. Restricting access to certain defined geographic areas.

4. Curfew, loitering or crowd formation.

5. Closing down or restrictions upon schools, places of amusement, public transportation, water usage, private aircraft and citizen band radio equipment.

6. Permit requirements for parades, assemblies and public events; and regulations upon size or material used in sign sticks.

F. *Review of Other Agencies' Methods as a Basis for Planning*

Observers should be sent to the scene of a disturbance, even if they must travel long distances to get there. The head of the police department in the disturbance area should be informed about the observers and his permission to have them obtained.

After the disturbance is over and the observers have returned there should be:

1. An evaluation of the observers' experience.

2. A sharing of this experience in department staff meetings.

IV. INTELLIGENCE

The chief of police must possess all available intelligence regarding conditions in the community and in his department relative to community tensions and potential or ongoing disturbances. Intelligence is not the same as mere information. Intelligence is derived from information through a special process or system. Items of information, taken singly, are not much more than simple data. Through simple and continuous examination of these individual items — considering their time and space relationships — we very often gain insights into their larger and more significant meaning. This process is intelligence.

Decisions must be made and action taken based upon intelligence, not mere information. The decision maker must not be burdened with a constant, confusing flow of small pieces of data. The service provided by the Intelligence Officer or Unit is to review the flow of information and forward to the decision maker the estimates of the larger meaning.

A. *Information*

1. The function of an *Intelligence Officer* or *Unit* is to gather, record, evaluate and analyze information which, when converted

to intelligence estimates, supports the readiness of the department and aids actual operations within the department.

2. It is a staff and not an enforcement function.

3. Although they are sometimes interrelated, there is a distinction
between criminal intelligence and intelligence regarding the
social state of the community. Our emphasis here is upon
community tensions and possible or actual disturbances.

4. Through regular meetings the Intelligence Officer or Unit should
make every effort to maintain good communication and
cooperation with other units and individuals within the department.

   a. He (or they) should work closely with other agencies —
private and government — at the local, state and federal
levels.

   b. He (or they) should develop and maintain avenues for the
exchange of information and integration of intelligence data
from outside resources and surrounding communities.

B. *Operations*

1. All files should be kept within the Intelligence Unit and not
maintained as a part of other departmental records.

   a. Access to these files should be limited to members of the
Unit or members of the department approved by the chief
executive.

   b. These files should contain:

      (1) Information regarding individuals and groups who
constitute problems or potential problems.

      (2) Copies of all publications, pamphlets, newspapers,
articles, etc., that tend to influence public opinion in
both the *minority community* and the *majority
community*. These data can be correlated with similar
files in other government agencies.

2. Intelligence Officers should act as observers at public and private

meetings — observe individuals and groups participating in demonstrations and civil disturbances, both locally and in other jurisdictions.

C. *Resources*

1. All available sources and community channels should be utilized to discover tensions in the community, their probable causes and possible solutions and alternative police actions.

2. Information sources include:

    a. Uniformed beat and traffic men.

    b. Detective, Juvenile and Community Relations personnel.

    c. Community leaders.

    d. Community organizations and agencies.

    e. Minority group leaders.

    f. Public news media staff.

    g. Labor and trade union personnel.

    h. Businessmen.

    i. School officials and students.

    j. Allied agencies such as parole, probation, welfare, etc.

    k. Informants (money should be available, if necessary).

    l. Rumors.

D. *Community*

In preplanned incidents, intelligence estimates regarding the community should provide data on:

1. Probable causes of disturbances.

2. Composition of groups who will be involved.

3. Locations of disturbances.

4. Known leaders or organizations involved.

5. Estimated number of people who may become involved.

6. Organizations and individuals, both private and public, who are active in the community.

7. Prominent individuals living in the community who may influence the crowd.

8. Possible locations of arms, equipment and supplies available to groups.

9. Temper of groups.

10. Objectives or purposes of groups.

E. *Preplanning for Disturbance*

The Intelligence Officer or Unit should assist by determining:

1. Locations of assembly areas for crowds.

2. Types of buildings in area.

3. Type of area involved, topographical features.

4. Location of all important buildings.

5. Location of fuels, explosives, arms, equipment and supplies, which if left unguarded, may be seized and utilized by rioters.

6. Conditions of streets and routes into the area (blocked, passable, widths).

7. Location of premises vulnerable to looting.

8. Access routes – primary and secondary.

9. Medical facilities in the vicinity.

10. Night illumination available.

11. Diagrams of public utility systems.

12. Fire stations.

13. Likely screening or check points.

14. Potential command post sites.

15. Possible escape routes for crowd or officers.

16. Location and type of traffic control devices in the vicinity.

17. Possible sheltered mobilization, staging, or rest areas for disorder control personnel – police, fire, military, etc.

18. Vital or sensitive institutions requiring protection.

F. *Actual Disturbance*

1. In spontaneous eruptions the ongoing collection of reliable information is necessary as the Field Commander bases his decisions and the development of courses of action primarily on the intelligence developed from the information he receives from the various sources available to him. The channeling of verified information to the chief of police enables him to evaluate departmental needs and to implement measures required to control the incident, while providing continuing police coverage of areas not affected by the emergency.

2. The officers assigned the normal responsibility for intelligence information should continue in this capacity and utilize additional officers and supervisors as they become available. The intelligence officers must receive and forward information and handle requests for information by the Field Commander. These tasks can be accomplished by:

   a. Assigning individuals to specific sectors or specific incidents for information on conditions or occurrences there. Prior to their assignments, these individuals must be briefed on the current known status of the situation and should be given any necessary equipment – walkie-talkies, binoculars, maps, etc.

   b. Establishing or continuing undercover observation in

disturbance areas in order to:

(1) Establish the cause of the disturbance.

(2) Identify leaders and members of known groups involved.

(3) Identify and arrest the persons agitating or inciting the crowd and violating the law. These arrests might best be made by an officer on normal uniform duty or in an arrest detail assigned to disturbance in casual clothing.

(4) Gather information of evidentiary value in order to effect warrants and future arrest to agitators and leaders.

c. Additional duties of intelligence personnel could include:

(1) Infiltration of crowds, meetings and public gatherings to collect and forward information.

(2) Continuous observation of known troublemakers and agitators.

(3) Checking out of alleged sniper reports.

(4) Operation of photographic equipment, recording devices or video-tapes during disturbances and/or during arrest procedures.

(5) Distribution of any known agitator's pictures.

(6) Debriefing the officers returning from disturbance areas.

(7) Coordination of intelligence among all agencies involved in combatting disturbances.

3. Utilization of the following persons in the disturbance area to obtain and report information should be considered:

a. Community relations officers, detectives and juvenile officers who have established effective contacts with neighborhood leaders and private or public agency personnel.

b. Community people and private or public agency people to identify participants and persuade others to return to their homes.

   c. Police cadets to mingle with younger groups active in the area.

   d. Staffs of private fire and burglar alarm companies to assist in locating problem areas and disturbance patterns.

G. *Rumors*

During a civil disturbance rumors are frequent and may aggravate and possibly increase the disorder. Some rumors may be started in a deliberate effort to confuse the police department and other agencies concerned with control of the disturbance. Intelligence functions concerned with combatting rumors would include working closely with a rumor center which has been established, preferably outside the police department to receive and confirm or deny rumors. A special telephone number announced by public news media would greatly assist the rumor center in their work. The work of the rumor center would include:

1. Passing on received rumors for evaluation and information.

2. Giving the news media facts continuously through appropriate channels.

3. Using church, private, public, civic and fraternal organization members to dispel false rumors.

4. Attempts to determine the sources of rumors.

5. Keeping police intelligence officers informed in order to establish base of rumors.

6. Maintaining a rumor log for evaluation.

7. Stopping rumors as ₄ ˙ₖJᵛ as possible by documenting their falsity.

8. Display on television of pictures of leaders who are rumored to have been beaten or killed.

V. LOGISTICS

The police department's plans for the provision, maintenance and security of personnel, communications, transportation, equipment and facilities necessary for dealing with civil disturbances must be reviewed frequently. Policy should be established for frequent revision of personnel lists (department and other individuals involved), rotation and replacement of supplies, testing of equipment and inspections of facilities.

A. *Personnel*

1. An inventory should be set up of department personnel who have received specialized training or possess certain skills (linguistics, weapons, mechanical) useful for specific assignment during a disturbance.

2. During a disturbance a record of the following types of people might be considered:

   a. All department personnel assigned to disturbance.

   b. Outside personnel involved in handling the disturbance.

   c. Individuals responsible for procurement and distribution of equipment and supplies.

   d. Individuals responsible for maintenance and security of equipment and supplies not currently in use.

   e. Personnel assigned to guard utilities, public buildings, gun shops and hospitals and to do general escort and protection duties for firemen, public officials, etc.

3. Positive, workable agreements and plans concerning the availability and utilization of nonpolice personnel for disturbance assignments should be formulated. Such personnel include:

   a. Retired police and firemen.

   b. Police reserves.

   c. Private guard and watchman services.

   d. Civil defense personnel.

   e. Correction institution personnel.

   f. Parole and probation personnel.

    g. Court personnel.

    h. Government employees.

    i. Utility company employees.

    j. Civil Air Patrol.

    k. Community leaders.

    l. Clergy.

    m. Medical personnel.

B. *Communications*

  1. An inventory and analysis should be done of the need for procuring and/or improving:

    a. Regular or emergency radio frequencies.

    b. Telephone equipment both base and mobile.

    c. Portable base stations.

    d. Walkie-talkies and accessories (earphones, microphones).

    e. Emergency power transmittors for base and remote sites.

    f. Portable radios.

    g. Scrambler gear.

  2. Emergency or cooperative use of existing frequencies and personnel currently employed by the following establishments should be considered:

    a. Fire department.

    b. Government agencies.

    c. Public works.

    d. Bus and cab companies.

    e. Utility companies.

    f. Other commerical users.

  3. Citizen-band operators, mobile and stationary, could be contacted for assistance.

  4. Monitoring of citizens band and walkie-talkie channels being used by rioters might be needed.

C. *Transportation*

  1. All police department transportation methods and manpower necessary to operate those used during the disturbance should be considered:

    a. Motorcycles.

    b. Squad cars, stationwagons and ambulances (tops numbered for aircraft direction).

    c. Trucks and buses.

    d. Aircraft and boats.

  2. Use of transportation facilities owned by other public and private agencies (buses, cabs, trucks) should be arranged.

  3. Vehicle maintenance — fueling, battery replacement, tires, minor repairs — and necessary towing of department and private vehicles should be provided for:

    a. By existing department equipment and personnel.

    b. Through authorization of commercial garages and gas stations to perform needed services.

D. *Equipment*

  1. Procurement of following additional equipment should be considered:

    a. Riot or regular batons.

b. Smoke and gas grenades, gas guns, gas masks, smoke pots.

c. Riot guns, carbines, rifles.

d. Rifle telescopes and infra-red sniperscopes.

e. Sufficient ammunition (for department and personal weapons).

f. Helmets with face shields.

g. Protective sheilds and body armour.

h. Boots, gloves and replacement uniforms or clothing.

i. Fire extinguishers.

j. Hand lights and batteries.

k. Loud speaker systems and battery powered megaphones.

l. Portable tape recorders.

m. Photographic equipment.

n. Flares and fuzees.

o. Rope, crowbars, jacks, bolt cutters, axes, shovels, saws and entry tools.

p. First-aid kits, stretchers and resuscitators.

q. Handcuffs and restraining devices.

r. Portable fingerprinting kits.

s. Sign-making materials.

t. Binoculars.

u. Windshield screens for vehicles.

v. Walkie-talkies.

2. Prior arrangement should be made for community sources to supply following as needed:

   a. Heavy-duty equipment and rescue apparatus with operators.

   b. Trailers (house and van).

   c. Barricade materials (ropes, barbed wire).

   d. Floodlights and mobile generators.

   e. Board-up services.

   f. Special tools and acetylene equipment.

3. Command post needs include:

   a. Fire extinguishers.

   b. Typewriters and office supplies.

   c. Situation maps, tackboards, overlays and blackboards.

   d. Recorders and tapes.

   e. Status logs.

   f. Standby communication equipment.

   g. Emergency food and water.

   h. Gas masks.

   i. Defensive weapons.

   j. Personnel rosters.

   k. Signs.

E. *Facilities*

1. The pre-arranged establishment, identification and security of the following must be considered, with appropriate supplies and materials:

    a. Mass detention facilities to provide separate and appropriate accommodations for men, women and children.

    b. Field command post.

    c. First-aid stations with medical personnel.

    d. Automotive pounds for recovered, damaged or towed vehicles.

    e. Recovered property pound.

    f. Equipment and supply distribution area.

    g. Parking for assembly and staging areas.

    h. Parking area for private vehicles of personnel on duty.

    i. Refugee area for homeless with provision for food, clothing, social services and location of lost and injured family members.

    j. Helicopter landing area.

2. Food, shelter, bedding and sanitary facilities needed by police and other personnel officially assigned to the disturbance must be provided, possibly through cooperation with:

    a. Airlines, Red Cross, Salvation Army and caterers.

    b. Hotels, motels and school boards.

    c. Commercial suppliers of food, bedding, jiffi-johns, etc.

VI. STRATEGY

A. *Introduction*

The civil disorders of the recent past have caused law enforcement agencies to take a hard look at police strategies and tactics that have been designed to bring order out of disorder. The riot situations experienced, particularly in the large cities, have taken on a different form and dimension from that which has been described in the most current police literature on *How to Control a Riot.*

Thus, the textbook riot has not occurred to any great degree, and the textbook control measures have thus proven unusuable. The squad formations, with their well-defined uses, have failed to provide the police field commander with a sufficient range of tactical maneuvers to deal with the operational problems of control that have confronted him. These squad formations and other crowd control techniques are still useful in the special crowd situations for which they were developed and should remain in the basic police curriculum for crowd control. However, this curriculum must now be expanded to include some of the measures proven effective in recent civil disorders where control strategy and street tactics were developed and tested almost simultaneously. Any good plan should provide for flexibility. However, as a general rule police should do the following:

1. *React quickly with enough strength to overwhelm the rioting group.* This principle is so basic it appears almost unnecessary to state, but experience has shown that the police have not always reacted quickly enough nor with sufficient force. This, of course, is not always possible because of the size of the group and the area involved. However, it should be a basic policy so that the field commander will not vacillate in ordering the size or response of his control task force. A force of insufficient strength may only aggravate the situation. A cardinal rule is to commit your force only when reasonably confident that they can achieve their mission.

   The secret of sufficient strength in minimum time is the ability of the organization to switch from normal to emergency posture. As stated in an earlier section, if an extreme emergency such as a riot takes place, there should be no question that all nonemergency functions would be immediately curtailed.

2. *Establish control in all parts of the involved area.* The police must establish control quickly and decisively. There should be no area of the disturbance to which they are denied access because of external pressures. There are, however, often significant reasons to remain out of a particular area for a *period of time* — such as during negotiations.

3. *Arrest all law violators and apply reasonable force when necessary to make an arrest.* The immediate implementation of this decision is contingent upon the availability of sufficient personnel to effect it and to process arrestees. It should be done

as soon as possible. This policy decision will accomplish two things: First, it gives direction to the field commander and the officers in his task force; it mitigates against indecisive action. Second, it tells the field commander that he must *gear up* immediately for processing and accepting large numbers of prisoners.

4. *Arrest law violators without relaxing present legal requirements.* Failure to observe the rules of evidence, laws of arrest and other elements of the criminal law will lead to obvious consequences. Police should make only those arrests which can reasonably be presumed to lead to a successful prosecution. Otherwise, violators will be unconcerned about being arrested, and police officers may become careless in their arrest and evidence procedures. One of the principal roadblocks to successful prosecutions in the past has been that the police, because of the exigencies of the immediate situation, have not taken ordinary care to assure that the arrestee can be identified with the act for which he was arrested. Order must be established under law.

5. *Remain in the affected areas after order is restored.* One of the most important lessons learned has been that the police must remain in the area in force after establishing control. This can be an expensive process in terms of manpower, but it is vital to continued order. With assistance from the National Guard or Federal troops through foot and motorized patrols, you may demonstrate the presence of authority and control capability. Reduction of the control force should be accomplished gradually, while a constant flow of intelligence information from which to assess the field situation is maintained.

B. *General Considerations and Principles*

1. Once mobilization has begun and the operational posture of the police agency has shifted from a normal to an emergency mode command, decisions must be made concerning control strategy and tactics.

2. It is imperative that if the initiative has been lost to the rioters it be swiftly recaptured by the police. The tactics and strategy employed should point to this end. Experience has shown that rioting spreads quickly and that any successes gained by the rioters at the expense of constituted authority, or any apparent reluctance of the police to put down rioting, will only encourage

the forces of disorder and inspire others to join them.

3. All lawful measures should be taken to restore law and order as quickly as possible. Strict impartiality must be observed and every police officer must control himself against his own private inclinations to respond to jeers or epithets. A quiet, purposeful demeanor is essential to prevent a situation from deteriorating. When action is decided upon, it should be pressed forward with determination, and no sign capable of interpretation as weakness should be permitted to appear.

4. No more force should be used than is reasonably necessary to achieve the objective. The application of force should cease once the objective has been achieved. When force is reasonably necessary and lawfully applied during the early stages of a disturbance, there should be no hesitation in its use. It is better to bring the rioting to an early conclusion than allow it to spread with the possibility of many casualties, much damage and loss of public confidence. In this connection each department must be guided by clear policy and by the laws under which it operates.

5. The ability to clear the streets as soon as possible is essential to the early suppression of any serious disturbance. If a curfew can be legally employed, it should be proclaimed as early as possible, then enforced rigorously. Failure of the police to act in this manner from the outset will only bring the curfew into contempt and encourage further disobedience.

6. Since a disturbance must be suppressed quickly, it requires determined and resolute leadership at all levels of command. While much has already been said about the need to quickly adjust the organizational structure of a police agency, there must also be a rapid mental readjustment on the part of every officer regardless of his rank. The police should have the initial advantage and should seek to hold it. Command and supervisory officers must be decisive in their actions, and indecision will only lead to loss of confidence among the police rank and file and be an encouragement to further disorder.

C. *Unit Structure*

1. The basic unit for riot control is a *squad* consisting usually of nine men and a supervisor. The squad moves about only on direction of its leader. Its officers act as a unit and not as individuals.

2. Next are the *platoons*, consisting of three squads and the *company*, consisting of two or more platoons. Most control measures will require no more than the deployment of a platoon. However, in the initial strike against a heavily concentrated group of rioters it may be necessary to deploy by company.

3. Light-striking forces or *brush fire units* consist of highly mobile platoons. Transportation may be provided by bus or personnel carrier. This kind of force has a number of effective uses and should be a part of any riot unit structure.

4. *Special weapons and tactics teams* consisting of four officers may be combined into squads which are equipped and trained for use against sniper activity and other special problems. In the initial stages, they are invaluable for establishing high ground control, security for the field forces and reconnaissance of forward areas.

D. *Riot Control Planning and Deployment*

1. The police field commander must set up and implement a plan which will restore order. Because there can be no delay in taking action in the field, a plan should be formed and ready for implementation at the time the first units are assembled and ready for assignment. Command and operations officers should be completely familiar with information available on the kinds of action that can be taken, should be able to fit the proper action to the kind of situation found on the streets and should discuss and criticize possible courses of action routinely and not wait until a disturbance occurs.

2. Before a plan can be formulated the field commander and/or operations officer must have current estimates on:

a. Area involved.

b. Indicated reason for disturbance.

c. Estimated strength of the rioters.

d. Actions, such as looting, rock throwing and burning.

e. Make-up of crowd (militant, indigenous).

f. Weapons in evidence (molotov cocktails, bricks).

g. Sniper activity — where?

h. Mobility of the crowd — direction?

These kinds of estimates should come from the field intelligence and reconnaissance units.

3. To properly utilize this data, the field commander should have available maps and photos of the area showing:

a. Street pattern.

b. General topography.

c. Building structure, use and composition.

d. Natural barriers.

e. Sensitive installations.

Combining this *at hand* information with the estimates received from field intelligence and reconnaissance will aid greatly in setting up missions and the overall control strategy.

4. If the sequence of events is normal, there will be a number of regular field units already engaged in control activity prior to the shift in organization and the forming-up for riot control. As quickly as possible, these units should be disengaged and brought to the staging area for riot control formation or sent back to their districts to police the remainder of the city, depending upon the pre-set plan.

Officers involved in the initial response usually are acting individually and sometimes remote from communications. There should be a careful accounting of all units responding to the initial call. If the communications division is unable to contact them by radio for reassignment, the field commander must try to contact them.

E. *Command Strategy*

Planning-Intelligence-Control

One of the most important concepts in planning the deployment of control units is the integration of the planning, intelligence and control functions (P.I.C.). The *planning* phase of the operation is based on the estimates supplied by the *intelligence* function. *Control* is applied through monitoring the progress, success or failure of each mission. Without a full implementation of this concept, operational planning will lack flexibility and the control measures will lack optimum efficiency. For example, a mission carefully planned and aimed at dispersing a large group may, upon reaching the scene, find the group has already dispersed. Unless the mission is monitored, valuable time may be lost before the control force is directed toward another mission. Or, a much lighter or heavier control force than originally planned may be necessary. Adjustments will not be made quickly unless the mission is monitored and the control ingredients of P.I.C. applied.

Squad and/or platoon leaders given specific control missions must report back on their progress so that deployment adjustments can be made in a timely and effective fashion. Reporting back will not be consistent unless the monitoring system demands a periodic situation report from the mission. Personnel involved in control measures are quick to become involved and slow to report their progress.

1. Mission briefings should be conducted in a concise and well ordered manner. In most cases it is unlikely that the field commander will be able to issue detailed information. However, he should provide the following minimum information for briefings.

   a. Size and location of crowd.

   b. Mood and action of crowd.

   c. Direction in which crowd is moving.

   d. Direction crowd should be dispersed.

   e. Approach route.

   f. Other incidents in the area of disturbance.

   g. Special instructions (closing streets, cordoning area).

2. A squad or platoon leader should provide the following information to those under his command.

   a. Situation — disposition of police and rioting forces and a general picture of the problems to be encountered.

   b. Mission — a concise statement of what the squad or platoon is to accomplish.

   c. Specific duties — squad or individual assignments.

   d. Special instructions on arrest and booking facilities.

VII. CONTROL TACTICS

A. *Basic Plan*

Before going to the scene of an incident, it is essential that the unit leader (squad or platoon) have a basic plan of what he intends to do. For example, it may be essential that rioters be dispersed in a northerly direction, and in order to achieve this, the unit leader must place his forces to the south of the rioters. In planning his approach he must also consider the possibility that the crowd might move to block the approach route of his unit.

1. The unit leader should always maintain a position which allows him maximum control over his unit, and his position must be visible to the officers of his unit.

2. The unit leader must control his unit and cannot become embroiled in the action.

B. *Riot Control — Tactics*

Riot suppression tactics fall into the following general categories and occur in approximately the same sequence:

1. Dispersing the rioter's attack.

2. Gaining high ground security and control.

3. Sweeping the area — mop up.

4. Establishing mobile and foot-squad patrols.

5. Sealing off the area — perimeter control.

A field commander may have a difficult time planning the sequence of the above tactics. He may be guided somewhat by the numbers and type of personnel responding, the actions of the rioters and the size of the area involved.

C. *Dispersing the Rioters' Attack*

If there are large groups of rioters looting, throwing rocks, burning or causing extensive injury to life and property, the first order of business must be dispersal.

1. A unit leader given a dispersal mission should not permit his unit to deviate from that mission. The tendency is to become embroiled in incidents that are observed enroute to an assignment. They should be reported, but there should be no engagement of the unit unless the deviation is authorized by the field commander.

2. Upon arrival at the scene, the unit leader may find that the original information upon which the mission was planned is insufficient or exaggerated. For this reason he may send out a reconnaissance group to update his information before effecting a dispersal. If at all possible, the unit leader should be a part of the reconnaissance. A hasty or ill-considered plan based on inaccurate information or no information is not only likely to fail but may also waste more time than that used for a reconnaissance.

3. In appraising the situation, the unit leader should determine the direction in which he intends to scatter the crowd. A riotous crowd should not be dispersed into a business district or other area containing attractive looting targets. It should be driven away from such targets and toward an area where the physical features tend to break it up into small parties or into open spaces where little damage can be done.

As the unit moves in, the leader should note the direction the rioters are scattering in. Also, he must be alert to the possibility of rioters going into buildings and reforming to attack the rear of the unit.

4. There are no firm rules concerning the type of formation to be

adopted for dispersal. The principle underlying any plan is to bring to bear in a coordinated effort as many squads, platoons or companies as appear necessary to break the resistance of the crowd and disperse it.

5. Attacking a disorderly crowd from two or more directions at once makes dispersal easier because each section being attacked fears for its own safety, and the common purpose linking the rioters is broken.

    a. Two possible methods of such attack are:

        (1) *Pincer Attack:* Delivered from the front and *both* flanks. This method tends to drive the crowd before the frontal attack.

        (2) *Flanking Attack:* Delivered from the front and *one* flank. This approach tends to drive the crowd toward the open flank.

    b. An attack from both front and rear may allow some rioters to escape to the rear of the advancing units. Such an escape is highly undesirable.

    c. When deciding between a *Pincer* or *Flanking* attack, the unit leader should consider wind direction, in case gas must be used.

6. It is better to involve too many policemen in the attack than too few. This tactic contradicts the usual admonition to keep about one-third of the personnel in reserve. The decision to commit or hold back is not an easy one, but the police executive must consider the most likely consequences. An unsuccessful dispersal attack can prove extremely costly in lost time and increased disorder.

7. A crowd cannot be bottled up completely. They must be given an avenue of escape, otherwise they may have no alternative but to stand and fight.

8. Dispersal and attack tactics may require the greatest exertion of police force. Since these tactics are directed at the main body of rioters engaged in the most violent and destructive action, dispersal and attack must be the first order of business in the

control plan. An attack such as this can be accomplished upon a small but violent group as well as a large group. While the attack is in progress, control of elevated positions must be attempted.

D. *Gaining High Ground Security and Control*

Control of high ground (roof tops and vantage points) must be gained as quickly as possible in the initial stages of the action.

1. Helicopter patrol can assist in gaining high ground. In the early stages, the only control may come from the helicopter. Helicopters can be used to spot rioters operating on top of buildings and other high structures and also to spot stores of rocks, bottles and other missiles.

2. Until squads are available for deployment to high ground, assigning the mission to *Special Weapons and Tactics Teams* should be considered. The SWAT Teams can thus guard against sniper fire and, if it does occur, will be in an advantageous position to attack the sniper positions. (See Appendix 1.)

3. Officers positioned properly on roof tops will also be in position to spot potential problems. For example, rock throwers are often found to the rear of a crowd or hiding behind a building where they cannot be spotted by the ground units which are being bombarded. Roof-top control can spot these rock throwers and direct ground forces in a strategic approach.

E. *Sweeping the Area — Mop Up*

After a successful attack, the elements of the dispersing crowd should be followed up, hurried and prevented from re-forming. Rioters should be driven off the streets but not onto property or into buildings where they do not belong. Agitators should be arrested.

1. Mopping up can be accomplished by deploying squads to sweep through the riot-affected area on a broad front.

2. Sweeping tactics should be used to clear an area infested with small and elusive groups of rioters or when it is apparent that the crowd is giving way and breaking easily into small groups.

3. Small groups remaining in the disturbed area can be dispersed by

bringing squad pressure to bear on the specific locations of these groups. Sweeps can be expedited by assigning them to mobile units that dismount only when necessary to engage a group of rioters.

4. Sweeps are particularly effective in ferreting out rioters who have remained behind to cause additional damage or violence.

5. If a sweep is conducted on foot, squads should be moved in single file next to buildings for protection. The skirmish line moving down the center of the street with no one confronting it accomplishes nothing and provides snipers with excellent targets.

6. The sweep should be a steadily advancing force which disperses small groups and arrests violators. The pace should be slow enough to observe inside buildings, side streets and alleys. Officers should not break ranks to chase rioters. If units are deployed properly on the flanks, rioters escaping one sweep unit will undoubtedly run into a flanking unit.

F. *Establishing Mobile and Foot Squad Patrols*

Almost simultaneously with preparation for a dispersal or attack, plans should be laid for establishing mobile and foot-squad patrols.

1. If at all possible, a mobile squad patrol should be implemented along the periphery of the affected area at the same time the dispersal is made. A mobile squad patrol consists of nine policemen and a sergeant working in three cars operating together.

2. The area to be covered by a mobile patrol should not be too extensive. If this area is densely populated, there may be a need for foot patrol in squads. If foot patrols are employed, they should be linked with the mobile patrols.

3. Ultimately, mobile and foot-squad patrols should develop a tight net over the entire affected area. These patrols should handle calls for emergency service, gather and report information preventing groups from forming and handle all emergencies in their assigned area. Patrols from other areas should not respond on their own volition to calls for service. Any movement out of the assigned area should be at the direction of the field commander only. If a patrol squad finds a buildup of rioters it

cannot handle, it should call for a response from a light striking force or *brushfire unit.*

4. As long as a mobile patrol unit makes regular checks of foot patrols within its area, it should not be tied to a regular schedule. Instead, it should be permitted to use its own initiative and thus introduce an element of surprise to make its coverage more effective.

5. In addition to its assigned duties, a mobile patrol can:

   a. Act as a communications link with foot patrols.

   b. Act as a mobile reserve to assist foot patrols which clash with rioters before a light striking force is employed.

   c. Act on its own intiative against small groups.

   d. Patrol between strong points which form a cordon around the affected area.

   e. Patrol access routes.

   f. Escort prisoners or injured persons from the scene.

   g. Enforce a curfew.

6. If it is found that a mobile or foot squad patrol cannot adequately handle the problems confronting the unit, the area should be reduced and an additional patrol added.

G. *Light Striking Forces — "Brushfire" Units*

These units are the mobile reserve, once the main groups of rioters have been dispersed, mop-up sweeps have advanced through the affected areas and mobile and foot squad patrols have been put into effect.

1. These units consist of up to three squads or a platoon transported in a bus or personnel carrier. Any problem the mobile squad is incapable of handling would be dealt with by these units. There should be enough men to accomplish the job and enough mobility to depart quickly to the next assignment.

2. An additional use for these units is deployment into shopping centers and industrial complexes that might be in the path of the rioters.

H. *Sealing Off the Area — Perimeter Control*

Once some of the more vital control problems have been taken care of, it may be necessary for the police to seal the disturbed area by establishing a perimeter control. The area is best isolated by an extended line of roadblocks surrounding it.

1. Units deployed to seal an area should be connected by either mobile or foot patrols responsible for patrolling within a reasonable distance from the strong points. These patrols are then in position to deal with small groups intent upon harassing a roadblock. Four men in a vehicle on constant patrol will help to create an *omnipresence* of the police.

2. Even before perimeter control is established, certain key intersections should be blocked in order to:

   a. Retain access routes.

   b. Prevent assistance from forming to aid rioters.

   c. Prevent innocent people from wandering into the area.

   d. Keep the traffic flow to a minimum within the affected area.

   e. Prevent unauthorized persons from entering and aggravating the disorder.

VIII. MISCELLANEOUS TACTICS

A. *Linear Riot Strategy*

In the American city *riot* of the 1960's, the aggressors operated in a highly mobile and fluid state. In their day to day operations, the American police also operate in a highly mobile and fluid state. When matched against the fluidity and mobility of the police, the fluidity and mobility of the arsonist and looter give the rioter a decided arithmetic advantage for success in evading apprehension.

Policemen are accustomed to working as individuals, not as

members of groups. This propensity projects up into the top ranks of police departments. Large-scale deployment of policemen classically overlooks the importance of a more highly organized police deployment and operation in a riot situation. The organization of policemen for riot duty into effective field operating units is frequently a slow process. During this process, many officers wait in staging areas which are usually remote from the active site of operations.

A linear riot strategy could be designed to provide a combination staging area, headquarters area, personnel relief and feeding area and a blockade along a major, arterial highway. The establishment of a long line of static force has as its objective the isolation of the rioters from as-yet-untouched looting objectives. For example, if rioting were to break out south of the business area of a city, it is logical to assume that the business area would ultimately be a prime looting objective. A major street north of the riot area and south of the business area could be chosen as a linear area along which policemen can be deployed to prevent the flow of traffic in all directions. This deployment might consist only of two or three policemen per intersection for a distance of several miles. However, officers newly reporting to the area could be deployed at various segments of the chosen area, officers being briefed for missions could be briefed in this area and officers resting from missions could be fed in this area. This linear area and the areas at right angles to it in both directions could constitute a tactical area of responsibility for a sector commander. Other such linear areas would be constituted throughout the riot-potential area, with a general objective of boxing in a disturbed area so that rioters cannot freely move to loot and burn.

As each linear area is established, it would be placed under a sector command, and the field commander would delegate the detailed mission-planning and execution to the sector commander. The field commander would reserve to himself the monitoring of all sources of information, the assignment of tactical areas of responsibility and the assignment of general missions. Proper reporting would be made by the sector commander and his subordinates on the progress and completion of all missions so that proper distribution of personnel could be made among the various areas.

Linear strategy has the advantage of decentralizing personnel along the line, even while they are taking breaks or eating. However, it requires well-coordinated logistical support and should not be attempted until the support problems are considered and resolved.

The riots experienced in the major cities showed that the great bulk of the rioters were indigenous to the neighborhoods and attacked objects within their general area. Mobility was not a major factor except by those who participated with apparent organization. It is believed that a new wave of rioting could show a greater movement among the rioters. Hit-and-run guerrilla tactics by highly mobile units may be the order of the day. For this reason, linear riot control strategy is provided as a possible tool for the future.

B. *Sniper Control*

Police departments have not had a planned approach to sniper control. Reports of snipers are *generally* exaggerated. The result has been that when sniper activity has occurred or has been reported, there has been an overreaction by the police. The police response has been uncoordinated, with little or no fire control, resulting in injuries to innocent persons and firing at non-existing snipers. Sniper control should therefore be assigned to specially equipped and trained teams.

When sniper activity is reported or observed, the responding mobile patrol squad should:

1. Determine the validity of the report.

2. If the report is valid or sniper fire is observed, the squad should:

   a. Call for the SWAT Teams.

   b. Isolate the area.

   c. Determine the direction of fire and location of fire, if possible.

   d. Do not return fire unless absolutely necessary to protect life and property.

C. *Reports of Fire and Emergency Calls for Service*

Experience indicates that called-for services, especially of the emergency type, increase considerably during a civil disturbance. Most of these calls emanate from within the affected area. A large number of emergency calls prove to be unfounded, even though careful screening may take place in the communications facility. Intelligence reports indicate that placing unfounded requests for emergency service by the police and fire departments is a well accepted tactic of rioters to add to the overall confusion, diffuse the police control effort and, in the extreme, bring the police to an area where they may be effectively annihilated. Rioters may also put in *an officer needs help* call as a diversionary tactic.

Since this is an accepted technique, the police should attempt to provide verification in the field of each emergency call prior to sending in a massive control force. Within their assigned beats, the mobile patrol squads are in a perfect position to make this verification. They may approach each call as a reconnaissance unit. If the call is verified and exaggerated, the mobile patrol squad may be able to handle it. If it is verified and not exaggerated, the mobile squad can request the assistance of a light striking force. Consideration could be given to having a police unit respond to fire alarms with a fire department unit. If the call is bonafide, the fire unit would summon equipment and the police unit standby to protect the firemen. If possible, responding units should avoid the use of warning devices such as sirens, lights and bells.

Helicopter patrol can be of great assistance in making these verifications, particularly on fires or incidents that can be observed from the air. The helicopter can quickly make a reconnaissance and direct the activities of the fire units, the mobile patrol squad and/or the light striking force. It can also airlift men and equipment to the scene.

D. *Deployment Against Rock, Bottle and Missile Throwers*

In many civil disturbances, the police and innocent victims have been assaulted by barrages of rocks, bottles and missiles. Persons engaging in this kind of assault usually are in the background of a crowd, positioned behind some type of cover, utilizing hit-and-run tactics. The police reaction in many cases has been to stand and confront the crowd, make a frontal attack or retreat outside the rock-throwing range. Squad and platoon leaders should recognize that in order to apprehend the rock-throwing assailant, special deployment tactics must be used. It is impossible to describe the exact method of deployment that will prove successful because of the miltitude of situations that will arise. However, some simple techniques are suggested:

1. Since rock throwers usually operate from the back of a crowd or from cover, a detail detached to flank the crowd and to watch for and apprehend them should be deployed prior to a frontal attack. However, the flanking tactic should not be executed unless it is an acceptable movement under the conditions present.

2. Spotters from roof tops and high-ground security forces can also determine the identities of rock throwers and direct the ground forces in their apprehension.

3. Another technique is the deployment of undercover officers who would infiltrate the crowd in the vicinity of the rock throwing and either direct uniformed or plainclothes officers to the violators by signal or wait for the opportunity and effect the arrests themselves.

4. All officers committed to riot situations should be provided with helmets. Officers engaged directly in crowd control should have protective head and body gear.

IX. THE COMMAND POST

A. *Introduction*

There is a tendency to treat the concept of a command post as a novelty which is reserved for periods of great strife or emergency. The command post in civil disorders merely represents a decentralization of authority and command in the same manner as precinct operations in larger cities.

If the chief of the department decides to allow a subordinate to make meaningful decisions at or near the scene of a civil disorder, then a *field command post* should be established under the command of the designated individual. However, decisions of this nature are based upon information or intelligence reports concerning the incident, and a field commander isolated by lack of radio and telephone communications cannot make well-founded decisions. *Under these limitations,* a field command post is generally inappropriate. In this situation and in most medium-sized and smaller cities, the ideal location for a command post is in the police headquarters which would have the maximum communication capability. A subordinate might be placed in charge to handle the immediate situation within the command post to allow the

department commander time to plan and coordinate with the chief
executive and other officials.

B. *Field Command Post*

In larger cities *where facilities are available* or in those situations
requiring their establishment, a field command post would allow a
field commander to implement and direct control plans near the
incident. In a minor disturbance, the field commander should
ordinarily position himself within view of the incident (while
maintaining radio communication with the field command post),
thereby affording himself the opportunity to take immediate
remedial action based upon a current evaluation of the problem.
During a serious civil disorder, the field commander will undoubtedly find it necessary to devote much of his time to
decision-making at the field command post, substituting his
intelligence reports for personal observations. His periodic observations from an automobile or helicopter would suffice to maintain a
proper perspective of the situation.

1. The magnitude of the disturbance determines how complex the
   configuration of the field command post should be. Operations
   often can be effectively conducted from a properly-equipped
   vehicle.

2. Large parking lots, open fields, parks or athletic fields are
   preferable for a field command post location; they afford
   adequate space for the assimilation of personnel and equipment.

3. Rather than a vehicle, a conveniently located permanent facility
   such as a police station, school, armory or multi-story parking
   lot might be utilized as the field command post.

4. Other factors to be considered in the selection of a location for a
   field command post are:

   a. The area the disturbance activity encompasses.

   b. Areas likely to be the target of riots.

   c. Security from attack and, if possible, protection from public
      view.

   d. Area to be utilized for a staging area (sufficient space for equipment, assembly area, helicopter pad, etc.)

   e. Accessibility to responding units.

C. *Staging Area*

The staging area location must be close to the command post or the field command post, whichever is to be operated, for the collection, storage, maintenance, disbursement and accounting of personnel, vehicles, supplies and equipment used or held in reserve. The staging area may also be used for the temporary storage of booked property and impounded vehicles. In the event a large logistic support is required to meet the demands of the emergency, a field store unit and field transportation unit could be established with the staging area where material arriving at the scene could be assembled and reassigned. A method of accounting for and controlling assignment of equipment should be provided.

1. The field commander is responsible for protecting life and property in his assigned area and for the command of all police operations within his area.

   a. The establishment of a command post may also require that the following be considered:

      (1) Perimeters around the command post; using a pass system or authorized personnel list to screen persons entering.

      (2) Elimination of public parking in the immediate area.

      (3) Good exterior lighting completely around command post; maintaining an emergency generator.

      (4) Adequate supplies (refer to logistics section).

      (5) Adequate rest room facilities for adults.

      (6) Accommodations for eating and sleeping.

      (7) Security of communications centers. These centers should be located so as to be readily accessible to field commander.

(8) Facilities or a briefing location for press. The press should be restricted to specific areas within the command post.

(9) Logging incidents and marking map overlays.

b. News Media

(1) A public information officer should be part of the field command staff. In major disturbances he should have a counterpart at headquarters to whom he will feed information as quickly as it becomes available.

(2) For press releases, the public information officer should arrange a specific schedule and a point of dissemination. He should not deviate from this procedure unless a major event occurs.

(3) The public information officer should act as a *buffer* between the press and the field commander, so that the commander can devote maximum time and attention to the disturbance itself.

(4) Reasonable limitations should be set for press entry into high hazard areas. Contacts by the press with police personnel in the field should be minimized. Press interviews should be confined to the command post area and should be approved by the officer in charge.

(5) News media representatives should be required to produce bonafide credentials in order to enter the area.

(6) In major disturbances, the issuance of special press cards by the public information officer should be considered.

(7) The types of news media equipment (floodlights, etc.) brought into the disturbance area may have to be curtailed.

X. ESTABLISHMENT OF EMERGENCY CONTROL CENTER

A *larger* police department should consider the establishment of an *emergency control center* to assist in the *control* of any serious unusual occurrence. The emergency control center serves as a headquarters for the department commander during the emergency and ordinarily is located in the main police administration facility, near or within the communication center.

A. The purpose of an emergency control center is to provide as many auxiliary and support resources as possible for the field commander and his staff, thereby freeing them for field operations directly related to controlling the disturbance. The particular responsibility of an emergency control center is to manage the resources of the department to insure that the field forces in the affected area receive adequate support.

B. A serious or major unusual occurrence places an overwhelming strain on a police department's radio communication facilities. Therefore, the major portion of the radio frequencies available to a particular department should be reserved for the exclusive use of the units involved in the disturbance. For a police department with only one radio frequency, the problem will be solved partially when non-emergency services are discontinued. A strict radio discipline must also be observed.

C. For police agencies with two or more available frequencies, it is suggested that at least one be designated for use as a tactical frequency during riots. Existing equipment might have to be modified, but in most cases the cost of such changes will be comparatively low. All vehicles should be equipped with the tactical frequency capability.

D. Another advantage of an emergency control center is that the control of two or more unusual occurrences, or a civil disturbance which is of the *hit-and-run* or *guerrilla* type, can more readily be managed, and resources more effectively allocated. The field commander (or field commanders) may then concentrate his efforts on field operations necessary to control the particular problem he is assigned to and need not concern himself with unassociated problems.

E. Personnel assigned to the emergency control center would have intelligence, personnel, logistics and press relations functions and would maintain communications with their counterparts in the field command posts.

F. Other considerations include:

1. Keeping of an up-to-the-minute, accurate log of every

occurrence — fires, sniper activity, personnel status, movements of crowds, etc. This log could be the duty of a secretary assigned to the center.

2. Installation of telephone equipment with flashing lights rather than bells to keep down unnecessary noise and confusion.

3. Representatives present from other public agencies to provide assistance in deploying their personnel and equipment as required by the field commander.

XI. ARREST PROCEDURES (See Appendix 4.)

The problems of arrest and processing are not dissimilar to problems arising in other areas of disorder control. The police are confronted with a situation far beyond that for which they are equipped and trained. Facilities geared to normal, routine operations are inadequate to handle the influx of prisoners, complaints and required services. Time elements are suddenly compressed by the urgent need to keep a maximum number of police officers on the street to deal with the disorders in progress, and standard procedures for arrest, processing and investigation often make unacceptable demands upon the time of operational personnel.

Certain alternative methods can be used to overcome or reduce the *time loss* aspects of arrest processing during a civil disorder. While not recommended for normal police activity, such alternatives can be built into emergency procedures, so long as the basic criteria of legality and subsequent prosecution are retained.

A. *Mass Arrests*

The problem of mass arrests seems to center around two sub-problems — prisoner handling capacity and the identification of arrested persons with specific violations of the law. Seriously outnumbered and thinly spread law enforcement personnel confronted by massive disorder and lawlessness must make arrests when possible, but the practicality of arresting large groups of people often becomes difficult or impossible. Even when police can safely make arrests in large numbers, such numbers frequently tax prisoner handling facilities to the point of inefficiency and confusion.

The need to have the arresting officer return to the street from the booking area as soon as possible is critical. Under difficult conditions field personnel are often tempted to arrest violators in large numbers with little thought to subsequent prosecution just to remove them from the disorder area. While this expedient appears to solve an immediate problem for the police, it results in serious legal problems and severe criticism of control operations. In the recent riots, arresting and removing large numbers of largely unidentified riots just to *get them off the street* was found to create more problems than it solved.

Other cities with major disorders required arresting officers to accompany their prisoners to the central booking station at the city or county jail for processing in the normal manner with the standard booking forms and procedures. Under this system, a much more satisfactory rate of post-riot convictions was obtained. However, the arresting officer was lost from duty on the street for lengthy periods. Another alternative for handling prisoners seems to have been the most effective – field booking station(s).

B. *Field Booking*

The principal function of field booking is to provide the fastest and most efficient method of handling prisoners and return of the arresting officer to duty at the scene of the disorder. The field booking process incorporates time-saving arrest, processing and transporting features that should be used only during disorder periods.

The field booking station consists of a reasonably secure location adjacent to the disorder area where police officers can deliver and process prisoners. A public or private building with telephone communications is suitable. Radio communications are desirable but not absolutely necessary. The field booking station should be provided with a minimum of equipment to facilitate movement as disorder patterns change. Recommended essential equipment includes:

1. Polaroid-type cameras with film and portable light source.

2. Arrest holding memos.

3. Handcuffs.

4. Evidence containers.

5. Office supplies.

The station should be manned by a staff of police technicians with nonpolice government employees as assistants, and, when available, military personnel to guard and transport prisoners. Assigning a first-aid team to each booking station to treat minor injuries of police officers and prisoners might also be considered.

In the first step of field processing, the arresting officer brings his prisoner to the field booking station where a photograph of the officer and prisoner is taken. The photograph, which should be made with polaroid-type equipment, will include any evidence seized during the arrest. While the photograph is being taken, the prisoner or the arresting officer should hold a card with the assigned case number displayed in large figures.

After the photograph has been taken, the arrest holding memo should be filled out (if this has not been accomplished earlier). The arrest holding memo is an abbreviated arrest form. Upon completion of these steps, the arresting officer retains his copy of the arrest holding memo, is issued additional handcuffs as required and is released for return to street duty. A copy of the arrest holding memo is attached to the photograph and accompanies the prisoner and his personal property to the central booking facility. Another copy of the memo is attached to the container which holds all evidence seized in connection with the arrest.

For curfew violations, certain deviations from these procedures may be applicable. Through coordination with court officials, procedures may be instituted to accept the arrest memo in lieu of the actual appearance of the officer. In these instances, it may be adequate for the officer to fill out the arrest memo at the scene,

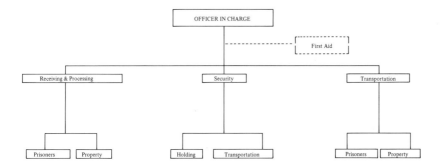

Figure 5: ORGANIZATION OF FIELD BOOKING STATION: Processing Teams (as needed): 1 Photographer; 1 Recorder.

retain his copy and turn the prisoner over to roving jail wagons or patrol cars for transportation to either a field booking station or the central facility.

Another procedure for processing minor offense arrests would be the summons or citation in lieu of actual taking into custody.

C. *Arrest Reporting*

The standard arrest forms used by field personnel are somewhat limited in adaptability and are often too time consuming during civil disorders. Officers cannot easily be spared from the field to complete the lengthy standard form or forms for every arrest they make. Thus, a number of departments have developed short arrest forms or arrest holding memos. These forms are applicable in most arrests resulting from the disorder. However, it is recommended that the standard form be used, and the normal booking procedure be followed in certain major offenses. A person arrested for homicide, sniping or arson should be processed in the normal manner regardless of the time involved.

When the short arrest form is used, personnel at the central booking facility should be able to complete the details of the standard form when the prisoner is brought in from the field. The standard form, with the accompanying short form, should provide all necessary information. The short arrest form should contain the following minimum amount of information required to identify the prisoner with his specific offense and with the arresting officer:

1. Name of the person arrested.

2. Arrest or case number.

3. Offense.

4. Location of offense.

5. Date and time of offense.

6. Brief details of arrest.

7. Name and number of arresting officer(s).

8. Space for thumbprint.

9. Space for information regarding evidence transfer.

D. *Control of Evidence and Property*

Cities experiencing major civil disorders with accompanying mass arrests have indicated serious problems in the control of evidence and property. These problems of evidence control are parallel to those of arrests. Because of the volume of evidence and the relatively short time that officers can be spared to fill out the necessary evidence or property forms, much evidence was collected which could not be identified with specific cases. To solve this problem, a number of different methods were developed.

1. In one city, all evidence was turned over to an evidence team which was responsible for recording, tagging and storing all evidence taken during the disturbance. The evidence teams maintained control of all evidence until it was called for by the courts. A photograph of all evidence seized during each arrest was taken with the arrested person and the arresting officer. This picture was attached to the arrest report. At each field booking station, evidence teams worked with the assistance of non-police government employees.

2. In cities experiencing lesser disorders, each arresting officer maintained control of his own evidence. This appears to be impractical in situations in which a large number of arrests are effected.

3. Evidence bags, which can be stapled shut, marked with a case number and to which a property receipt can be attached, should be considered.

4. In many cases, the volume of evidence and property found was too great for the property room to transport or store. Other handling facilities were utilized, such as large moving vans, semi-trailers, warehouses and basements of public buildings. The important factor is to have all evidence at a central location, secured, marked well and separated.

E. *Prisoner Transportation*

Transportation problems developed in all cities experiencing major disorders. A serious shortage of prisoner transportation vehicles produced delays in removing prisoners from the riot scene, and frequently, sharply limited the number of arrests that officers could make in connection with the disorders. To some extent, this shortage of transportation can be avoided by planning to utilize commercial vehicles and buses and by borrowing prisoner wagons from adjacent jurisdictions and state correctional institutions. Military support forces can often assist in transporting prisoners as well as providing necessary security.

The transporting of juvenile prisoners remains a time-consuming problem because the majority of cities have laws or regulations restricting the transportation of juveniles to special juvenile bureau cars or regular patrol cars. Departments should consider the possibility of suspending such restrictions during civil disorders to permit the transportation of juveniles in patrol wagons, jail vans or other prisoner transportation vehicles.

F. *Detention Facilities*

Cities encountering a massive prisoner influx reported that their city detention facilities were inadequate to process and hold persons arrested during the disorders. To handle overflow, they used county jails, work farms or makeshift detention facilities. The use of these secondary facilities, which were often some distance from the central booking station, created new problems in transportation and record keeping.

When secondary detention facilities are utilized, persons arrested for felony violations should be confined at the city jail, while those arrested for lesser offenses should be held in the less-secure temporary facilities.

In many cities, photographing and fingerprinting all incoming prisoners became impossible during peak periods. Therefore, in several cities only those arrested for major violations were fingerprinted and photographed to reduce the strain on identification facilities. The departments using polaroid-type camera systems along with the short arrest form at field booking stations appear to have overcome this problem. However, even though a polaroid-type photograph is made at the field booking station and a thumbprint is placed on the short arrest form, routine identification photographs and full fingerprinting should be completed at the central booking facility as soon as time permits.

Another problem encountered at the central booking facility was the inability to check the records on all or even a majority of prisoners processed. Most cities indicated that they checked their records for outstanding warrants and wanted notices only in those cases where such a search was specifically requested. In other cities, a record check was made on the arrested person after he appeared in court for the preliminary or bail hearing. The limiting factor appeared to be the availability of personnel in the records section.

With a minimum of planning and organization, it should be possible to make routine records checks on all felony arrests during periods of heavy prisoner influx, with a more thorough check made on other prisoners at a later date, but prior to their release from confinement.

G. *Prisoner Services*

Legal counsel can be made available through the cooperation of the courts and the local bar association. Representatives from the public defender's office can be stationed near the detention section to provide defense assistance for any person who cannot afford to hire counsel.

In most cities, prisoners can be fed without major difficulty. For preparing food, jail kitchens, school cafeterias or catering services should be considered for prisoners, refugees and police alike. Also, assistance can be obtained through Civil Defense channels. Advance planning and coordination would eliminate the use of sworn personnel to prepare food during emergencies.

Medical treatment for sick and injured prisoners can be handled in a number of different ways. In cities where medical facilities and physician services are available in the jail, prisoners will be treated on location. Patients requiring more specialized treatment can be sent to the local hospital and returned to jail as soon as possible. In communities where medical service is not available at the detention facility, prisoners requiring medical attention must be sent to the local hospital by ambulance. This creates an extra drain on manpower, as officers must accompany the ambulance and stay with prisoners until they can be returned to detention.

Emergency disorder control plans should include provisions for administering as much medical service as possible within the detention facility. Both police manpower and ambulance equipment are at a premium during civil disorders, and both should be conserved.

In department planning for the possibility of mass arrests during a civil disturbance, the following summary list should be given consideration:

1. Development of special mass arrest forms for ease of processing.

2. Methods of expediting arrest forms through routine procedure.

3. Necessary changes in identification operations concerning fingerprinting, photo and record checks.

4. Special procedures for handling of juvenile and female offenders.

5. Utilization of special equipment such as cameras on the scene, transportation vehicles, restraints, video tapes, etc.

6. Availability, for consultation on the scene, of representatives from state attorney's office.

7. Pre-arrangement for special facilities to be used in processing for detention.

8. Review of role of National Guard or Federal troops in terms of arrest powers and holding prisoners on the scene.

9. On-the-scene procedures for proper evidence and prisoners' property handling and marking.

10. Availability of public defenders and volunteer defense counsel at detention facility.

11. Means of advising prisoners of their rights at detention point.

12. Availability of first-aid and medical personnel at the detention facility.

13. For minor offenses, selected supervisory personnel authorized to release prisoners without charge after review of circumstances at arrest.

14. In minor cases, selected personnel to issue summons or notice to appear in lieu of detention.

15. Assignment of prosecuting attorney at booking point.

16. Provision for telephones to allow for calls to attorneys and families.

17. Emergency judicial procedures with additional judges, court and detention personnel. Formulated bond procedures or *no cash* bail.

18. Planned food, water, bedding and sanitary facilities for prisoners.

19. Centralized information on prisoners to answer inquiries regarding name, charge, location of detention and status of disposition.

20. Release to news media of names on all persons held.

XII. RECOVERY AFTER DISTURBANCE

A. *Restoration of Order*

1. When the major disturbance appears to have ended:

    a. Following a critique, outside agencies should be withdrawn from the area and their assignments.

    b. Department patrol strength should gradually be de-escalated, based on assignment and time in the disturbed area.

    c. All emergency regulations — curfew, liquor sales, etc. — should be reduced and gradually rescinded.

2. Local services should be reestablished.

    a. Public transportation.

    b. Public utilities.

    c. Reopening of private and public buildings.

    d. Normal traffic movement.

3. The area should be restored by the following measures:

    a. Removal of all barricades.

    b. Sending cleanup services into the neighborhoods.

    c. Restoration of normal services and deliveries into the area.

    d. Recovery of abandoned or surplus police equipment and supplies.

4. Police should proceed with the following functions:

    a. Recovery of stolen property and return to its lawful owners.

    b. Prosecution of criminal offenders.

    c. Reports on deaths, injuries, property loss, damages, etc.

5. Complaints about police conduct should be investigated:

    a. Investigation of all complaints.

    b. Complaints should be examined and evaluated with a view toward policy revision.

    c. The press should be notified for full public disclosure of findings on allegations, accusations, etc.

B. *Return to Normal Police Operations*

1. Personnel should be returned to their regular assignments.

    a. Provision for time off should be provided, based upon amount of personnel time involved in the disturbance.

    b. If overtime pay is provided, the payments should be expedited.

2. Disturbance should be evaluated.

    a. Critique and intelligence information should be investigated and analyzed to determine the causes of the incident.

    b. Responsibility should be fixed with a view towards prosecution of those responsible.

    c. The department's success in dealing with the disturbance should be analyzed.

    d. The department's failures should be analyzed in terms of:

        (1) Need for additional training.

        (2) Improved techniques.

        (3) Required policy changes.

        (4) Revision of operational procedures.

        (5) Need for improved community liaison and intelligence.

    e. Any critique should not be limited to supervisory and command levels:

        (1) Attempt to obtain the valid reaction of the entire department.

        (2) Attempt to obtain the reaction of other agencies, private and public, involved in incident.

    f. Inform press, community and city government of findings.

        (1) Implement needed corrections and modifications.

        (2) Explain fully to personnel the need for revisions.

    g. Review the entire planning process and actions in the field in order to avert any recurrence.

C. *Restoration of Community Relations*

All community groups should be met with and their reactions to the disturbance should be obtained in terms of:

1. Causes of the disturbance.

2. Response by the city government.

3. Appropriateness of police action.

4. Community conduct.

5. Corrective measures needed.

APPENDIX NO. 1

SPECIAL WEAPONS AND TACTICS
SWAT TEAM CONCEPT

The SWAT Team program was developed by the Los Angeles Police Department. It is introduced here only to guide the police administrator who has not included the concept in his riot control procedure. Some of the following points are at variance with the Los Angeles SWAT program but should be considered before a final decision is made.

1. The SWAT Team concept may be employed with as little as a one-man team. It is the special weapons capability — not the number of men involved — that marks the importance of the concept.

2. Normally it is composed of four permanent team members, including at least one rifleman, two shotgun men and one observer. SWAT Team members operate as a team (or combined with other SWAT Teams as squads or platoons) to perform special tactical missions requested by the field commander. All individuals should be armed with shoulder weapons and have necessary equipment available such as walkie-talkies, lights, binoculars, etc.

3. The elimination of snipers may require superiority of firepower in order to get within reasonable distance of the snipers. Street-fighting often requires covering fire by one member of a team as the other members move foreward. Because a shotgun is ill-suited to provide covering fire under these conditions, a trained rifleman should be assigned as part of a SWAT Team.

Purposes of SWAT Teams

A. To assist and protect police and fire personnel regularly engaged with rioters.

1. In response to individual requests by the field commander regarding barricades, arsonists, snipers or molotov-cocktail throwers.

2. In response to forces needing assistance by application of special tactics.

3. For station and command post defense.

B. To perform control point missions by securing a commanding position and keeping desired areas clear of special problems.

C. To perform rescue operation missions — assisting other officers, firemen and endangered citizens.

CHEMICAL AGENTS

SWAT Teams (or special teams) should be provided with *tear gas* and related equipment.

1. Team members must be familiar with procedures concerning use of protective gas masks, gas grenades, smoke grenades and other riot control agents.

2. Tactical operational training would include use of smoke grenades for cover operations, utilization of smoke and gas grenades against unruly groups and application of gas to discourage looting of business establishments.

3. All department members should be made aware of decontamination methods to deal with accidental discharge and to assist citizens in their request for information regarding the decontamination of their premises.

APPENDIX NO. 2

NOTES ON THE USE OF
THE CHEMICAL AGENT *CS* IN CIVIL DISORDERS

We invite your attention to the riot control agent CS. About ten years ago, after a testing and evaluation period, this chemical agent replaced the well-known conventional *tear gas* or CN in the military services. Additional testing and evaluation of the effects of prolonged dosage in confined spaces is currently in progress. The National Guard and the Army are equipped to use this agent if called upon to assist local police in controlling a civil disturbance, since available evidence indicates it is more beneficial and less harmful than any currently available riot control agent. It can minimize the numerical superiority that the mob has over the police force. It is an effective and humane means of achieving temporary neutralization of a mob with a minimum of personal injury.

CS is a riot control agent that can be regarded as an improved *tear gas*. It is a white powder that can be dispensed in several ways: (a) by prepacked containers such as grenades or small projectiles, (b) by a spray from a pressurized container such as a properly modified dry chemical fire extinguisher or (c) in bulk form with compressed air dispersion. It is immediately effective on contact with the eyes, the respiratory tract and the skin and will render the receiver incapable of concerted aggressiveness while he is in contact with it.

This nonlethal agent permits police officers to control a larger unruly crowd. Properly used, CS can discourage looting of business premises when released inside the buildings under attack. For the same quantities of CS and CN, CS produces more intense effects over a larger area.

CS is used in the same manner as the conventional *tear gas* CN has been used for many years. It is applied in the form of a smoke-like cloud so that persons engaging in a disturbance come in contact with it. The CS is released so that advantage is taken of any air currents or moderate breezes to move the cloud toward the rioters and away from those applying it.

CS is used when the numbers of rioters and the intensity of violence is beyond the capability of the available police to prevent the endangering of public safety and security; it is used to prevent property damage and to deter looting. Furthermore, it is a much-desired alternative to physical force. CS can be used in streets and in other open spaces and sparingly inside buildings.

Precautions in the Use of CS

Those who employ CS must wear protective masks to avoid personal incapacitation, either inadventently or in the case of a sudden wind shift. If utilized in grenade form, inspect the area as soon as practicable to see that a fire is not started. CS should be applied with a knowledge of where it will go; locations such as air intakes of buildings and subways must be identified for cleanup activity later. Special attention should be paid to the use of CS in the vicinity of hospitals and schools.

Decontamination of persons who have CS on their skin is carried out by washing with *cool* water; the respiratory tract is cleared in 10 to 20 minutes by breathing fresh air. Flush the eyes with *cool* water — this tends to relieve the sensation. Clothing, drapes, rugs and furniture should be aired out for several hours. Vacuum cleaners will pick up large quantities of CS but may redistribute some of it if proper filters are not used. Floors should be flushed with water if possible. Ordinarily, exposed foods should be destroyed. Canned and bottled foods should be washed. Fans used to remove smoke from fire-damaged buildings also may be used to ventilate stores and other places of business where CS has been used. Streets, sidewalks, floors and walls can be washed with water solutions of common and readily available chemicals such as: (a) non-ionic detergents and monoethyl alcohol (MEA), (b) washing soda and a detergent, (c) lye and a detergent.

Members of a decontamination team should be protected with masks and gloves. Exposed skin area should be minimized. Decontamination personnel should wash thoroughly after completing their duties.

APPENDIX NO. 3

EXAMPLES OF A DEPARTMENT IMMEDIATE EMERGENCY PLAN AS COMPILED BY THE CHICAGO POLICE DEPARTMENT

GENERAL ORDER NO. 67-12   Effective date: 12 May 1967

IMMEDIATE EMERGENCY PLAN

I. PURPOSE

The purpose of this order is to establish procedures for the immediate control of emergencies.

II. DEFINITION OF EMERGENCY PLAN

A. The Immediate Emergency Plan is really a series of *Plans* tailored to meet the needs of varying degrees of emergencies, while at the same time providing continuing police coverage of areas not affected by the emergency. The following plans are to be used as a guide, but any other arrangement of vehicles that the emergency calls for may establish the *Plan:*

1. Plan I utilizes one supervisor's car, four squad cars and one squadrol.

2. Plan II calls for one supervisor's car, six squad cars and one squadrol, in addition to the vehicles in Plan I.

3. Plan III calls for one supervisor's car, six squad cars and one squadrol, plus the vehicles in Plans I and II.

4. Plan IV calls for one supervisor's car, eight squad cars and one squadrol, plus the vehicles in Plans I, II and III.

5. Plan V calls for one supervisor's car, twelve squad cars and one squadrol, plus the vehicles in Plans I, II, III and IV.

B. Additional squad cars or squadrols may be requested to augment any one of the plans without calling for additional plans; however, any additional plan may be requested if the circumstances require it.

III. PROCEDURE FOR IMPLEMENTING EMERGENCY PLAN

A. The first vehicle to arrive at the incident will contact the Communications Center, if additional help is required, give its vehicle number, beat number and location and specify the *plan number* or the number of vehicles or men believed necessary to bring the situation under control. The Communications Center will accept this recommendation as authorization to put into effect the *plan* called for.

B. The commanding officer of the Communications Center will immediately notify the office of the Bureau of Field Services of the plan to be put into effect.

C. Any police officer, regardless of rank, is authorized to call into effect any plan which, in his opinion, is required to bring the situation under control.

D. The responsibility of designating vehicles to be utilized in the various plans is placed with the Communications Center. When assigning vehicles in *any plan,* dispatchers may make their selection from any district. If the emergency intensifies, the dispatcher will extend the area from which assignments are being made, always exercising caution not to strip any district of its entire vehicular complement.

E. In Plans I through V, the City-Wide III frequency may be used. Personnel in the vehicles involved in a plan will switch frequencies at the discretion of the dispatcher and only on the dispatcher's orders.

F. The use of mobile relay on the City-Wide III frequency *may* be requested by any member involved in an Immediate Emergency Plan or may be activated at the discretion of the dispatcher.

G. Detective and Traffic Division vehicles and men may be utilized as required. In addition, in those instances when the emergency situation is going to extend over a long period of time and when uniformed Task Force units are in operation in the general vicinity of an emergency, they will be utilized in lieu of district vehicles either at the onset of the emergency or as a relieving force as the situation warrants, depending upon the number of Task Force personnel and vehicles in use at that particular time and area. Any of these units, when needed, are to be requested by the ranking supervisor at the scene of the emergency through the Communications Center dispatcher.

H. The Communications Center will designate as Communications Car one of the assigned units from the affected district. When practical, the first car from the affected district will be the Communications Car. All radio communications will be handled by the chauffeur of the Communications Car. He will remain with his vehicle at all times and maintain a log of all vehicles reporting to the incident and their locations. He will also keep the Communications Center informed of the name and rank of the officer in charge.

I. The Communications Center will announce by radio the vehicle number and location of the Communications Car. When additional vehicles are assigned, they will be directed to report to the Communications Car unless detailed to locations on the perimeter of the incident. If vehicles cannot be driven to the Communications Car, they will be parked as close as possible (without obstructing traffic), and the crews will proceed on foot to the Communications Car for assignment.

J. The first supervising officer to arrive at the incident will assume command and remain in charge until relieved by a supervising officer or commanding officer from the district in which the emergency occurs. All supervising officers responding to the emergency will assist the officer in charge at the scene.

K. The Communications Center will notify the field lieutenant of the district concerned as soon as any Emergency Plan is implemented. The field lieutenant will respond to any plan and remain until relieved by a superior or until the emergency is over. The watch commander will proceed to the scene of any Plan IV or higher. He will take command until relieved by the district commander or other superior officer, or until he feels that his presence is no longer required. The watch commander may exercise his own discretion as to whether to proceed to the scene of a Plan I, II or III.

L. All vehicles in the proximity of an incident not specifically assigned will obtain clearance from the Communications Center before proceeding to the incident.

M. Any officer who participates at the scene of an emergency in civilian clothes will pin his star in plain view of his shirt or coat.

IV. OPERATIONS AT EMERGENCY SCENES

A. The initial responsibility of any officer taking command at an emergency scene is to evaluate the extent of the emergency situation and take immediate steps to ensure that adequate manpower and equipment are being made available.

B. What action is taken at the scene will necessarily be determined by the individual situation, but in any case, the officer in charge at the scene must take decisive action to keep onlookers away. The officer in charge will deploy personnel to ensure that onlookers will be kept at such a distance that they are out of danger, they are kept from destroying evidence and they do not interfere with official actions.

C. Officers in charge at emergency scenes will assign the personnel and vehicles necessary to keep access and egress lanes open so that the movement of ambulances, police or fire equipment, etc., is not hampered.

V. TERMINATING AN EMERGENCY PLAN

In any emergency situation to which more than one police unit responds, the supervisor or command officer in authority on the scene will have the responsibility for ordering police units back to regular assignments when there is no need for them at the scene of the emergency. Units ordered back to regular duty will immediately switch back to their radio zone frequency and report to their dispatcher. When units are relieved, the officer in charge will notify the City-Wide III dispatcher. When the emergency itself is terminated and all units are to leave the scene, the officer in charge will notify the Communications Center.

James B. Conlisk, Jr.
Superintendent of Police

APPENDIX NO. 4

DISCUSSION OF ARREST AND POST ARREST PROCEDURE TAKEN
FROM BAR LEADERSHIP AND CIVIL DISORDERS
THE AMERICAN BAR ASSOCIATION SECTION OF CRIMINAL LAW

A. *Arrest and Enforcement Procedures*

Any emergency plan for civil disorders should provide clear guidelines for police on when to arrest and the use of alternatives to arrest. The question of timing is all important and must be a judgmental decision on the scene based upon all available information with consideration of all factors. While time can be of the essence at the very outset of a disturbance in quelling and containing it, there can be instances where overreaction can escalate, rather than restore law and order.

Police action in an isolated instance is routine and normal. In a disturbance of widespread proportions, the police in many instances will require orders of higher authority. The guidelines should contemplate the exericse of this authority, and the emergency plans should provide for its prompt exercise, as there can be no vacillation when prompt and decisive action is required.

The following guidelines and checklists should be considered:

(1) Consideration should be given as to when and on what basis arrests are to be made, i.e. for major offenses, minor offenses, to clear an area and related matters.

(2) The object of the arrest, in addition to law violation, can also be to remove an agitator from the scene or to effect temporary detention to clear the streets or to prevent persons from entering or leaving the riot area. Obviously, persons in the riot area should be permitted to go back to their homes or, if they live outside the riot area, to return home absent overt law violation.

(3) The plans should also include alternatives to arrest and detention such as the issuance of a summons or notice to appear (like a traffic ticket) or to adopt station house summons and release procedures such as used by the New York Police Department. These alternatives to arrest need to be operational before the emergency arises. In the event of mass violations making many minor offenses, the alternative to arrest can become an important aid to prevent the overburdening of existing facilities in a crisis, particularly if coupled with the condition of not returning to the riot area. Training and preparation in the use of these alternatives is necessary. Experience has demonstrated that in many instances, such as curfew violations not attended by any offense, a summons would be valuable in relieving congestion in detention facilities.

(4) Existing legislation on arrests should be reviewed and a legal basis worked out in advance of the emergency with steps taken to

expeditiously seek any corrective action necessary through the legislative process.

(5) The nature of probable violations can be anticipated in the event of civil disorders. Consideration should be given to outlining for the police the elements of each offense and the minimum evidence necessary to support an arrest and subsequent prosecution.

(6) Adequate evidential and administrative support for arrests, i.e. identification, pictures of persons arrested, fingerprints where appropriate, identity of witnesses, statements of witnesses and arresting officers and the preservation of physical evidence, are a necessary part of emergency plans.

(7) The plans should provide procedures which will not unduly delay arresting officers in turning over persons arrested so that maximum police manpower can be kept at its main function of maintaining order and protecting the law-abiding citizens. Likewise, emergency plans should make provision to augment local police with other law enforcement officers, i.e. county officers, officers from neighboring communities and state police.

(8) When the National Guard has been called out, police generally should be assigned to make arrests even when state laws specifically give the power of arrest to the National Guard because practical problems will subsequently arise at later trials when Guardsmen may not be available to testify. (Part IV, page 6, the Report of the National Advisory Commission on Civil Disorders, March, 1968, in its supplement on Control of Disorder has helpful information on the use of military forces as does Department of the Army Pamphlet 27-11, December, 1966, "Military Assistance to Civil Authorities." Chapter 13, of the report of the National Advisory Committee on Civil Disorders, March, 1968, entitled "The Administration of Justice Under Emergency Conditions," is also most helpful.)

(9) The emergency planning should also include guidelines on the use of equipment, force to be employed, the justification and availability of equipment with provisions for uniformity in action by civil police and military forces.

(10) Emergency transportation should be provided to take persons arrested to the booking location and from there to the detention site as expeditiously as possible. An inventory of transportation vehicles should be made in advance and a procedure set up to mobilize the

equipment on short order when needed, with provision to deputize drivers as custodial personnel.

(11) Booking procedures under normal circumstances are wholly inadequate in any widespread disorder resulting in thousands of arrests. Hence, there is a need to provide a simplified procedure providing minimum information. A multiple-use form devised by the U. S. Department of Justice for larger protest demonstrations could be readily adapted in advance planning to any jurisdiction. The form is filled out at the processing station where the arrested person is taken by the arresting officer who swears to it and then returns to his post. A polaroid picture is taken of the arrested person with the officer and attached to the form. A docket number can be assigned to the form in consecutive order, thus providing the number of persons arrested at all times. Single copies can be sent to key points in the process through which arrestees pass.

B. *Post-Arrest Processing Facilities*

The all important processing starts following the arrest. In each instance, local laws, facilities and the gravity of the situation will dictate the procedure. If existing facilities can stand the burden, this would be preferable. Booking at the precinct station and detention in the established center would be desirable. But emergency plans must assume the worst, as has now been amply demonstrated. In most situations, a single processing center can be set up near the scene of the action and has the benefit of centralizing overall control of procedures and a central source of information on those arrested. A nearby school, church, garage, warehouse or large office lobby could very well be hurriedly staffed for booking, initial processing and then movement to detention quarters.

The emergency plans should consider:

(1) Location of adequate facilities for booking and initial processing of a potentially large number of arrestees in areas easily accessible to any contemplated scene of disorder with adequate sanitary facilities and provision for humane treatment.

(2) Inventorying and having readily available necessary office equipment, office supplies and means of prompt delivery to the designated site.

(3) Providing available personnel to man the booking center with police officers, bailiffs, custodial personnel and medical assistance, including female custodial personnel. In most instances, offical personnel will

need augmentation which can be recruited and trained in advance from other agencies not normally associated with law enforcement.

(4) Provision should be made for the assignment of representatives of the District Attorney's office to be available for consultation in the booking process.

(5) An orderly, predetermined method of handling records should be provided and centralized so that at all times dispositions in the booking process will be readily available.

(6) Procedures should be provided in the emergency plans on whether persons arrested will be deprived of personal effects other than dangerous weapons or physical evidence which should, of course, be seized. Experience has demonstrated that most persons arrested in an emergency will be released soon after arrest. Such a procedure will facilitate processing and hold down the necessary paper work.

(7) Consideration should be given to having available at the booking center representative community leaders and a member of the bar not associated with either prosecution or defense to serve as observers to avoid allegations of abuse and to inform the community about the treatment of those arrested. Likewise, the emergency plans should make provision for access by representatives of the news media to the booking centers under safeguards which will not prejudice any prospective defendent in a criminal proceeding to a fair trial.

(8) The emergency plans should also anticipate a central telephone number which can be publicized so that all calls from family and the potential defense attorney for the person arrested can go to one place and be expeditiously serviced. Various alternatives should be considered, based upon availability of service. If telephone service at the booking or central records center is not available, calls could go to a central police number and communication could be had by walkie-talkie or short wave radio to the central records center.

(9) Likewise, a public announcement should be made as quickly as possible once an emergency starts as to the procedure of booking and detention, along with facilities to assure all interested parties that those arrested are being properly treated and cared for medically, legally, socially and in every other way. This likewise could have a deterrental effect once it was known that law and order would be maintained.

C. *Post-Arrest Screening and Release*

The emergency planning for the post-arrest screening and release must start with a review of existing law and a determination of the adequacy of legislative and administrative provisions relating to the post-arrest release, the issuance of station house summons, special processing of juvenile offenders and possible outright release of minor offenders. Here again the intensity of the strain on the judicial machinery must be an important factor in the plans.

(1) Guidelines should be worked out in advance on the prosecutive policies to be followed, the offenses to be charged and the ability to handle mass arrests, all of which must ultimately be determined by the gravity of the offense and the validity and quantum of the evidence, the background of the arrestee, his roots in the community, absence of a criminal record, along with the intensity of riot conditions at the moment and the role of the arrestee in the riot.

(2) In making the plans, it is necessary to establish administrative procedures to implement the guidelines which will be applied in initiating prosecutive action and some form for release procedure, i.e. available means to check previous criminal records, identity, residence, means of support, where the arrestee will go upon release, identity of groups who will supervise him upon release. Obviously, release should be considered either by issuance of a station house summons or outright release if the riot has subsided, and there is doubt that evidence will support prosecution.

(3) The emergency plans should consider the issuance of summons and station house release, as contrasted to posting cash collateral, for minor offenses to avoid adding to the burden of police officials in holding cash and additional paper work. Experience has demonstrated that cash collateral is invariably forfeited while a summons can either be pursued or subsequently dismissed if investigation justifies it after the riot has subsided. Under the unique emergency conditions prevailing during a riot, it seems almost inevitable that persons suspected — but innocent — of minor offenses may be arrested. To charge them what amounts to a fee for their release, when it is recognized that their unfamiliarity with legal procedures is likely to result in forfeiture of the cash collateral, only imposes an additional hardship in such cases.

(4) Since the most important function of post-arrest screening is to separate different classes of arrestees and make a preliminary determination of their subsequent handling, it is important that both prosecuting and defense attorneys be present in sufficient numbers at

the processing center to expeditiously handle the disposition of preliminary screening. Obviously, there must be a difference in the treatment of a person arrested for homicide, arson, sniping, robbery or possession of explosives and a minor offender caught in a dragnet, a curfew violator or a couple entering the riot area on the way home with minor children.

D. *Detention Facilities*

Detention facilities in most communities already are over-burdened, and any civil disorders of any proportion will necessitate emergency detention facilities. Existing detention facilities should first be used to capacity, and custodial officials should have plans to move regular inmates together and, insofar as possible, keep arrestees of a riot separate from other offenders. The great majority of arrestees in riot situations will require only minimal security facilities.

It is of utmost importance that the facilities of an area which might be converted to emergency detention facilities should be surveyed in advance. In addition, detention facilities in surrounding areas might be considered.

In considering emergency detention facilities, the following factors should be considered.

(1) A preference should be given facilities as accessible as possible to the areas where emergencies might occur. The facilities should approximate as nearly as possible the minimum standards of detention which will provide accommodations without over-crowding, the segregation of detainees by age and sex, the provision of housing, feeding, bedding and sanitary facilities.

(2) Provision should be made in advance to quickly mobilize custodial personnel, both male and female, maintenance and service personnel. Minimal medical facilities should be provided with a medical staff on duty at all times, along with social and probation workers. Police officers should be used to a minimum, as their services are needed elsewhere in the emergency. Ordinarily, catering services are available in the larger areas, but when not available, other food services should be provided.

(3) Provisions should be made to enable detainees to communicate with their families and lawyers.

(4) Facilities need to be provided for privileged communications with defense counsel.

(5) The emergency planning should locate and inventory sources of supply of beds, bedding and other materials to provide at least the minimum comforts. The same emergency planning which the Red Cross has done so effectively in meeting disasters, or civil defense workers have done to meet disasters, can well be applied to providing for emergency detention.

(6) Transportation facilities need to be readied in advance to expeditiously move persons from the booking and processing areas to the detention facilities.

(7) Plans should be made for record keeping to keep track of detainees, as well as to furnish information to all appropriate government agencies, the public and news media.

(8) Once an emergency detention center is operable, provisions should be made for inspection by community leaders as well as representatives of news media under proper safeguards which avoid premature publicity prejudicing a prospective defendant's rights.

(9) Provision should be made for proper advice to the public, detainees and their families as to appropriate legal procedures with signs on desks to identify officers and clerical personnel, along with their function to hold frustrations to a minimum and simplify operational procedures.

(10) Many of those detained will not have been taken before a judicial officer. It is, therefore, of prime importance to provide easy availability to the courts, district attorneys, defense counsel, social workers and probation officers. Consideration should be given to moving the courts, prosecutors and defense lawyers to the detention facility, certainly during the period of arraignments and preliminary hearings, if such a procedure would expedite the administration of justice. In the event that arrests are occurring in large numbers over several days, the need to start bail, arraignments and preliminary hearings becomes apparent and, depending upon the gravity of the situation, should be handled on a shift basis, if necessary utilizing all available judicial, prosecutive and defense personnel.

(11) The importance of emergency detention facilities cannot be over-

emphasized. Minority groups who riot because of frustrations, inequities and deeply-seated emotional rebellion against what they consider as injustice, can only have deeper feelings if not treated humanely with justice and fairness. Where riots occurred without previosuly prepared emergency plans, the machinery for the administration of criminal justice was shockingly inadequate and survived only through loyal, sacrificial dedication of civic-minded public officials and citizens.

APPENDIX NO. 5

DEFINITIONS

Civil Disturbance. Group actions of violence or disorder prejudicial to public law and order.

Demonstration. An assemblage of persons exhibiting a public display of sympathy with, or against, an individual, political, economic or social condition or movement.

Department Commander. The chief of police, or a senior officer acting in his stead.

Field Commander. A police department officer having line command over a given geographic area of responsibility. The responsibility could include the riot control and the routine police problems within a given area. If the commanding officer has responsibility for only the riot problems in his area, his title could be changed to Task Force or Riot Commander so as to be more specific. If the riot conditions are widespread, and it is necessary to divide the city into several independent areas, the title given to the individual commander could be Area, Precinct or Sector Commanders.

Mob. A disorderly crowd whose members, under the stimulus of intense excitement or agitation, lose their sense of reason and respect for law and follow leaders in lawless acts.

Riot. A breach of the peace committed by persons in furtherance of a common purpose to execute some enterprise by concerted action against anyone who may oppose them. (A branch of the peace is an unlawful disturbance of the peace by an outward demonstration of a violent or turbulent nature.)

Task Force. That part of the department involved in the control of an unusual occurrence.

Unusual Occurrence. (UO). An unscheduled physical event involving potential or actual personal injury or property damage arising from fire, flood, storm, earthquake, tidal wave, landslide, wreck, enemy action, civil disturbance or other natural or man-caused incident requiring exceptional police action.

a. *Minor Unusual Occurrence.* (Blue Alert). A UO which can be handled by the present facilities of the on-duty patrol division with the assistance normally available from other on-duty divisions.

b. *Serious Unusual Occurrence.* (White Alert). A UO of such proportion that the facilities usually available to the on-duty patrol division are inadequate to establish control and which requires temporary modification of the Department organization.

c. *Major Unusual Occurrence.* (Red Alert). A UO which threatens the safety of the city to such an extent that in the opinion of the Department Commander it is necessary to activate the entire department for control purposes.

CHAPTER V

THE RESERVE FORCE CONCEPT

IT has been demonstrated by experience that the normal day-to-day personnel strength of a police department is not equal to the demands of a disaster situation when it becomes necessary to implement or put into operation a police emergency plan. Conscientious police administrators recognize the tactical advantage of a reserve force to supplement the line power resources of the department in the emergency. Circumstances may arise where the available personnel strength of the department is inadequate to cope with the problem, and the availability of a well-organized and trained reserve force may provide the difference between success and failure.

The Auxiliary Police Unit

Known generally as auxiliary police units, these supplementary forces are recruited from among the responsible citizens in the local community. Their duty assignments may involve traffic regulation and control, crowd control, assisting in surveillance, civil disturbance control, service under disaster conditions, roadblock operations, Civil Defense assignments and other functions. In some instances, air squadron units, scuba diving units, boat flotillas and rescue squads have been organized as a part of auxiliary police activities.

Auxiliary police units must be recruited, organized and trained under the closest supervision by regular officers in the department who possess the necessary capabilities for this important assignment. The Sheriff's Department of Alameda County (Oakland), California, operates eight platoons of male reserves, two platoons of female reserves, two underwater rescue platoons, fire units, rescue units, a posse and an air squadron. The 266 hours of training required by the sheriff's department for reserve officers

238

exceed the required basic training for a regular peace officer in California, as set by the Commission on Peace Officer Standards and Training. The training curriculum is organized as follows:

1. Introduction to law enforcement (8 hours). History, functions, purpose and concepts of law enforcement.
2. Criminal investigation (57 hours). Applicable investigative and interrogation procedures and techniques; an emphasis is placed on the essential elements of report writing.
3. Defensive tactics (19 hours). Use of defensive and offensive techniques, searching, handcuffing, crowd control and physical training methodology.
4. Patrol procedures (100 hours). Preparation and techniques of motor patrol procedures, public relations, types of criminal complaints, field observation and personal demeanor.
5. Traffic control (4 hours). Traffic control techniques and practical application of traffic safety, highway engineering, traffic enforcement and traffic accident investigation.
6. History, development and definition of civil, criminal, juvenile laws and procedures (24 hours).
7. Firearms (12 hours). Legal, moral and departmental policy concerning the use of firearms and force; use, function and firing of all departmental weapons.
8. First aid (7 hours). Fundamental principles of first aid; special classes in the emergency aspects of childbirth, life saving and water safety.
9. Administration of justice and criminal evidence (12 hours). Structure of justice at all judiciary levels; complaints, indictments, trial procedures, testimony and introduction of evidence.
10. Examination (3 hours).

Opinion concerning the desirability of these reserve forces varies somewhat among police administrators. Chief Jacob A. Jessup of the Department of Public Safety in Sunnyvale, California, conducted a survey among a number of American police departments and concluded that the formation and use of a police reserve in Sunnyvale would not be in the best interests of the public and the police service.*

However, as pointed out by Bristow, there is an organizational advantage in the use of police reserves; the field force commander may often deploy reserves to handle routine control problems, thus relieving his regular manpower for active crime control assignments.† Where a well-organized and well-trained reserve force is available, there are definite organizational advantages to the field force commander.

In addition, the economics of a reserve force must be given consideration. In a survey conducted by the California State College at Los Angeles to cover the states of Arizona, California, Colorado, Idaho, Montana, New Mexico, Oregon, Utah, Washington and Wyoming, many of the replies commented favorably with respect to the financial savings experienced in those communities where a police reserve force is used. One chief of police observed that he was able to save the city $50,000 a year through the use of reserves. Another chief stated that his reserve officers permitted him to replace regular officers on vacation, sick leave and noncompensated overtime to a total of 25,000 hours per year.**

Since reserve officers are usually unpaid in terms of a salary, the Alameda County Sheriff's Department was able to indicate in a recent annual report that its use of reserve deputy sheriffs provided the county with law enforcement support which would have cost $187,000 had that support been provided by regular officers. The Los Angeles County Sheriff's Department indicated that the monetary value of their reserve officer activities, had they been performed by regular deputies, was $1,035,658.00 for one year.

---

*Jessup, Jacob A.: A Study of the Use of Police Reserves or Auxiliaries. *Police,* January-February, 1960, pp. 26-29.

†Bristow, Allen P.: *Effective Police Manpower Utilization.* Springfield, Thomas, 1969, p. 41.

　See King, Everett M.: *The Auxiliary Police Unit.* Springfield, Thomas, 1969. This volume will prove helpful in the organization, staffing and operation of an auxiliary police unit.

**Gourley, G. Douglas and Bristow, Allen P.: *Patrol Administration.* Springfield, Thomas, 1961, p. 48.

The Highland Park (Michigan) Operation

A novel variation in the auxiliary police concept has been developed in Highland Park, Michigan. An unusual increase in juvenile crime in that city of 38,000 prompted the police to organize a Citizens' Night Patrol, consisting of five radio-equipped cars, with from two to three men in each car. On duty from 8:30 P.M. to midnight, they exercise no police power and engage in no police action of any kind whatsoever. Their function is to *prowl,* to observe and report any unusual or suspicious activity by radio to headquarters, whereupon one or more uniformed patrolmen move in and take over the situation.

Members of the Citizens' Patrol are unarmed and do not leave their cars under any circumstances. Radio-equipped cars of other city departments, which would otherwise be in the garage for the night, are used by the Citizens' Patrol. The essence of the plan is that it doubles the observation power of the patrol force, and the police of Highland Park report a sharp reduction in the number of incidents involving juveniles.

The Tactical Unit or Mobile Task Force

Closely related to the reserve force concept is the tactical unit or mobile task force. Although staffed by regular police personnel, it offers an alignment of line power for the duration of the emergency far above what would be possible with the normal deployment of police personnel. This becomes self-evident when the total work program of a police department is considered.

General Operations

Operations constitute the field work of a police organization, and they should be directed toward securing maximum efficiency with economy of resources in terms of money and effort. The line power of a police organization finds expression in two types of field operations. The first is *general operations,* and these are concerned with meeting the normal daily problems associated with crime, vice, traffic and the miscellaneous activities which are generally referred to in police circles are general duties. General operations concern the ordinary, stable disposition of personnel resources and equipment in the line.

With trained men, properly distributed, the striking power of the organization can be addressed in an orderly and effective manner to the routine problems associated with the general operations of the department. The degree of efficiency with which this end is achieved will determine in large measure the volume of special operations and the special assignment of manpower which this entails. However, even in the most efficiently organized and managed police departments, occasions constantly arise requiring special operational planning and execution.

Special Operations

Special operations are limited to the execution of temporary plans for the attack upon specific problems and emerging situations which arise at particular or irregular intervals. They are concerned with the execution of short-term plans designed to cope with critical situations of a temporary nature in order to permit an overwhelming concentration of striking power at a particular time and place to meet a specific problem.

In a small department, such situations may develop only a few times during a month; their frequency increases with the increase in the population of a community, and it is also influenced by the composition of the population, sociological and economic characteristics of the community and all other factors which condition social organization. In an average city from 100,000 to 200,000 population, these operational crises may follow in comparatively rapid succession during a twenty-four hour period and require almost continuous provision for the special deployment of manpower and equipment. Those departments where proper attention is given to special operational planning, can meet these crises as they arise without endangering general operations.

Routine duties occupy most of the time of police officers, and when these duties are carefully planned and personnel properly supervised, they can be discharged with a considerable degree of success. There are times, however, when these daily activities must be interrupted, either briefly or for a substantial period of time for the purpose of concentrating upon some problem which demands immediate action. Criminal emergencies and natural disasters such as earthquakes, hurricanes, tornadoes, conflagrations, explosions and other types of event occur when they are least expected.

Accordingly, plans must be prepared in advance so that the line power resources of the department can be brought into play with dispatch at the time and the place where they are needed. A part of the force or the entire organization may be used to cope with the problem. Parades, meetings, where there is a possibility of friction or uprising, visits by the President of the United States or other important personages, athletic events, riots, strikes, fires, disasters of any type or any unusual or extensive criminal activity or unusual traffic or vice conditions present operational difficulties which require special planning and direction. Increased criminal activities on the part of one or more persons may lead to an emergency situations, which continues until they are apprehended. As a result of their activity, there is created during the hours and in the areas in which they operate, a need for police service out of proportion to the year-around average.

These special situations require an orderly diversion of the striking power of the department in sufficient amount to bring about liquidation of the problem. Therefore, implementing the requirements of special operations, there must exist and be available at all times a *tactical unit* or *mobile task force* representing the mobile power of the department which can be concentrated in any quarter of the city at whatever hour or hours the circumstances may dictate. The tactical unit is not to be regarded as a reserve force held at police headquarters waiting for something to happen, although headquarters may be its base of operations.

Members of the tactical unit are, under normal conditions, patroling beats or carrying out the routine work of their regular positions in the detective, traffic or other divisions, subject to mobilization at a moment's notice for assignment on a special tactical operation. The number of men actually engaged on a tactical operation at any one time may and will vary from one to a hundred or more, depending upon the nature of the problem. In the larger departments, the uninterrupted succession of emergencies, one after the other, may require the maintenance of a tactical unit on a semi-permanent or permanent basis. The entire line strength of the organization may be involved, and in certain types of emergencies in the felony classification, police departments over a large area may be alerted into action where the perpetrator has escaped from the scene of the crime.

It is clear that the routine functions of the police must go on, but this can be managed during limited periods when action is indicated in terms of concentrating the power of the force on some objective which requires immediate attention. The striking power of a police department is amplified in this manner to a degree altogether impossible by routine assignment of personnel. Tactical unit personnel should be carefully selected on the basis of their personal qualities and performance records. The nature of the work may require moral courage, together with physical courage and endurance of a high order. This unit should be so organized and equipped that it can be moved rapidly from one point to another.

The operational pattern of the tactical unit is seldom the same on any two assignments and will depend entirely upon the nature and dimensions of the emergency problem or situation toward which its attention is directed at the moment.

Criminal emergencies command the major share of the attention of the police in the conduct of special operations. The number and variety of situations in this category calling for the emergency concentration of police strength cover the total range of the criminal spectrum. A flood of worthless checks descending upon the merchants of the community or a series of sex crimes are of short duration and come to an abrupt end through the operation of the tactical unit. Fluctuations in the need for police service may result from a series of safe burglaries, an unusual amount of car prowling, a series of robberies or an expanding series of house prowls. Information furnished by the Records Division, maps and field studies offer the basis for the planning of special operations.

In the field of traffic control, appropriate study of the available data will indicate the engineering, educational or enforcement operations that will liquidate a particular problem. Analysis of an abnormal rise in the traffic accident rate along a certain thoroughfare may indicate that moving violations are the major contributing cause. The situation may assume emergency proportions and warrant the operation of a tactical unit during the time and at the locations where these violations are occurring. Supplementing the work of the patrol force by application of intensive enforcement pressures on a selective basis, a concentration of striking power is effected, and in this manner the causes contributing to increased accident rates are modified and the situation relieved.

As previously indicated, deployment of personnel on a tactical operation means a temporary reduction in the strength of beat patrol and other line units for the purpose of dynamic offensive tactics. A skeleton patrol will have to suffice until the objectives are achieved. Obviously, this is attended with some danger, but nevertheless it must be done in certain instances if the police are to fulfill their obligations. It is utterly impossible to assume that the police can solve all the problems presented to them by merely placing the officers on beats.

The training of members of the tactical unit merits the best that can be given. Without training, plans are impotent. Without both plans and training, a police department courts disaster. It is a function of police administration to set up training programs for officers in the department and to formulate plans of operation in advance for all types of emergencies so that the officers may be prepared to meet every situation successfully. This is especially true of the Tactical Unit. Otherwise, there may be needless sacrifice of personnel and discredit reflected on the department because of the lack of preparation. Merely to dispatch a squad or a company of men to the scene of an emergency is to risk the lives of these men and at the same time expose the department to embarrassment.

Similarly, plans must be worked out in advance of a possible jail emergency. Police headquarters itself may also be the object of attack, as has been amply demonstrated during the past few years. An attempt may be made to liberate prisoners or to take custody of them for the purpose of lynching or for other reasons. Police buildings should be designed to withstand such attack, and plans should be developed in advance for assignments and operations in the event of such an attack. Most police headquarters buildings are far from ideal in this respect, and a premium is therefore placed upon preparation in advance for any emergency situation. The importance of advance preparation and planning for all police emergencies cannot be over-emphasized. During the emergency, there is no time to develop elaborate plans of action. The police are under a heavy stress at the moment and should be ready for immediate action.

In order to forestall or meet such attack, to safeguard firearms, departmental equipment and records, and to prevent the escape of prisoners, it is necessary to maintain maximum headquarters security at all times in all department buildings and offices. Records security is especially important. When exterior doors, including roof access points, are equipped with an alarm system wired directly to the desk, such alarm system should be tested at least once each month, and the desk officer should make an entry on the Police Bulletin of the results of such test.

Areas within department buildings which are open to the public should be separated from areas which are designated for the exclusive use of departmental personnel. Public access must be limited to those areas in which police business with the public is normally conducted. Areas ordinarily used only by departmental personnel are to be considered restricted areas to which un-authorized public access is strictly prohibited.

Quite apart from the catastrophe or calamity arising from physical causes, a tactical unit with operational plans worked out in advance will prove of great usefulness in severe social disturbances, such as prison outbreaks, race riots, mob situations, industrial disorders and similar man-made emergencies. When such disturbances involve widespread destruction of property, including the crippling of communications or other essential utilities in the community, the problems facing the police would be identical with those accompanying a destructive flood, earthquake or fire. The department should spare no effort in drawing the blueprints and outlining the details for such plans of operations.

All of the foregoing situations bring into sharp focus the need for a tactical unit or mobile task force superimposed upon the normal patrol power of a police organization. The International Association of Chiefs of Police has repeatedly emphasized that an adequate *show of force* insured efficient dispersal of a threatening mob, for example; whereas, delay, indecision and inaction at the first sign of trouble inevitably required the *use of force* to disperse the threatening mob, and such action invariably resulted in property damage and personal injury, in addition to embarrassment for the police department.

An increasing number of police departments are now making use of the tactical unit or mobile striking force to supplement routine patrol operations in the approach to emerging situations and the emergency. The number may be expected to continue to increase. The effective results which follow the concentration or saturation of an area or location with striking power sufficient in terms of personnel, training and equipment to assure liquidation of the problem have now been well demonstrated.

A random sampling survey of forty-seven police departments in the United States in various population brackets revealed that of the twenty-nine departments responding to a questionnaire, eighteen were using the tactical unit as a special phase of their line operations.*

Under the administration of George D. Eastman, Director of the Police Division of the Department of Public Safety in Pontiac, Michigan, a study of line operations indicated the need for a flexible unit with the capabilities for applying selective enforcement pressures in special crime situations.

Pontiac is a city with an area of twenty square miles and a population of 85,000. The personnel strength of the Police Division is 124 officers. One-man patrol cars are employed. When the division staff study clearly demonstrated the need for a special mobile striking force, the *Flexible Unit* was created, consisting of five experienced patrolmen under the immediate command of a Sergeant. The stated responsibility of the Flexible Unit was to serve as a compact, mobile and effective operational striking force in given locations at times where the records indicated the need for a special concentration of enforcement pressure.

---

*Arnwine, Major Henry B.: *A Study and Evaluation of Police Tactical Operations.* Master's thesis, Washington State University, 1963.

In order to maintain the unit intact, it only works five days a week. Due to the variation in need by hour of day, the unit may go on duty at any time, although it usually begins its work between 7:00 P.M. and midnight. Depending on the nature of the emergency, the Sergeant and five patrolmen may operate as a compact unit in uniform or plain clothes, or they may work in pairs or singly. Unmarked cars are used.

At one time, the Flexible Unit, equipped with walkie-talkies, may address its attention to the surveillance of known criminal offenders or stakeouts at known crime hazards. At another, they may be giving special attention to a series of residential burglaries or, in old clothes, walking a railroad track from which there is ready access to industrial and commercial installations for burglars. The unit responds to felonies-in-progress reports and renders assistance to the patrol force by closing all avenues of escape from the area. However, it does not answer any call that would be handled by the beat patrolman as a routine matter.

When not engaged in meeting criminal emergencies, the Flexible Unit gives its attention to the problem of selective traffic enforcement, with special reference to moving violations. In this manner, the selective application of force by a cohesive, mobile unit gives the line commander strong additional striking power without the necessity of adding more men to the force. The value of such a Flexible Unit in a disaster situation is self-evident.*

Similarly, in Oak Park, Michigan (integrated police and fire services), the departmental staff decided that one way to improve their capabilities in dealing with disorders and disasters was to organize and train a select group of officers as a tactical unit. These men would be the nucleus around which the department would build its emergency capabilities. The officials of Oak Park also felt that impending problems, purely local in nature, might need vigorous tactical police action in reducing the likelihood of disorderly group situations.

Eleven officers are assigned to the tactical unit, with five others held in reserve. The unit is commanded by a Lieutenant and is equipped with three shotguns, two rifles, two carbines, three

*Eastman, George D.: The Flexible Unit — A Unique Striking Force. *Police,* July-August, 1960.

sub-machine guns and one gas gun. Normally, the members of the tactical unit are on duty in their regular assignments in the patrol services, but subject to immediate mobilization when the need arises.*

In addition, a group of chiefs of police in the area had become concerned with the limited ability of the smaller departments to cope with a number of problems. Plans were developed for mutual aid in disasters, disaster identification procedures and in the implementing of area road blockade plans.

In Richmond, Virginia, a city of 230,000 population and a police department with a personnel strength of 422 officers, it was found advisable to create a mobile, flexible unit to supplement the routine patrol operations by having available, special striking-power capabilities to be used in applying selective enforcement pressures in emerging situations. Training emphasis is placed on crowd control techniques and on meeting the criminal emergency where the records indicate an abnormal increase in crime reports, particularly burglary and robbery.

As in Oak Park, Michigan, the tactical unit does not operate on a full time basis but is mobilized for service when the emergency need arises. Tactical operations are conducted on the precinct level, with a tactical unit of from ten to twenty officers available to each precinct.

An expanded concept of the tactical unit operation has appeared in England, where Area Crime Squads are organized and operated on an area basis in the larger urban complexes. In a typical arrangement, with Manchester (population 686,000) as the control center, seven police forces contribute personnel to the Area Crime Squad, serving an area with a combined population of approximately 2,000,000 people. Under centralized command, the activities of the squad are directed toward criminal offenders who operate throughout the area complex and who do not necessarily confine their activities to a single town or city.†

---

*Leonard, Glenford S.: Our Tactical Police Unit. *The Police Chief,* April, 1962.
†A letter dated July 2, 1963, from J. E. Colton, Chief Constable, Salford, England.

CHAPTER VI

TWO MAJOR DISASTER-ORIENTED ORGANIZATIONS

ALTHOUGH the United States continually works for peace and stability in the world, the nuclear threat continues to grow. President Nixon said in his State of the Union Message that peace in the last third of this century would hinge on relations between the United States and the Soviet Union. These relations are still clouded by uncertainty and secrecy. For example, it is known that the Soviets, over the past few years, have deployed more than 250 SS-9 missiles in the 10 to 25 megaton range. Those responsible for national defense must assume these weapons are deployed against U. S. Minute-man missiles. This threat to the U. S. retaliatory missile force is, in effect, a threat to the nation's survival.

Other threats to world peace darken the future. The Red Chinese work to become a world nuclear power. Furthermore, their border confrontations with the Soviets raise the possibility of escalation to the nuclear level and the involvement of other nations. Smaller nations may also acquire nuclear weapons.

In the face of the harsh realities of the world in which people live, it is essential that the United States maintain a strong Civil Defense system as part of the total defenses. An effective, nation-wide fallout shelter system is an essential component of our civilian defenses.*

The National Civil Defense System

The National Civil Defense System finds expression at the federal, state and local levels. Its responsibilities, programs and organization follow.

---

*Department of Defense, Office of Civil Defense: Annual Report, 1970, p. 7.

Responsibilities and Programs. The Federal Civil Defense Act of 1950, as amended (Public Law 920 — 81st Congress), states the intent of the Congress of the United States to "provide a system of civil defense for the protection of life and property in the United States from attack." The same Act also established a Federal agency to be responsible for a National Civil Defense Program.

The Office of Civil Defense (OCD), within the Department of Defense, acts for the Secretary of the Army in developing and administering the overall National Civil Defense Program, including:

1. A fallout shelter program.

2. A civilian chemical, biological and radiological warfare defense program.

3. Development and operation of civil defense warning or alerting and communications systems.

4. Planning for emergency assistance to state and local governments in a postattack period.

5. Guidance and assistance to state and local governments to increase their protection and emergency operations capability.

6. Programs for financial contributions and donation of federal surplus property to the states for civil defense purposes.

7. Developing systems to conduct nationwide assessment in event of attack to determine: (a) the nature and extent of damage, (b) surviving resources and (c) specific hazards resulting from the detonation or use of special weapons.

In support of the foregoing responsibilities, OCD conducts the following programs: Research and Development, Training and Education, Information Services, Emergency Information and Liaison Services. These are discussed later.

OCD also advises the Secretary of the Army on military support to civil defense, is represented at Headquarters, North American Air Defense Command (NORAD), at Headquarters, Continental Army Command (CONARC) and participates in emergency exercises involving elements of DOD and other Federal agencies and State and local governments.

Organization. The Office of Civil Defense is organized at the *Assistant*

Secretary level of the Department of the Army and is civilian in character and direction. OCD Headquarters is located at the Pentagon. In addition, there are eight OCD Regional Offices located at Maynard, Mass., Olney, Md.; Thomasville, Ga.; Battle Creek, Mich.; Denton, Tex.; Denver, Colo.; Santa Rosa, Calif. and Bothell, Wash. There is also an OCD Staff College at Battle Creek, Mich.

In attaining its program objectives, OCD works closely with state and local governments to develop their capability for taking effective action in time of emergency. This is in keeping with a declaration in the Federal Civil Defense Act that the responsibility for civil defense "shall be vested jointly in the federal government and the several states and their political subdivisions."

The concept of "civil defense" in the United States is that of the normal forces of federal, state, and local government being organized — with supplementary forces as required — to meet the effects of attack.

In the civil defense program, the Office of Civil Defense works with the 50 States, Puerto Rico, the Virgin Islands, the Canal Zone, Guam, American Samoa and the District of Columbia and through the States, with more than 3,000 countires or parishes, and more than 17,000 incorporated local governments.

In addition, OCD coordinates emergency functions with the Office of Emergency Preparedness and works with some 30 other federal agencies that have emergency preparedness responsibilities assigned by executive orders.

Liaison, including contractual arrangements for certain civil defense activities, is maintained by OCD with the National Association of State Civil Defense Directors, the United States Civil Defense Council (local member-ship) and various other technical and professional advisory groups.

The National Fallout Shelter Program

The objective of the National Fallout Shelter Program is to provide the people of the United States with protection from fallout radiation that could result from nuclear attack. The program is focused not only on providing fallout shelter but also on the preparations necessary for effective use of the shelter system in event of attack.

The Department of Defense has conducted exhaustive studies which show that with a minimum radiation protection factor (Pf) of 40 (radiation received in shelter would be only 1/40th, or 2 1/2 percent of that outside), more than 90 percent of the people surviving the direct effects of a nuclear

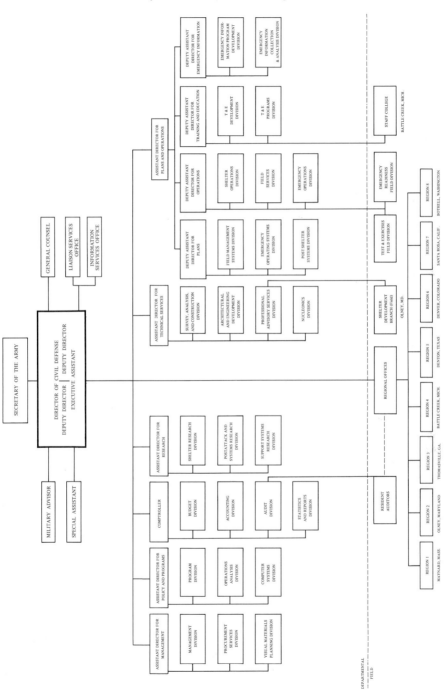

Figure 6: OCD Organization Chart

attack on the United States, *and who otherwise would die from the effects of fallout radiation without shelter,* could survive. OCD policy, therefore, is that standard public fallout shelter should provide a minimum radiation protection factor of 40 (Pf 40). (Where shelter meeting this standard is not available to citizens, local community shelter plans will provide for the use of the best protection available, pending development of shelter meeting the national standard.)

The National Fallout Shelter Survey. Under the Fallout Shelter Program, potential public fallout shelter facilities are located in existing buildings and special facilities (mines, caves, tunnels) through surveys conducted by the U.S. Army Corps of Engineers (CoE) and the Naval Facilities Engineering Command (NAVFAC). Eligible facilities are licensed and marked — and stocked with OCD-furnished supplies of a food ration, water-storage containers, medical and sanitation supplies, if needed, and radiation detection and monitoring equipment.

Home Fallout Shelter Survey. Despite notable progress in identifying public fallout shelter spaces through the nationwide survey, shortages still exist in many parts of the United States — particularly in residential areas. Because of this, OCD, in cooperation with the Bureau of the Census, sponsors Home Fallout Protection Surveys. Individual surveys are usually conducted for a state, upon request by the governor. The surveys collect data from householders on the type of house, materials used in construction and depth of basement. From this data, OCD advises the householder on the protection factor of his basement and, if required, how to improve the radiation shielding.

Shelter on Military Installations. Military installation commanders are responsible for fallout shelter surveys on their installations to determine protected spaces that may be used not only by military personnel, but also by the public in areas where it can be permitted. CoE or NAVFAC personnel can assist in military area surveys. Commanders are also responsible for preparations for effective use of fallout shelters on their installations in event of nuclear attack.

Community Shelter Planning. A system of public fallout shelters is essential to local emergency readiness. Also necessary is planning for most effective use of the total shelter resource of any community — both public shelters and private shelters. Therefore, OCD has developed a Community Shelter Planning Program (CSP). In this program, professional planners work closely with local civil defense directors and other local government personnel in preparing shelter-use plans. An important aspect of CSP is the development of emergency informational materials for the public. CSP also provides the basis for preparing the Emergency Operations Plan of local government which states the emergency responsibilities of all the departments — police, fire, public works, etc.

Shelter Development. The OCD Shelter Development program has focused on architects and their consulting engineers, who are encouraged to include dual-use shelter in their building designs to increase the national shelter inventory. Graduate-level courses for architects and engineers have produced several thousand fallout shelter analysts. OCD has developed radiation protection design techniques that apply to building design. It has also initiated a Direct Mail Shelter Development system whereby new projects and their architects are identified through construction reports; architect and owner are then contacted and asked to include shelter. A university advisory service is available to give architects advice on radiation protection design. Other programs to demonstrate shelter design include architectural competitions, design studies and awards programs. Results of these are published and disseminated to architects and engineers.

Civilian Chemical, Biological and Radiological Defense. OCD programs for civilian chemical, biological and radiological warfare defense stress protection from the radiological threat. Studies conducted by the Department of Defense indicate that the threat to the United States posed by chemical and biological agents is relatively less significant than the nuclear one. Chemical agents in particular are not considered a strategic threat, as they are effective mainly if used against a tactical target of limited area. However, the threat of biological warfare is under constant review, and research continues on methods of detecting, identifying, reporting and analyzing the threat and developing defenses against it.

A nationwide monitoring and reporting system has been designed for the collection, evaluation and dissemination of radiological information. Several thousand radiological monitoring stations have been established and equipped throughout the 50 States, and at least two radiological monitors have been trained for duty at each station. Monitoring information would be reported to authorities at all levels of government and in the military services. The information would provide a necessary base for decisions on emergency and recovery actions.

Emergency Operating Capability of State and Local Governments

Development of the emergency operating capability of state and local governments, and the protection of persons necessary to those operations, receives high priority in OCD guidance and assistance.

In this regard, OCD concentrates on:

1. Development of Community Shelter Plans (CSP's). (This forms the basis for the city or county Emergency Operations Plan.)

2. Development of Emergency Operating Plans including provisions for increased-readiness measures to become effective upon receipt of an official alert and for emergency actions to be instituted upon receipt of warning.

3. Development of Emergency Operating Centers including operating procedures and warning and communications facilities.

4. Development and improvement of the emergency operating capabilities of state and local departments (i.e. police, fire, public works, etc.). This involves planning and personnel, facilities, equipment and supplies.

Overall management guidance of state and local civil defense activities is provided by OCD through a system of annual program papers and semiannual progress reports submitted on computer-oriented formats. The periodically-updated information submitted on program goals, and on progress made, provides an effective management tool for the civil defense program — and thus results in more effective application of the civil preparedness effort.

Emergency Operating Centers (EOC's). Key officials would move to EOC's during a crisis or attack situation and from there would direct and control emergency operations. These operations would include the gathering and dissemination of official information to the emergency services of local government and to the public. Each operational EOC has a fallout protection factor (Pf) of 100 or better, adequate warning and communications facilities, emergency power sources and sufficient fuel, food, water and medical supplies to sustain a 14-day continuous operation. Many communities throughout the United States have operationally ready EOC's.

The Emergency Broadcast System. State and local EOC's are being tied into the Emergency Broadcast System (EBS), a system developed by the FCC and the broadcasting industry. In a crisis or attack situation, official information and directions would be broadcast promptly through EBS. As support to EBS, a broadcast station protection program is being carried out by OCD. This program includes provision of emergency power sources where needed and radio links between EOC's and key EBS stations. This would make it possible for these EBS stations to stay on the air in a fallout environment and would help assure effective nationwide coverage.

Civil Defense Warning and Communications

Warning. Federal warning systems are designed to disseminate warning to strategic points from which state and local governments are responsible for warning the public. A Civil Defense Warning System (CDWS) operates throughout the continental United States, including Alaska. Separate warning systems serve Hawaii, American Samoa, Guam, Puerto Rico and the Virgin Islands.

The Federal portion of the CDWS is the National Warning System (NAWAS). The North American Air Defense Command (NORAD) initially provides warning information. Then, from 3 civil defense warning centers, warnings and warning information can be passed within approximately one minute to the 8 OCD Regional Offices and to nearly 1,000 Warning Points throughout the United States. The three civil defense warning centers are continuously manned and operated for OCD by U.S. Army Strategic Communications Command (USSTRATCOM) warning officers. The primary National Warning Center is in Cheyenne Mountain, Colorado Springs, Colo. Alternates are the National Two Warning Center at the Federal Center, Denton, Tex. and the National Three Warning Center near Washington, D.C. The Warning Points are at key federal locations and in state capitals and other cities. From these points, warning is further transmitted via state and local warning networks.

State and local governments use a variety of communications facilities for sending warning and supplemental information from the Warning Points to thousands of local warning points. Telephone and radio are widely used for alerting local civil defense personnel and government officials. Local warning systems include both indoor and outdoor devices to alert the public. The siren is a preferred common outdoor warning device — although horns, whistles and voice sound systems are also used. Indoor warning devices include telephone, radio and various commercial communications facilities, such as public address systems and circuits for transmitting background music to public places.

The Civil Defense *Warning* and *Alert* signals are:

THE ATTACK WARNING SIGNAL

A wavering tone or short blasts for 3 to 5 minutes — actual attack against this country has been detected — take protective action immediately!

THE ATTENTION OR ALERT SIGNAL (optional for local use — not a
part of the national CD
system)

A steady blast or tone for 3 to 5 minutes for peacetime emergencies —
listen for essential emergency information!

Communications. Effective communications systems are required at all
levels of government for conducting civil defense operations on a nationwide
basis and for addressing the public during emergencies. The primary system of
communications between OCD national headquarters, the eight OCD
Regional Offices and the state civil defense offices is the Civil Defense
Telephone and Teletype System, designated *NACOM 1*. The system includes
both telephone and teletypewriter services. Its connections extend also to the
emergency relocation sites of selected federal agencies, and it can be
interconnected with commercial, military and other federal teletype systems.
NACOM 1 is backed up by the Civil Defense Radio System, designated
"NACOM 2." This is a high-frequency radio network which can be used to
transmit voice, code and radio-teletype messages. *NACOM 2* has been
installed in OCD Headquarters, in all OCD Regional Offices, in 46 states, the
District of Columbia and the Canal Zone. It can be used also to contact
Continental United States (CONUS) Army Headquarters and some AEC
installations.

The Emergency Broadcast System (EBS), already discussed in relationship
to the emergency operational readiness of state and local governments, is an
important aspect of civil defense communications. The order of priority in
EBS programing would be: (1) Presidential messages, (2) local instructions,
(3) state government messages and (4) regional and national programing and
news.

Military Support of Civil Defense

The military mission in event of a national emergency involving a nuclear
attack on the United States would be as follows: The Joint Chiefs of Staff,
the Military Services and Defense Agencies will be prepared to employ
available resources which are not engaged in essential combat, combat-
support or self-survival operations to assist civil authorities to restore order
and civil control, return essential facilities to operation, prevent unnecessary
loss of life, alleviate suffering and take other actions as directed to insure
national survival and a capability on the part of the nation to continue the
conflict. Military assistance would complement and not be a substitute for
civil participation in civil defense operations.

The Department of the Army has primary responsibility for military support of civil defense within the continental United States. Accordingly, the Army coordinates military defense plans with civil defense plans and provides such military information, consistent with requirements for military security, as federal, state and local agencies may require in developing their plans.

The Director of Civil Defense is responsible for advising the Secretary of the Army on policy and program aspects of military support to civil defense. Coordinated military support planning and compatibility of resulting plans with civil emergency plans are the objectives.

Each state Adjutant General works closely with the state Civil Defense Director (in 12 states the Adjutant General is also the Civil Defense Director), to insure that military support will be based on state and local civil defense plans; and, under the planning guidance of the Continental U. S. (CONUS) Army Commander, he plans for the postattack employment of military resources which may be made available by the services.

The Commanding General, U.S. Continental Army Command (USCONARC) and the CONUS Army Commanders provide preattack planning guidance to the state military headquarters in the performance of military support of civil defense missions in the 48 contiguous states. In Alaska, Hawaii and Puerto Rico, similar headquarters are guided by the appropriate unified commanders. The services have on-post civil defense responsibilities.

Postattack Assistance. In accordance with Executive Order No. 10952, as amended, "Assigning Civil Defense Responsibilities to the Secretary of Defense and Others," the Office of Civil Defense is charged with developing plans and operating systems "to undertake a nationwide postattack assessment of the nature and extent of the damage resulting from enemy attack and the surviving resources, including systems to monitor and report specific hazards resulting from the detonation or use of special weapons."

During and after an attack, damage assessments would provide to government – federal, state and local – the bases for informed direction of emergency operations; and later on, for most effective actions to speed recovery.

Federal agencies are responsible for maintaining damage assessment capabilities related to their normal functions and for providing pertinent data to OCD.

To make effective use of stored data in developing damage estimates during and following attack, OCD maintains a National Civil Defense Computer

Facility. Data bases at the facility are being continually expanded and updated. OCD has also developed a Manual Damage Estimation System which analysts can use to match preplotted data on selected resources with that derived from weapons strike reports.

Assistance to State and Local Governments. Postattack, the nationwide requirement for emergency measures to assist survivors and help restore essential facilities and services, would be extensive. The Office of Civil Defense would coordinate the gathering, analysis and dissemination of situation data received from throughout the United States. Broad operational priorities for deployment of Federal assistance would be progressively determined from information gathered.

Support Activities

In developing and maintaining an effective nationwide civil defense program, the major elements (e.g. shelter and emergency operating systems) require certain supporting activities. Among these are (1) Research and Development, (2) Training and Education, (3) Information Services, (4) Emergency Information and (5) Liaison Services. These, and some other support activities, are discussed below:

Research and Development. It is essential that civil defense planning, hardware and systems keep pace with rapdily changing weapons technology and delivery systems. OCD therefore maintains a Research and Development Program which applies scientific knowledge and principles to the solution of emergency operating problems. The program is carried out principally through contractual agreements with government, educational and private research organizations.

Training and Education. The OCD Training and Education Program supports civil defense activity nationwide at all levels of government and provides civil defense education to the public. Key personnel in government receive instruction on planning and directing civil defense operations, and others are trained in the skills needed to cope with civil defense emergencies.

To provide professional and technical civil defense training, OCD operates a Staff College at Battle Creek, Mich. and provides additional instruction through the following:

Community Shelter Planning (CSP) Training Program
Civil Defense University Extension Program (OCD/Extension Divisions of
    Land-Grant Colleges and Universities)
Civil Defense Adult Education Program (OCD/HEW)

Medical Self-Help Training Program (OCD/HEW)
Explosive ordinance reconnaissance training of local and state police by
  USCONARC
Rural Civil Defense Program (OCD/USDA)

OCD-produced training materials are used by local governments to train their personnel and auxiliaries in police, rescue and radiological defense skills. OCD also has developed and offers a home-study course entitled, "Civil Defense, U.S.A." The agency works with national educational associations for incorporation of civil defense concepts and principles into the nation's school system.

Information Services. Provides information concerning the ongoing and projected activities of the Office of Civil Defense.

Emergency Information. OCD Emergency Information activities are directed primarily to the preparation and dissemination of information that the public would need in a period of rising international tension or in an attack situation.

Liaison Services. A strong civil defense program depends, to a large extent, upon the support and readiness activities of industry, organizations of various types and voluntary services.

The industrial-readiness program concentrates upon (1) protection of personnel, facilities and equipment, (2) continuity of management, (3) protection of vital records and (4) development of mutual-assistance pacts.

The resources and organizational capabilities of industry and business are invaluable factors in overall local civil defense preparedness. Industrial protective services, in particular, are generally well organized and equipped and are ready for action at all times.

Industrial and business facilities contain much of the nation's public fallout shelters. Millions of persons receive civil defense education and skills training at the workplace. OCD works with other federal agencies, industry and business in developing civil defense informational materials to meet particular needs. OCD also sponsors industrial civil defense conferences, seminars and training sessions conducted primarily for civil defense purposes.

Other Support. OCD maintains various other support activities to help further the National Civil Defense Program. These include: (1) Community Services, (2) Labor Liaison and (3) International Activities.

Community Services seeks to increase understanding and involvement of public and private sector leaders and leadership groups in community action for civil defense. This involves work with fraternal and civic groups and organizations for voluntary support.

Through *Labor Support* representatives, OCD maintains liaison with labor and trade unions for support of the National Civil Defense Program. Special labor civil defense seminars, courses and informational materials have been developed and are presented or distributed throughout the United States.

International Activities of OCD involve exchange of civil defense information with other countries and mutual civil defense planning. In coordination with the Office of the Assistant Chief of Staff for Intelligence, Department of the Army and the Department of State, these activities are conducted cooperatively with the North Atlantic Treaty Organization (NATO), the Central Treaty Organization (CENTO) and the United States/ Canada Joint Civil Emergency Planning Committee (CEPC).

Training, emergency information and other special-purpose informational materials are developed by OCD. Policy and operational guidance of the agency is disseminated to other federal agencies, and state and local governments, by means of the *Federal Civil Defense Guide* and related publications. Technical publications are developed for selected professionals, notably for architects and engineers, as guidance in the nationwide shelter program. OCD publications and related informational materials are listed in OCD Miscellaneous Publications MP-20, *Publications Index*, available through state and local civil defense agencies or from the Office of Civil Defense, Department of Defense, Washington, D.C. 20310.

Financial Assistance

The Office of Civil Defense administers a Federal Financial Assistance Program to help state and local governments develop and maintain civil defense readiness within their jurisdictions. Federal surplus personal property may also be donated for this purpose.

Federal financial assistance may be granted for *up to* one-half of the total costs for eligible items. Categories for which funds may be granted upon approval of application include:

Personnel and administrative expenses
Supplies, equipment and training
Construction of Emergency Operating Centers (EOC's)

The four basic requirements for a unit of government to be eligible for OCD financial assistance are:

1. Civil defense organizational arrangements must be established pursuant to law.

2. There must be an OCD-approved operations plan.

3. There must be an approved program paper for the current federal fiscal year.

4. The state or local civil defense agency must comply with Title VI of the Civil Rights Act of 1964.

In addition, applicants for financial assistance for personnel and administrative expenses must (1) have an approved merit system for all of their civil defense employees and (2) submit a financial plan and staffing pattern along with an annual request for funds.

OCD also makes direct grants to state and local governments in the form of fallout shelter supplies and radiological instruments and for the professional services of architects and engineers, planners and administrative materials required in community shelter planning.

Fallout and Radiation

The nationwide fallout shelter system, an important part of the total defenses of the nation, can protect millions of persons from fallout radiation. Much of this system is in being — with shelters marked and stocked with survival supplies. Work is proceeding to expand the system. In event of impending or actual nuclear attack, people would move to fallout shelters.

To understand the need for fallout protection, one needs to become aware of the basic nature of fallout and of fallout radiation.

A nuclear weapon burst produces a blast wave, heat and radiation. When the detonation is close to the ground, large quantities of earth and other materials are mixed with radio-active material from the weapon. These materials are drawn thousands of feet upward with the rising fireball and the forming mushroom cloud. As the fireball cools, the radio-active materials condense on the soil and other particles.

These radio-active particles gradually fall back to earth. The heavier particles fall fairly quickly near the point of explosion. The lighter particles drift with the upper winds and fall in an irregular pattern that may extend for several hundred miles. This effect is referred to as *fallout*. The particles of fallout, which range in size from coarse to fine sand or table salt, are highly radio-active.

Time of Fallout Arrival and Distribution. The time of fallout arrival and distribution at various distances and directions from the point of explosion depends upon the winds. Significant amounts of fallout begin to arrive in the immediate vicinity of a blast area soon after an explosion. People some 20 miles away might have a half-hour or longer to seek protection. At a distance of 100 miles, the fallout may not arrive for 4 hours or more, depending on wind speed. The fallout will continue to spread over an increasingly larger area and may eventually cover several thousand square miles.

It is impossible to preduct with accuracy how large the hazardous downwind area of severe local fallout will be or what shape it will take. Too many conditions can affect it.

No Area "Safe". Assuming a random attack against a wide range of military, industrial and population targets, fallout would be distributed over very large areas of the United States. The actual area affected would depend on the season, wind conditions and other variables, but no area could be designated in advance as safe.

Kinds of Radiation. Fallout particles probably would be visible, especially if potentially lethal contamination levels occur. However, radiation given off by the particles cannot be detected by any of the human senses. *Radiation cannot be seen, heard, smelled, tasted or felt: special instruments must be used to detect and measure it.*

Fallout particles from a nuclear explosion emit one or more types of radiation, namely gamma rays and/or beta particles. Beta particles have a maximum range of only 10 to 12 feet in open air (average range 3 to 4 feet). They do not penetrate heavier materials easily. They pose some hazard, however, in that beta radiation from fallout collected on the person can cause severe burns.

Gamma rays pose the greatest threat, since they have a long range and are extremely penetrating. They are similar to X-rays. Gamma radiation is far more penetrating than beta. Ordinary clothing, which protects against beta, provides no protection against gamma. In a fallout area, the amount of gamma radiation reaching the body can be reduced to acceptable levels by putting enough shielding (mass) between a person and the source of radiation.

(This is the protective principle of fallout shelters).

Radioactive Decay. Radiation levels from fallout build up during the time the particles are being deposited. Radiation then decreases with time; that is, the radiation level, as measured in roentgens per hour (R/hr), drops lower and lower. The decrease is rapid at first and much slower later on. This falling off of intensity is due to *radio-active decay.* There is a sharp drop in radio-activity in the first 6 to 8 hours following a nuclear explosion, and then a gradual leveling off to a relatively low decay rate by the end of the first 48 hours.

It must be emphasized that the *radio-activity in fallout cannot be destroyed.* Neither boiling nor burning, treatment with chemicals or any other action will destroy or neutralize radio-activity. Because of radio-active decay, fallout will become less harmful with the passage of time, but there is no known way to speed up the decay process.

When large amounts of radiation are absorbed by the body in short periods of time, sickness and death may result. This is why fallout shelters are necessary for protection from fallout radiation.

Protection from exposure to radiation involves a combination of one or more of three things: Shielding, distance and time, defined as —

1. Shielding (shelter).

2. Distance (distance from radiation source) or removal of radio-active materials (decontamination).

3. Time (exposure control) (combination of 1 or 2 above, with time-scheduled exposures). (Radio-active decay is also a function of time.)

In a fallout area, shielding is the most dependable means of protection. Shelter provides mass between people and the source of radiation. By keeping the fallout particles outside, shelters also provide some protection by distance. The degree of intensity and the rate of decay to acceptable levels must be determined by specialists with special equipment.

Fallout Shelters, Public and Private

Identifying Public Shelters. Most communities now have public fallout shelters that would protect many of their residents against fallout radiation. Where there are still not enough public shelters to accommodate all citizens, efforts are being made to provide more. In the meantime, local governments plan to make use of the best available shelter.

Most of the existing public shelters are located in larger buildings and are marked with a standard yellow-and-black fallout shelter sign. Other public shelters are in smaller buildings, subways, tunnels, mines and other facilities. These also are marked with shelter signs or would be marked in a time of emergency.

Home Shelter. Public fallout shelters usually offer some advantages over home shelters. However, in many places — especially suburban and rural areas — there are few public shelters. If there is none near you, a home fallout shelter may save your life.

The basements of some homes are usable as family fallout shelters as they now stand, without any alterations or changes — especially if the house has two or more stories, and its basement is below ground level.

However, most home basements would need some improvements in order to shield their occupants adequately from the radiation given off by fallout particles. Usually, householders can make these improvements themselves with moderate effort and at low cost. Millions of homes have been surveyed for the U. S. Office of Civil Defense by the U. S. Census Bureau, and these householders have received information on how much fallout protection their basements would provide and how to improve this protection.

Shielding Material Required. In setting up any home fallout shelter, the basic aim is to place enough *shielding material* between the people in the shelter and the fallout particles outside.

Shielding material is any substance that would absorb and deflect the invisible rays given off by fallout particles outside the house and thus reduce the amount of radiation reaching the occupants of the shelter. The thicker or denser the shielding material is, the more it would protect the shelter occupants.

Some radiation protection is provided by the existing, standard walls and ceiling of a basement. But if they are not thick or dense enough, other shielding material will have to be added.

Concrete, bricks, earth and sand are some of the materials that are dense or heavy enough to provide fallout protection. For comparative purposes, 4 inches of concrete would provide the same shielding density as:

— 5 to 6 inches of bricks.

– 6 inches of sand or gravel
– 7 inches of earth
– 8 inches of hollow concrete blocks.
– 10 inches of water.
– 14 inches of books or magazines.
– 18 inches of wood.

May be packed into bags, cartons, boxes or other containers. (6 inches if filled with sand).

The national Civil Defense organization is geared directly to disaster or the threat of disaster, primarily in terms of military attack. However, it also plays a major role at the local level in disaster situations such as hurricanes, earthquakes, tornadoes, floods and similar emergencies. Local Civil Defense organizations function under the jurisdiction of the State Civil Defense Office. State offices, in turn, are structured into *regions* which come together as a national organization, operating under the Office of the Secretary of the Army – more specifically, the Department of Defense. Each State Civil Defense Office has a master plan of survival which is related to the Regional plan on the national level and to Civil Defense plans at the local level.

Planning and supply are the two major functions of the state offices. Plans at the state level involve the use of the capabilities of state agencies and those at the local level of government. This includes public safety communications in general and police communications systems in particular. Section 89.17 of the Federal Communications Commission's Rules reads as follows:

> A station licensed under this part may transmit communications necessary for the implementation of civil defense activities assigned to such station by the local civil defense authorities during an actual or simulated emergency, including drills and tests; PROVIDED that such communications relate to the activity or activities which form the basis of the licensee's eligibility in radio service in which authorized.

Local Civil Defense

Civil defense is a joint responsibility of the federal, state and local governments. Each has a distinctive role. Community preparedness, and actions by local governments in peacetime emergencies, form a solid base for readiness to meet the effects of nuclear attack. In disaster, communities often have to *go it alone*

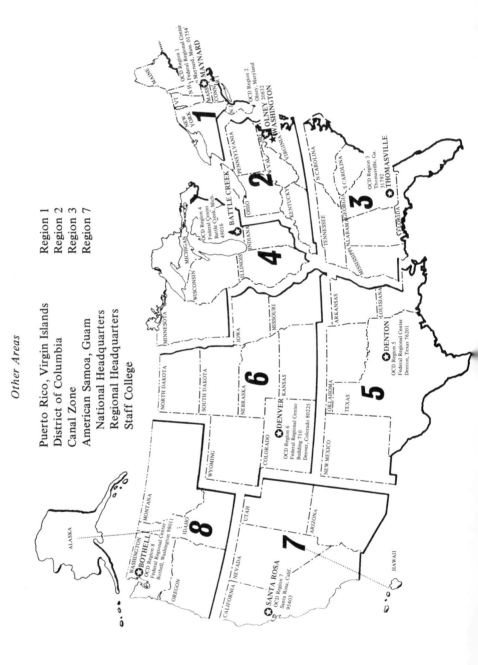

Figure 7: OCD Regions

Other Areas

Puerto Rico, Virgin Islands   Region 1
District of Columbia   Region 2
Canal Zone   Region 3
American Samoa, Guam   Region 7
National Headquarters
Regional Headquarters
Staff College

for awhile. This would be even more likely in the event of military attack — and for even longer periods of time.

In terms of clarification, *civil defense* and local government are very close to being one and the same thing. Civil defense operations occur when a local government responds to any massive emergency — a tornado, flood or other natural disaster; a major fire, explosion or industrial accident; a civil disorder or disturbance; or a nuclear attack.

News stories about a disaster may report that the police force cordoned off the disaster area and helped remove the injured, the fire department fought the blaze, the public works department cleared away the debris and doctors treated the injured. Some people ask, "Yes, but where was Civil Defense?" The answer is that civil defense was there. It was the police, fire, public works and other forces of government dealing with the emergency, *whether or not* they regarded themselves as engaging in civil defense operations or even thought of the two words — *civil defense.* And civil defense was the doctors and nurses and hospital staffs doing their job.

Civil defense is the concerted response to an unusual emergency situation — a response that calls for maximum use of community resources, with a greater need for coordination between emergency is the official who is always in charge — the mayor or

Civil defense is *not* a special unit or group of people standing by to save the day in the event of a major disaster. Local police, fire and other forces may on occasion need some trained auxiliaries to assist them in disaster operations. Some additional trained people may be needed to monitor radio-active fallout with special instruments or to serve as public fallout shelter managers. But the forces *responsible for* civil defense operations are the normal forces of government — plus non-governmental personnel with special skills, such as doctors and nurses.

The official in charge or in command during a civil defense emergency is the official who is always in charge — the major or other chief executive. He often has a key staff advisor or specialist called a *civil defense director* or *coordinator,* and there may be a staff office referred to as the *civil defense agency.*

One of the civil defense director's major responsibilities is to take the lead in assisting the operating departments of government — the police, fire, engineering and other departments — to make plans and preparations for major emergencies of all types.*

A related function, to allow local forces and resources to be used most effectively in a major emergency, is to provide the means and procedures for the chief executive and his cabinet — the chief of police, fire chief, city engineer and other key executives — to make rapid and coordinated decisions. The civil defense director should lead in this government-wide effort to provide for *direction and control* in emergencies.

This usually involves a plan for operations at a control center, at which the key officials of government will get information on the emergency situation and can make decisions rapidly after coordinating with each other as conditions may require. This control center (or Emergency Operating Center) should have the necessary communications facilities to transmit orders to local government forces.

The Office of Civil Defense has prepared a home study course of programmed instruction that is open to everyone — *Civil Defense, U.S.A.* It requires approximately 15 hours of study and consists of five units: (1) need for civil defense, (2) nuclear weapons effects, (3) shelters, (4) warning and (5) governmental responsibilities for civil defense. Enrollment may be arranged through the local civil defense agency or by sending a request with return address, including ZIP code, to *Civil Defense, U.S.A.,* Box 2000, Battle Creek, Michigan 49016.

The American Red Cross

"Since time whereof the memory of man runneth not to the contrary," the name *American Red Cross* has been synonomous with disaster relief in the United States and all over the world. No disaster plan anywhere fails to mention its important role in meeting human needs, and without cost, when calamity strikes.

---

*See Appendix B, *Maintenance of Law and Order during Civil Defense Emergencies, Planning and Programs, Orientation and Training,* Federal Civil Defense Guide, Part E, Chapter 9. Prepared in cooperation with the International Association of Chiefs of Police and the National Sheriffs' Association, November, 1968.

The authority under which the American Red Cross undertakes its activities for the relief of persons suffering from disaster is stated in Section 3, Paragraph 5, of its Congressional charter in which the organization is charged with the responsibility to

..... continue and carry on a system of national and international relief in time of peace and apply the same in mitigating the suffering caused by pestilence, famine, fire, floods and other great calamities and to devise and carry on measures for preventing the same. *

When any question arises as to the scope and activities of the American Red Cross, it is to be remembered that its Charter is not only a grant of power but an imposition of duties. The American Red Cross is a quasi-governmental organization — operating under Congressional Charter, officered in part by governmental appointment, disbursing its funds under the security of a governmental audit and designated by Presidential Order for the fulfillment of certain treaty obligations into which the government has entered. It owes, therefore, to the government which it serves the distinct duty of discharging all those functions for which it was created.

Not only is it constrained by these considerations growing out of its organic character, but there is also a moral obligation resting upon it to its membership and to the American people who have so freely and generously contributed to its support. Therefore, in the field of disaster relief, the Red Cross has both a legal and a moral mandate that it has neither the power nor the right to surrender. The Red Cross may determine the scope, policies and methods of its disaster relief program within the framework established by the Congressional Charter, but the organization must comply with the charge to mitigate the suffering caused by disaster.†

The legal grant of power to and the imposition of duties on the Red Cross in time of disaster are clear. Its jurisdictional lines with

---

*Public Law 4, 58th Congress, 3rd Session, January 5, 1905 (33 Stat. 599), which appears in *Handbook for Chapters* (ARC 550), "Charter and Bylaws."

†See The American National Red Cross: *Disaster Action, Chapter Preparedness,* Manual A. Washington, September, 1966, copyright 1966 by the American National Red Cross. Pages 9 to 15 are reproduced with permission.

respect to coordinated efforts with federal agencies have been assured by federal statute but are not intended to encroach upon or substitute for the authority and responsibility of federal, state, municipal and other local governments to provide assistance to their people in time of disaster.

However, the authority vested in the Red Cross makes unnecessary the issuance of special permission or license by state or local governments for the organization to activate and carry out its disaster relief program. Nor can any state, territorial or local government deny the Red Cross the right to render its services in accordance with the Congressional mandate and its own policies and under its own administration.

Clarification of the respective roles of the Red Cross and state and local governments in disaster relief activities has been accomplished by state and local laws and ordinances, executive proclamations and formal and informal understandings. The Red Cross welcomes cooperation from other organizations in carrying out its responsibilities and seeks to serve as a channel for the generosity of the American people.

The Red Cross Disaster Relief Program. Basically, disaster victims are responsible for their own recovery and are expected to use their own resources in this effort. When recovery is beyond the capability of an individual or a family, resources within the community, including those of the local Red Cross chapter, are mobilized to assist the family. Since the American Red Cross is a nation-wide organization, the combined resources of all chapters, through the national organization, can be drawn upon to meet disaster-caused needs that are too great for a single chapter to handle.

The objective of the Red Cross Disaster Relief Program is to mitigate the suffering caused by disaster, and the assistance rendered is designed to bridge the gap between what the victims are able to accomplish for themselves and what they actually need to resume normal family life in the home and the community.

The needs of victims can be separated into those of such an urgent nature that they must be met immediately and those that can be met after appropriate planning can be undertaken by the family and the Red Cross. Immediately following a disaster, food,

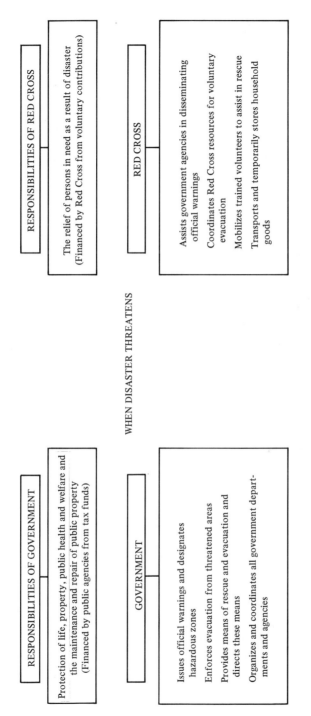

RESPONSIBILITIES OF GOVERNMENT

Protection of life, property, public health and welfare and the maintenance and repair of public property (Financed by public agencies from tax funds)

RESPONSIBILITIES OF RED CROSS

The relief of persons in need as a result of disaster (Financed by Red Cross from voluntary contributions)

WHEN DISASTER THREATENS

GOVERNMENT

Issues official warnings and designates hazardous zones

Enforces evacuation from threatened areas

Provides means of rescue and evacuation and directs these means

Organizes and coordinates all government departments and agencies

RED CROSS

Assists government agencies in disseminating official warnings

Coordinates Red Cross resources for voluntary evacuation

Mobilizes trained volunteers to assist in rescue

Transports and temporarily stores household goods

Figure 8: RESPONSIBILITIES IN NATURAL DISASTERS: Local Government Authority; Disaster Coordinator.

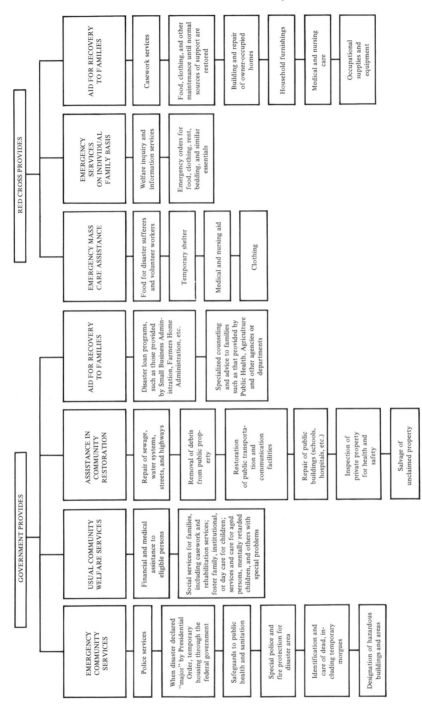

Figure 9: WHEN DISASTER STRIKES: This chart shows how distinct and yet how closely related are the responsibilities of Red Cross and of goverment in natural disasters. Red Cross and government are both needed to perform disaster functions.

clothing, shelter and medical and nursing or hospital care are provided to numbers of people on a mass basis or on an individual or a family basis. After these urgent needs have been met, the victims can begin to analyze their situations to determine how they can recover from the effects of the disaster.

The amount and kind of recovery assistance needed in each family situation is determined, in keeping with Red Cross policy, through joint planning by the disaster vicitim and the Red Cross. This assistance may include food, clothing and maintenance, the repair or rebuilding of owner-occupied dwellings and the provision of essential household furnishings, medical, nursing and hospital care and occupational supplies and equipment. The Red Cross considers only those needs created or aggravated by the disaster and does not undertake the replacement of total losses.

All disaster assistance given by the Red Cross is on a grant basis, with no obligation for repayment on the part of the recipient. Red Cross disaster is financed solely through funds donated by the American public.

Red Cross-Government Teamwork. Government responsibility in disaster remains the same as in normal times — the protection of life, property, public health and welfare and the maintenance and repair of public property. Disaster *increases,* but in general *does not change,* government responsibility. The Red Cross supports and assists the work of government authorities in alleviating the distress caused by disaster but does not assume responsibility for governmental functions.

Red Cross Chapter Responsibility. Each chapter board of directors is responsible for the development and maintenance of its chapter disaster readiness plan. For the purposes of coordinated planning and action, there may be developed mutual arrangements with other chapters in a defined geographic area. This, however, does not relieve the individual chapter board of its own disaster responsibility.*

In every disaster situation, the chapter must take immediate action to render the assistance and services that are required under the circumstances. Chapter responsibility encompasses all aspects

---

*See Appendix B for typical Red Cross Chapter disaster plan.

of the disaster operation, including immediate action to meet urgent needs, recovery planning to meet needs beyond those met in the immediate emergency, the recruitment and training of volunteers to work with staff throughout the operation, financing the operation and reporting to the national organization through the appropriate area headquarters.

In those disaster situations when the financial needs created by the disaster are greater than the provision made in the chapter operating budget together with funds contributed at the time of disaster, the chapter may request financial assistance from the national organization, establishing the basis for the request. The chapter may also request the assignment of national staff to assist in an advisory, supervisory or supportive capacity, with the chapter continuing to carry out the required disaster relief functions utilizing chapter volunteers, career staff and other community resources.

When a disaster is of such proportion that needs are created beyond the resources available to the chapter, the national organization will supplement the resources of the affected chapter with such supplies, equipment, volunteer and career staff and funds as may be required. Although volunteer and career staff may be assigned by the national organization in administrative and supervisory roles on major disaster operations, it is essential that chapter leadership — including volunteers and staff — continue in active, authoritative and responsible roles throughout the entire operation.

The services of the Red Cross are world-wide in scope and have been for more than one hundred years.* For example in March, 1965, the International Committee of the Red Cross announced that for the first time, the Viet Cong was accepting letters and parcels for captured Americans in South Vietnam. Delivery of food, vitamins, first aid and medical supplies was made with the assistance of the Red Cross of neighboring Cambodia as a neutral intermediary. Delivery of similar parcels and of mail from home for Americans held prisoner in North Vietnam had been arranged earlier through the North Vietnamese Red Cross.

*The American Red Cross, *International Services,* National Headquarters, 17th and D Streets, N. W., Washington, D. C. 20006.

Examples of the international character of Red Cross services in disaster and other critical situations to meet human needs are legion. Backed by the Geneva Conventions, which is consented to by nearly all the nations of the world, it reaches across political barriers to serve people everywhere.

The Role of the Federal Government in Natural Disasters

The federal government has a vital role in disaster relief. In order to provide more orderly assistance by the federal government, the 81st Congress passed Public Law 875 on September 30, 1950. This law, more commonly known as the Federal Disaster Act, forthrightly declares:

> It is the intent of Congress to provide an orderly and continuing means of assistance by the Federal government to the States and local governments in carrying out their responsibilities to alleviate suffering and damage resulting from major disasters, to repair essential public facilities in major disasters and to foster the development of such State organizations and plans to cope with major disasters as may be necessary.

Section 4 of the law states:

> In providing such assistance hereunder, Federal agencies shall cooperate to the fullest extent possible with each other and with State and local governments, relief agencies and the American National Red Cross under the Act approved January 5, 1905 (33 Stat. 599) but nothing in this Act shall be construed to limit or in any way affect the responsibilities of the American National Red Cross.

The law further provides for the President of the United States to designate to a federal agency the responsibility for the administration of the Federal Disaster Relief Act. The administrator of the agency coordinates the activities of federal agencies in providing disaster assistance and may direct any federal agency to furnish such assistance as he deems appropriate. The President has delegated to the Director of the Office of Emergency Planning (OEP) the responsibility for coordinating Federal disaster assistance under the Federal Disaster Act. The Red Cross maintains a working agreement with the OEP.

Upon the declaration of a major disaster by the President of the

United States, federal funds may be made available through the Federal Disaster Act to assist state and local governments in carrying out work essential for the preservation of life and property, in clearing debris and wreckage and in making emergency repairs to and temporary replacement of public facilities of local government damaged or destroyed in a major disaster. None of the funds made available through the Act can be used for direct grants-in-aid to individuals or to families affected by the disaster.

Federal disaster assistance is *supplementary* to and not in substitution for relief afforded by the states and their political subdivisions. Primary responsibility for disaster relief rests with the state and local agencies. Federal assistance is provided only when state and local resources are clearly insufficient to cope with the effects of the disaster.

Disaster Services Under Federal Agencies' Own Statutory Authorities. * Many federal agencies have statutory authority to provide disaster assistance to states and local governments prior to or in the absence of a *major disaster* declaration by the President. A few examples are:

The Department of Defense can provide military assistance to prevent starvation, extreme suffering or loss of life when local resources are clearly inadequate to cope with the situation.

The Corps of Engineers has authority to assist in flood fighting and rescue operations and to repair and restore flood control works threatened or destroyed by flood.

The Bureau of Public Roads can provide assistance to restore roads and bridges.

The Department of Agriculture can provide many services to meet the emergency needs of agriculture. These include the provision of available surplus food to relief organizations, the sale of feed grains at or below the support price and loans to disaster-affected farmers.

The Small Business Administration can provide both direct and bank participation disaster loans to individuals and business concerns to restore or rehabilitate damaged or destroyed property.

*See Office of Emergency Planning: *Federal Disaster Assistance Handbook for Local Government Officials.* Washington, D. C., U. S. Government Printing Office.

The Public Health Service can provide assistance to states and local communities for emergency health and sanitation measures.

The foregoing assistance is available without a major disaster declaration. Details concerning the type of disaster services which may be provided by federal agencies prior to or in the absence of a major disaster declaration are available from the Directors of the OEP Regional offices.

Assistance Available Following a Major Disaster Declaration. When a "major disaster" declaration has been made by the President, the available resources of all federal agencies may be used, as necessary, in combating the effects of the disaster. The Office of Emergency Planning will, when conditions warrant and the state requests, direct the appropriate agency to perform any or all of the following services:

1. Make available to states and local governments federal equipment, supplies, facilities, personnel and other resources.
2. Distribute through the American Red Cross or otherwise, medicine food and other consumable items.
3. Donate or lend surplus federal equipment and supplies.
4. Perform protective and other types of work essential for the preservation of life and property.
5. Clear debris and wreckage and make emergency repairs to, and provide temporary replacement of, essential public facilities of states and local governments.
6. Provide temporary housing or other emergency shelter.

Specific examples of the services that some of the federal agencies can provide at the direction of the Office of Emergency Planning are:

The Department of Agriculture can donate Commodity Credit Corporation-owned feed grains (1) for a limited period for livestock commingled and unidentified as a result of the disaster or (2) for an extended period for livestock owned by individual farmers who have suffered severe property loss as a result of disaster and cannot afford to buy feed.

The Bureau of Public Roads can survey damage and make emergency repairs and temporary replacement of roads, streets and bridges for states and local governments.

The Federal Housing Administration can provide temporary housing for disaster victims in such defaulted FHA-insured housing owned by the Commissioner as may be available in the disaster area.

The Veterans Administration can authorize the temporary suspension of payments on loans made or insured by the VA to assist borrowers in the retention of their property. It can also permit lenders to make advances on existing VA-guaranteed loans to repair disaster damage.

The Corps of Engineers can survey damages; perform debris clearance, protective measures or other emergency assignments; and inspect completed disaster projects.

The General Services Administration can make surplus Federal property available to States.

When a Presidential declaration of a *major disaster* is accompanied or followed by an allocation of funds from the President's Disaster Fund, the Office of Emergency Planning may provide financial assistance to *states and local governments* for the performance of protective and other types of work essential for the preservation of life and property, clearance of debris and wreckage, making emergency repairs and temporary replacement of essential public facilities of states and local governments and provisions for temporary housing or emergency shelter.

Requests for Federal Disaster Assistance. When a disaster occurs, local authorities take immediate steps to alleviate suffering and protect life and property. Most states assign, by law, the responsibility for disaster relief coordination to the state Disaster Office or the state Civil Defense Agency. Police, fire, civil defense, highway, sanitation and health departments are called into action. The Red Cross and other relief organizations provide emergency care for victims of the disaster. Local forces may be augmented by personnel from county departments and neighboring communities.

If further help is needed, state police and National Guardsmen may be sent into the area. Other state resources are committed as the situation demands. Federal establishments — particularly military installations — located in or near the disaster area provide immediate lifesaving assistance. When the combined efforts of local and state forces are insufficient to cope with the effects of the disaster, the state may ask for assistance from Federal agencies having statutory responsibilities for disaster relief.

Requesting a "Major Disaster" Declaration. If the magnitude and severity of the disaster clearly warrant assistance beyond that available under the statutory authorities of individual federal agencies, the governor may request the declaration of a *major disaster* by the President. While the governor may rely on state and local officials for information needed to support his request, *only* he can originate the request, certify the need for assistance and assure reasonable expenditure of state and local funds.

The Federal Disaster Assistance Regulations specify certain essentials which must be included in the governor's request to the President for a *major disaster* declaration. These are:

1. A certification by the governor that the total of state and local expenditures and obligations for disaster relief purposes, for that disaster and for all disasters during the twelve month period immediately preceding the request, exceed the amount published in the federal register by the Director of the Office of Emergency Planning as the minimum for that state.

2. An estimate of the severity and extent of the damage resulting from the disaster, and the overall total of funds and resources required to alleviate the damage. The estimate should include the type and duration of the disaster, the extent of damage and a list of affected counties. Public property damage should be listed separately from private property, with dollar amounts assigned to each category.

3. A statement of action taken or recommended to be taken by state and local executive and legislative authorities with regard to the disaster. Examples of such actions are emergency legislative sessions convened in connection with the disaster and special appropriations made or pending before state or local legislative bodies.

4. An estimate of state and local funds, personnel, equipment and material and other resources utilized or to be made available to alleviate the damage.

5. A statement of the extent and nature of federal assistance needed for each of the affected counties, including an estimate of the minimum federal funds, personnel, equipment, material or

other resources necessary to supplement the efforts and available resources of the state and local governments.

It is recognized that estimates made immediately following a disaster usually will be based on fragmentary and incomplete information. The full extent of damages probably will not be determined for days, and the cost of recovery may not be available for weeks. In most instances, however, sufficiently accurate estimates of damages and needs can be made to support the governor's request for a declaration and, where appropriate, an initial allocation of funds. Firm estimates are not required initially but are needed to support an allocation of funds at a later date.

Local government officials can assist the state in preparing the request for a *major disaster* declaration by providing the following information as soon as possible to the State Disaster Coordinator:

(a) An estimate of the nature and extent of public and private property damage with dollar amounts assigned to each category.

(b) A statement of local resources and funds committed to the disaster operation.

(c) An estimate of the type and extent of state and federal assistance required.

The governor's request is addressed to the President and presented to the Director of the Office of Emergency Planning through the appropriate OEP Regional Director. Upon receipt of the request, the Regional Director will insure that it contains the required information and forward it to the Director of OEP with his report and recommendation. The Director of OEP, in turn, will forward the request to the President, together with his recommendation.

The President then determines, whether the conditions constitute a *major disaster* within the meaning of the Federal Disaster Act and notifies the governor accordingly. The state Disaster Office advises local government officials in the affected area of the President's action.

Procedures for Providing Federal Assistance:

1. *The Declaration.* When the President makes a declaration of a *major disaster,* the Office of Emergency Planning immediately acts to provide federal assistance in accordance with the terms of

the declaration. Federal agencies having disaster responsibilities are notified of the Presidential action so that their disaster assistance programs may be initiated as necessary.

2. *Allocation of Funds.* An allocation of funds may be made by the President at the same time as the declaration. However, if the nature of the disaster precludes rapid damage assessment, only an initial allocation may be made, or the allocation may be delayed until cost estimates can be sufficiently refined to provide a reasonable basis for action. The allocation is made to the OEP Director for reimbursement of states and local governments for eligible costs and for reimbursement of federal agencies performing disaster relief operations.

3. *The Federal-State Disaster Assistance Agreement.* Upon the declaration of a *major disaster,* the state and the federal governments execute a Federal-State Disaster Assistance Agreement which provides for the manner in which federal aid is to be made available and used.

The agreement contains a statement that the governor has certified that the requirement of minimum expenditures and obligations for disaster purposes has been met. It also includes an assurance by the state that a reasonable amount of state or local funds will be expended to alleviate damage caused by the disaster. In addition, it lists the areas within the state eligible for assistance under the Federal Disaster Act and specifies the period during which such assistance may be provided.

4. *Project Applications.* Funds for reimbursement of specific projects are provided on the basis of project applications submitted by states or local governments and approved by the OEP Regional Director. Applications may be made by states or counties, cities, townships, school districts or other units which qualify as separate governmental entities within the geographical confines and under the laws of the particular state concerned. The project application describes the work for which federal assistance is requested and lists the basic categories of work required and the estimated cost of each item of work to be performed.

State officials furnish local applicants with information on eligibility requirements and the preparation of project applications. Standard application forms are also supplied by the state office. Project applications must be submitted to OEP through the state office within 90 days following the date of the *major disaster* declaration.

Each project application must be reviewed by the state. In approving the application, the governor or his authorized representative must certify that federal financial assistance applied for has been, or will be, spent in accordance with the Federal-State Disaster Assistance Agreement. The OEP Regional Director's approval of the project application is based on engineering inspections and reports by state and federal agency personnel and a review of the state's recommendation.

5. *Field Offices.* After the declaration of a *major disaster*, the Office of Emergency Planning, in collaboration with the state, may establish temporary field offices within the affected area. Such offices are staffed with representatives of appropriate state and federal agencies having disaster relief functions within the area. Staff is available to advise state and local applicants on eligibility of projects and to assist in the preparation of project applications.

By this procedure, correspondence relating to the approval of project applications can be kept to a minimum. Also, the OEP representative assigned to the field office can usually inform the applicant's representative of the amount of federal assistance which he will recommend. Thus, the applicant has an indication of the amount of federal assistance likely to be granted to cover the cost of eligible work and can proceed with some certainty pending notification of approval by the OEP Regional Director.

6. *Advances of Funds.* When a project application has been approved, funds may be advanced to the state for that project upon written request of the governor or his authorized representative, where the financial condition of the state necessitates such an advance or state statutes do not permit the advance of state funds to local governments to meet emergency requirements.

The request for an advance must stipulate the percentage of the approved project application amount to be covered by the advance. Advances are normally limited to 75 percent of the approved project application. The state makes the advance available to the local applicant immediately upon receipt.

7. *Audit and Final Payment.* Final payment on approved project applications is made after the work has been completed and the necessary audit has been made. The applicant must notify the state promptly when all work described in the project application is completed and must make available for state inspection records of expenditures and evidence of payment. State staff will instruct local officials in the preparation of claims for payment.

The state will perform such site audits and other review as are necessary for a certification by the state of each claim for reimbursement. The Office of Emergency Planning will make such additional audits as it deems necessary. All funds advanced to the state for individual project applications which audit shows to be in excess of approved actual expenditures must be refunded to the Office of Emergency Planning.

CHAPTER VII

COLLATERAL ASPECTS OF
PRE-DISASTER PLANNING

Mobile Emergency Headquarters

ON June 27, 1957, Port Arthur, Texas, was directly in the path of tropical hurricane Audrey. At the last minute, the storm by-passed Port Arthur and struck Cameron, Louisiana. The chief of police and the fire chief in Port Arthur both sent personnel to Cameron to assist in every way possible and to provide badly needed communications facilities.

When the men returned from Cameron, the Port Arthur police and fire chiefs arranged for a meeting with the city manager, the mayor and the city commission to discuss the work, especially communications relief work, that was performed in Cameron. In this meeting, it was decided that Port Arthur was in urgent need of some type of emergency communications system. Plans were formulated for a communications trailer to serve the police and fire departments and the Department of Public Works in grave emergency and disaster situations.

Funds were appropriated, and the city of Port Arthur purchased a Spartan House Trailer, twenty-seven feet long and eight feet wide. The interior of the trailer was wired and equipped for emergency operations. The front of the trailer provides space for the police and fire chiefs to direct operations. The rear of the trailer is designated as the communications center. It provides radio equipment for the Police Department, the Fire Department, the Street and Bridge Department and for the Jefferson County Civil Defense Disaster Network. There is also space for amateur radio operators.

There are six telephones, six circuits and a mobile telephone. Storage space is provided between the front and rear of the trailer for radio parts, flood lights and other necessary emergency

286

equipment. Across from the storage space is a fresh water tank with a capacity of seventy gallons, with a counter on top and a stainless steel sink at the end of the counter. There are six antennas mounted on top of the trailer to accommodate the various radio frequencies.

The mobile emergency headquarters unit is towed by a GMC pick-up truck which is equipped with a five kilowatt power plant, gasolene tank and a rack on top to carry two antenna poles that will raise to a height of fifty feet. In addition, the city of Port Arthur has purchased eight 150 watt gas driven power plants with an output of 110 volts AC and eight/25 watt mobile radio units to be used in the Civil Defense Disaster Network. These power plants and radio units will be used at Port Arthur school buildings designated as shelters for disaster relief.

The Port Arthur mobile emergency headquarters unit received its first real test and proved its worth on November 7, 1957, when a tornado struck Groves, Texas. The unit was put into immediate service and remained on duty through November 9.*

Similarly, the Michigan State Police placed in service sometime ago a new field office and communications center on wheels equipped for use as a mobile emergency headquarters in time of need. The plans were developed following the experience during the Port Huron and Flint tornadoes, when such a unit would have been of great value in directing rescue efforts and maintaining control of police operations.

The thirty-three foot trailer contains four radio transmitters and a telephone switchboard with a capacity of five trunk lines and twelve extensions. The transmitters will provide communications with the regular networks of the state police and conservation departments, local police and sheriff's departments. Telephone extensions can be rigged to other emergency headquarters, such as the National Guard and Civil Defense.

The office section is complete with desk, typewriter facilities and telephones. A public address system with four speakers is mounted on the roof top. An antenna tower with a height of 45 feet compresses into a length of 20 feet and tips over so that it can

---

*Leonard, V. A.: *Police Communications Systems.* Springfield, Thomas, 1970, p. 70.

be carried flat on the roof. If regular power is not available, auxiliary power for both radio and lights can be supplied by a 5,000 watt generator carried in the truck tractor which pulls the trailer. The telephone system, installed by the Michigan Bell Telephone Company, may be operated over commercial central office facilities or by local battery power supply.

All of the work of building desks and installing equipment, with the exception of telephones, was performed by state police personnel with little new equipment being used. The Michigan State Police forsees a broad use for the mobile emergency headquarters unit, not only at disasters but whenever a large number of police are mobilized for any purpose.*

Following a similar pattern, the Vermont Department of Public Safety converted a thirty-five foot bus into a specially built mobile emergency headquarters. The unit is based at Vermont State Police headquarters and is available for use where needed by the department throughout the state. It will enable the state police to operate at an emergency or disaster scene with facilities equivalent to those of a troop headquarters. It can readily serve as a temporary command post at the scene of any emergency, disaster or major crime, and it has an office for the officer in charge, as well as for a communications officer.

The mobile headquarters contains an array of emergency equipment, including complete first aid equipment, spotlights, rope, extension cords, axes, shovels, a portable crime laboratory and photographic darkroom. Latest telephone, teletype and radio equipment was installed, including a radio transmitter and receiver on the regular state police network; two-, six- and eighty-meter amateur radio band equipment; Civil Defense RADEF network equipment and the well-known citizens band communications unit. Through the cooperation and assistance of the New England Telephone and Telegraph Company of Vermont, provision has been made for six telephone lines and a teletype line into the mobile unit.

At the rear of the mobile unit, there is installed a 10 kilowatt alternating current generator which will provide 110 volt current

---

*International Association of Chiefs of Police: *THE POLICE CHIEF,* July, 1954, p. 29.

and also power for two 750 watt and one 1500 watt floodlights. In addition to the stationary generator, there is also a smaller, portable generator which can be taken from the unit and set up at a different location. A public address system is also included in the equipment.

The mobile headquarters has provision for sleeping five men so that the emergency headquarters may be manned during entire 24-hour periods whenever necessary. A small galley can provide food for the men in the event that the emergency headquarters unit is isolated from accessible eating facilities.

The Vermont Department of Public Safety feels that the mobile unit provides Vermont with an organized rescue and first aid headquarters, as well as an efficient operative control post in large scale disaster and major crime situations. The unit is available to all local police agencies, including the county sheriff's department.*

The obvious value of a mobile emergency headquarters unit in disaster and other major emergency situations suggests that an increasing number of police organizations will avail themselves of this important emergency equipment.

Increasing Apprehension Capability

The Alarm System. Burglary and hold-up alarm systems wired directly to police headquarters hold a key position in the *operating time interval — the time elapsing between the moment that a criminal attack is imminent or under way and the arrival of officers at the scene.*† There is no lifting of a telephone receiver. Upon excitation of the alarm circuit, contact with the police is instantaneous. This can become a very important factor in times of disaster and other major emergency situations when the opportunity for looting and other forms of theft become a real hazard.

In terms of the protection of valuables, it is interesting to note

---

*International Association of Chiefs of Police: *THE POLICE CHIEF,* August, 1961, p. 28.

†For an extended analysis of the operating time interval, see Leonard, V. A.: *Police Organization and Management,* 3rd ed. Mineola, Foundation Press, 1971, p. 333.

that man has found it to be physically impossible to construct an enclosure that cannot be penetrated by a burglar, given the time, the tools and the secrecy. The first true safe was introduced in New York in the early part of the nineteenth century, and soon afterward, the race began between the safe builders on the one hand and the safe burglars on the other. For a half century, safe and vault construction remained almost unchanged in terms of protective strength. Some modifications were made to offset the introduction of nitroglycerin as a weapon of attack. Then, the appearance of the cutter burner, the fluxing rod, the electric drill, chisel and hammer and the oxygen pipe introduced the need for revolutionary changes in the structural design of these protective enclosures.

In 1920, preparatory to its program of branch bank construction, the Federal Reserve Bank began a series of tests under the direction of Alexander B. Trowbridge, their consulting architect, in an effort to establish the relative resistance to attack of all known types of vault wall and lining construction and to rate these resistances in terms of cost.

The test walls were constructed by a reputable contractor under careful supervision, and the linings were built and submitted by leading vault manufacturers. Concrete consisting of carefully graded fine and coarse aggregates and fairly rich cement were found to offer some resistance to all three methods of attack — drills, explosives and the flame — provided that steel reinforcement extended entirely through the walls and at right angles to the direction of attack.

Further experiments were conducted the following year and details of vault wall construction were developed which provided increased protection, *but in all of them, penetration was effected under time tests.* It is therefore a matter of record that the most modern bank vault, representing as it does the ultimate development in protective enclosures, is vulnerable to penetration by the burglar, given the time and the tools.

It isn't necessary to go very far afield in order to discover that burglar-resisting materials can never be more than burglar-delaying materials. If the burglar has time enough — and by that is meant no more than a few hours — and the tools, it is safe to say that no commercially practical construction is impregnable against him.

Nevertheless, what ingenuity can devise to delay the burglar must be applied. But the mere prolonging of the safe-cracker's task is not protection. This delay must be exploited to the end that completion of the offense is interrupted by apprehension. Therefore, a first prerequisite of burglary protection is an adequate alarm system which will deliver a signal to the principal source of help — *the police.* With an efficient alarm system, a pasteboard box can be made more nearly burglary proof than a modern bank vault not so protected.

Banks, theaters, super-markets, jewelry stores and other locations which classify as police hazards* should be covered with this effective form of protection. Engineering an alarm system is a comparatively simple affair. Many devices are now available that will pass the word quietly to police headquarters that a criminal attack is under way.† These include the open and closed circuit triggered by a simple electrical contact, sound sensitive detectors, heat sensitive detectors, the photo-electric cell, radio frequency circuits, magnetic fields, circuited currency trays and cash register drawers, and other devices which offer almost endless approaches to the matter of *setting the trap.*

The Police Roadblock. Closely related to the alarm circuit and the apprehension process is the police roadblock operation. Numerous cases demonstrate clearly the value of the police roadblock in bringing to an abrupt halt the activities of a criminal offender. The irony of it all is that altogether too few police departments are prepared to put into operation at a moment's

---

*A police hazard is any person, place, situation or thing possessing a high potential for criminal attack or for generating a demand for police service.

†Important sources of security information concerning alarm circuit engineering include the following: Alarmtronics Engineering, Inc., 154 California Street, Newton, Massachusetts 02195; American District Telegraph Co., 155 Sixth Avenue, New York, N. Y. 10013; Babaco Alarm System, Inc., 723 Washington Street, New York, N. Y. 10014; Ruphonics Marketing, 202 Park Street, Miami Springs, Florida 33166; Mosler Safe Company, 1561 Grand Blvd., Hamilton, Ohio 45011; and Pyrontronics, Inc., 2343 Morris Avenue, Union, New Jersey 07083.

See Post, Richard S., and Kingsbury, Arthur A.: *Security Administration.* Springfield, Thomas, 1970.

Also see Steiner, Richard V.: Advantages of Police Monitored Alarms (alarm system wired directly to police headquarters). *Police,* March, 1972, p. 44.

notice this effective tool of apprehension. This is strange in view of the fact, as will be seen later, a relatively small amount of thinking and planning is required.*

As a case in point, in 1946, the Midwest was terrorized at some length by two murderers, Daniels and West, who had been released on parole a short time before from the Ohio State Reformatory at Mansfield. After their release, they separated for a brief time and then came back together to launch a series of wanton murders without parallel in the annals of the police. During this time, the highways of the Midwest were virtually deserted.

It all began with the holdup of a downtown restaurant in Columbus, Ohio. During the commission of this robbery, the proprietor attempted to dash through the front door for help, and a bullet from Daniels' gun brought him down with a fatal wound. Realizing that they were now *hot* again, they laid low for a few days. Then, at about 2:00 o'clock one morning, they decided it was time to go out to the Mansfield reformatory and take care of a guard at the institution that they had learned to dislike.

Fortunately, they were unable to find him. Then they thought of an alternative. They rang the doorbell at the warden's home outside the walls, and when he appeared, they said they were having car trouble and wondered if they could use the telephone. Once inside, they asked the warden where the rest of his family was, and he replied that his wife and daughter were upstairs asleep.

They ordered the warden upstairs. All three, the warden, his wife and daughter, were marched in their night clothes out to the car. They drove down the highway about four miles and then turned off on a country road, pulling to a stop in an isolated area alongside a cornfield. The warden and his family were ordered through a barbed wire fence into the field where they were told to stand abreast. The daughter was the first to go. The mother and then the warden fell to the ground.

After the sixth and seventh murders of a salesman and his wife (they wanted his car), the Ohio State Police pulled a plan from their files and put it into operation — a police roadblock covering parts of three states.

---

*See Schwarz, J. L.: *Police Roadblock Operations.* Springfield, Thomas, 1962. This book should be in the library of every police department.

At about 2:00 one morning, the two fugitives, wondering how they could get through the police cordon, came upon a truck loaded with new cars parked at the side of the road where the driver was getting some needed sleep. They awakened the driver, ordered him through a fence into a nearby field and shot him in the head. The truck loaded with new cars would serve as a perfect disguise in getting through the police roadblock.

In their plans, they failed to reckon with a sheriff, a former Pennsylvania police lieutenant, and Sergeant Cohn from a nearby police department, who were manning a roadblock at the intersection of two highways in southern Ohio.

The truck grinding to a halt, the sheriff walked up to the cab and asked the driver if anyone was with him, and the answer was "no". The sheriff instructed Sergeant Cohn to cover the cab while he climbed up to check the cars. He found the other fugitive asleep in one of the top cars. As they climbed down, the driver of the truck came out of the cab shooting, a bullet striking Sergeant Cohn in the chest (he recovered later in the hospital.) As the Sergeant went down, he pressed the trigger of a Thompson machine gun which was set on automatic, and a bullet hit the driver between the eyes. The other fugitive was later executed in the Ohio State Penitentiary.

In disaster and other grave emergency situations, a roadblock operation may be indicated at any time. In addition to blocking off the disaster area itself, criminal emergencies may arise that would require the operation of a roadblock. Therefore, it is essential that police departments develop roadblock operation plans in advance so that when the emergency strikes, there will be no delay and confusion in covering the situation.

The Indiana Law Enforcement Blockade System has attracted considerable attention. It was devised to coordinate the efforts of all law enforcement agencies in Indiana in setting up police blockades for the apprehension of a fleeing criminal offender and to prevent an offender from seeking refuge in another section of the state. There are 262 municipal, county and state police agencies who participate in the blockade plan and have predetermined blockade points to cover. The system covers 36,291 square miles.

In establishing a basis for dividing the state into blockade sections, the counties were discarded as being too irregular in shape and size. It was decided that the best approach would be equually spaced horizontal and vertical grid lines (about 17 miles apart), dividing the state into equal areas. The center of each of these areas was designated as the center of a blockade plan, given the prefix X and numbered consecutively X-1 through X-109. This established 109 blockade plans. The horizontal grid lines were labeled alphabetically A through $P,$ and the vertical lines were labeled "1" through "11".

The intersection of the grid lines were designated the center of a blockade plan and given the letter and number designation of the intersecting grid lines, B-2, G-8, etc. This established 130 additional blockade plans for a total of 239 state-wide. A crime committed anywhere in the state of Indiana is within 8 miles of the center of an established blockade plan.

After establishing the locations that should be covered, such as highway intersections, etc., and the police agencies that would cover them, the information was compiled into a Master Blockade Book. There is only one copy of this book which lists every blockade plan and all departments participating in each plan, along with their responsibilities. Each participating agency has a blockade book covering only those plans in which they play an active part.

It was necessary to establish a central point from which to disseminate blockade information in a criminal emergency. Because of its central location and access to state-wide police communication facilities, the Operations Center of the Indiana State Police at Indianpolis was designated as the control point. The Master Blockade Map and the Master Blockade Book are kept at the Operations Center.

Disaster and the Computer Sciences. A new and powerful weapon for law and order was begun in September, 1965, when the Federal Bureau of Investigation embarked on the development of a national electronic criminal information system to be known as the National Crime Information Center (NCIC). State and local computer installations already operational by 1965 provided the foundation for a nation-wide criminal information system. Always pacing the field, the Federal Bureau of Investigation has now mounted the computer-based National Crime Information Center at FBI Headquarters in Washington, D. C.

On the operational side, the central computer in Washington is capable of furnishing needed information concerning crime and criminals in a matter of seconds, so that the officer on the street has a national bank of information at his command at all times. The individual patrolman in the field, and the detective as well, can now make inquiry of stored criminal information and get a *real time,* up-to-the-minute response *in a matter of seconds.*

Records data in storage at the National Crime Information Center include stolen vehicles, vehicles used in the commission of felonies, stolen engines and transmissions, stolen or missing license plates when all plates issued for a specific vehicle are missing, stolen guns and other items of stolen property which are serially identifiable and wanted persons. The latter category included all federal fugitives and individuals wanted on lócal felony or misdemeanor charges, provided the municipality or state involved will extradite from any point in the United States.

Response times by the NCIC computer have more than exceeded expectations. Responses are averaging less than 15 seconds from the time the last character of the incoming message is received until the first character of the reply is on the way back to the transmitting terminal. Actual incidents have demonstrated that an inquiry from the street by an officer over radio or telephone to a dispatcher at an NCIC terminal can be answered back to the street in 90 seconds.

A New Mexico State Trooper, for example, observed two men asleep in a car parked alongside the highway near Gallup. He asked for their names and other information and then made a routine check through his headquarters in Santa Fe to the NCIC. In a matter of seconds, the officer received back the information that the two men were suspects in the slaying of four Cincinnati women during a hold-up the week before.

As was anticipated, highly mobile fugitives wanted in one state are *brushing* with the law in other states. In most instances, police agencies in remote states are arresting these individuals for new violations, and through the NCIC they obtain immediate information on warrants outstanding in other states. The fugitives are then held for extradition.

In another example of the use of the system, an automobile dealer in San Antonio, Texas, after completing some service on a 1966 Pontiac, called the FBI office, stating that he was suspicious as to the status of the car. An immediate check through the Texas Department of Public Safety to the NCIC identified the vehicle as being registered in Florida and as having been stolen in Atlanta, Georgia, on November 17, 1966.

The Kansas City Police Department reported that it made 80 *hits* on all files in a single month, with 55 percent of these hits against the Wanted Persons File. One interesting hit involved the arrest of a man in connection with a stolen car investigation with a resulting NCIC check revealing that he was a fugitive from Ogden, Utah, where a warrant was outstanding for him on a charge of armed robbery.

As of March 1, 1969, the records on file in the computerized National Crime Information Center totaled 823,904, with the breakdown showing 272,788 vehicles, 83,357 license plates, 31,864 wanted persons, 186,667 stolen or missing guns, 150,498 serially identifiable articles and 98,730 securities. The value of this centralized facility is readily apparent in view of the increased opportunities for looting and other forms of criminal offenses in a disaster area.

Developing Emergency Medical Services

In the context of medical services, the emergency can be of any magnitude, from the single traffic casualty or cardiac arrest to the mass victims of a fire, an explosion, tornado, earthquake or a hurricane. A good, emergency medical services system will be capable of marshaling the necessary health resources available in the community to meet such emergencies, whatever the magnitude. Once the basic system capable of meeting the smaller, day-to-day emergencies is established and operating, it is primarily a matter of phasing in more community resources when the number of casualties increases.

According to the American Medical Association, there are four basic components to a good emergency care system:

1. Broad-based training for on-the-spot first aid.
2. A communications system which assures prompt response to the need.
3. Well-equipped emergency vehicles, staffed by emergency medical technicians — ambulance personnel trained and equipped to provide all necessary life support at the scene and during transportation.
4. High quality emergency care facilities, staff and equipment at the hospital level.

Obviously, the first step in the development of an adequate emergency medical services system is to secure the cooperation and involvement of all appropriate community agencies and health facilities. Therefore, to the above four, the AMA adds another:

5. An emergency medical services council to bring together the leaders providing care for planning, education and funding.*

---

*American Medical Association: *Developing Emergency Medical Services — Guidelines for Community Councils.* Chicago, 1970.
American Medical Association: *First Aid Manual.* Chicago, 1970.
American College of Surgeons: *Essential Equipment for Ambulances.* Chicago, 1970.
American Society of Anesthesiologists, Committee on Acute Medicine: *Community-Wide Emergency Medical Services.* Pittsburg, 1970.

APPENDIX A

CORPUS CHRISTI HURRICANE AND EMERGENCY PLAN

INTER-OFFICE COMMUNICATION

Dept. ____Public Safety - Police____

*To*____All Supervisory Officers____

*From*____J. H. Avant, Chief of Police____ *Date*____July 6, 1971____

*Subject*____Hurricane and Emergency Plan____

The 1971 Hurricane or Emergency Plan is attached. It is actually a revision of the 1970 plan but must be studied very carefully due to numerous changes in assignments. The plan will be reviewed periodically by the Operations Coordinator to assure that all supervisors are familiar with the assignment changes.

The main function of the plan is to provide a well coordinated police operation during a hurricane or other emergency situation.

The assignment of officers to the various positions was determined by previous experience, position of rank and present shift assignments.

Each supervisory officer is instructed to study the entire plan so that his assignment will be familiar to him in the event circumstances force changes in assignments.

Each supervisory officer should be thoroughly familiar with his assigned duties and also to instruct personnel under his command regarding their responsibilities. Coordination is most important in order to realize the desired results during the confusion of a disaster.

Each employee obtain *Foul Weather* gear and other essential equipment *NOW,* instead of just before emergency.

Since all police officers will be on duty during a disaster, their families and homes can become a major personal concern. Officers should plan ahead and

299

not wait until an emergency is imminent, before making arrangements for the protection of their families. This will allow the officer to have peace of mind, which will improve his performance.

Do not delay; give this Emergency Plan your immediate attention.

J. H. Avant
Chief of Police

INTER-OFFICE COMMUNICATION

Dept.   Public Safety - Police

To   All Police Officers

From   J. H. Avant, Chief of Police   *Date*   May 5, 1971

Subject   Personnel Assignments for Hurricane and Other Emergency Situations.

I. Supervisory personnel assigned with specific duties for hurricane and other emergency situations.

   A. Director of Public Safety
   B. Chief of Police
   C. Operations Coordinator
   D. Assistant Operations Coordinator
   E. Field Commander
   F. Liaison Officer at Civil Defense Headquarters
   G. Personnel Assignment and Records Officer
   H. Pass Officer
   I. Shelter Officer
   J. Identification Officer
   K. Automobile and Equipment Officer
   L. Food and Supply Officer
   M. Police Reserve

   1-A   *Director of Public Safety* — works at staff level

   2-B   *Chief of Police* — works in cooperation with staff

   3-C   *Operations Coordinator* — Police Commander, operates directly under the Chief of Police. Coordinates overall operation. Has one (1) assistant assigned. Shall operate from the Technical Services Office near radio room.

4-D *Assistant Operations Coordinator* — Operates directly under the Operations Coordinator. Assists these officers in the overall operation. Has one (1) assistant assigned. He shall operate from the radio room.

5-E *Field Commander* — Operates directly under the Operations Coordinator. He is responsible for all field operations. Works in coordination with the Assistant Operations Coordinator. He has four (4) supervisory personnel assigned to him.

6-F *Liaison Officer at Civil Defense Headquarters* — Operates under direction of the Chief or Operations Coordinator from the Civil Defense Headquarters, to coordinate the activities of the police with those of other services. This position is valuable in that it allows the Police Division to receive information rapidly.

7-G *Personnel Assignment and Records Officer* — Operates under the supervision of the Assistant Operations Coordinator and will be stationed in the Criminal Investigation Office, room 108, in the police building. He is responsible for the dispatching of all police personnel and equipment where and when needed and keeping an accurate log of each, as to the time dispatched, where sent and type of assignment. He is assigned one (1) assistant.

(a) Personnel needed for the handling of food will be assigned by the Assistant Operations Coordinator through the Personnel Assignment Officer.

(b) Personnel will be assigned by Assistant Operations Coordinator, through the Personnel Assignment Officer, to act as liaison using communication equipment, between Civil Defense Headquarters and police radio.

(c) Clerical assistants will be assigned by the Assistant Operations Coordinator through the Personnel Assignment Officer.

(d) Assignment Officers will relieve one hour before shift change.

8-H *Pass Officer* — Operates under the supervision of the Assistant

Operations Coordinator with office located at Public Counter in lobby of police building in area of Central Records, room 101. He is responsible for the issuing of passes granting access to restricted areas. The alternate Pass Office, if needed, is located at # 1 Fire Station at Weber and S. Staples Streets. He is assigned one (1) assistant.

9-I   *Shelter Officer* — Operates directly under Field Commander. He is responsible for regular checks of designated Red Cross Shelters. He will be assisted by a ranking officer of the police reserve.

10-J   *Identification Officer* — Operates under direction of the Assistant Operations Coordinator. He shall be responsible for the identification and tagging of the dead and for all other duties which the facilities of his bureau affords.

11-K   *Automobile and Equipment Officer* — Operates directly under the Assistant Operations Coordinator. He shall be responsible for the service and repair of police vehicles and other equipment. He will have two assistants on day shift and one on the night shift. He will operate from the Traffic Office, room 105, as it is on ground level.

12-L   *Food and Supply Officer* — Operates under the supervision of Assistant Operations Coordinator. He is responsible for obtaining such food and supplies needed to support all personnel working in the police building and all the field command. The details concerning this function will be found in detail sheet attached to this directive. He will have one (1) assistant. He will operate from room B-7 in police building.

13-M   *Police Reserve* — Operates under the direction of the Assistant Operations Coordinator. A reserve officer with rank of Inspector, Deputy Inspector or Captain will be assigned to the Personnel Assignment and Records Officer. He will operate from the Criminal Investigation Office, room 108.

II. Ranking officers have been assigned the following shifts and duties:

8 AM to 8 PM	*POSITION*	*8 PM to 8 AM*
Cmdr. H. R. Hewlett	Operations Coordinator	Cmdr. N.C. Baumann
Cmdr. W. J. Smith	Assistant Operations	Cmdr. T. J. Despain

	Coordinator	
Lt. J. L. Jones	Assistant	Lt. R. W. Glorfield
Sgt. E. E. Kiddy	Assistant	
Lt. H. H. Hicks	Radio Communications	Lt. J. L. Mathis
Lt. K. A. Bung	Intelligence	Sgt. E. Ramirez
Sgt. L. L. Sherwood	Assistant	

NORTH OF AYERS

Cmdr. F. E. Holder	Field Commander	Cmdr. C. C. Hagan
Capt. H. E. Green	Assistant	Capt. J. M. Vines
Lt. W. C. Crisp	Assistant	Lt. L. S. Smith
Lt. R. R. West	Assistant	Lt. J. O. Casbeer

SOUTH OF AYERS

Cmdr. L. E. Melton	Field Commander	Cmdr. C. W. Tackett
Lt. C. F. Wimbish	Assistant	Lt. T. J. Smith
Ltd. J. A. Bright	Assistant	Lt. O. B. Bell
Lt. R. J. Sullivan	Assistant	Lt. R. D. Tatum
Capt. T. L. Bullard	Liaison Officer	Lt. J. C. Whidden
Capt. W. C. Banner	Personnel Assignment	Lt B. E. Blount
Lt. F. F. Graham	Assistant	Lt. O. B. Wilson
Res. Officer	Assistant	Res. Officer
Capt. C. P. Rachal	Pass Officer	Lt. W. E. Wilkins
Lt. C. B. Mauricio	Assistant	
Lt. H. C. Moore	Shelter Officer	Capt. D. G. Grizzell
Lt. W. C. Lowenstein	Auto & Equipt. Officer	
Sgt. H. J. Erkert	Assistant	Patrolman R. B. Cook
*Sup. J. J. Bagwell	Identification	*Lt. J. M. Solis
Capt. B. C. Freeman	Food & Supply	Capt. W. T. Jackson
Lt. R. F. Miller	Assistant	

*Identification Officers will be Pass Officers unless an emergency exists requiring Identification Services.

III. Shifts and instructions for other personnel not specifically assigned to other duties as follows:

A. The entire traffic section, excluding officers assigned to traffic investigation between 4 PM and 8 AM, and also four motorcycle officers (selected by Commander) will be consolidated with the day and swing shifts of Patrol Section and the Tactical Squad to form the uniform division on duty between 8 AM and 8 PM. They will be under the supervision of the Field Commander. All officers will report to the Personnel Assignment Officer for assignment.

B. The graveyard patrol shifts and the three relief shifts will be consolidated to form the uniform division on duty between the hours of 8 PM and 8 AM, under the supervision of the Field Commander. All officers will report to the Personnel Assignment Officer in the Patrol Office.

   All traffic officers who are regularly scheduled on traffic investigation units from 4 PM to Midnight, and from Midnight to 8 AM, will be assigned to the 8 PM to 8 AM shift under the Field Commander. They will report to the Personnel Assignment Officer in the Patrol Office for their assignments.

C. All officers from Criminal Investigation, Special Services and Identification regularly assigned to the day shift will be on duty from 8 AM to 8 PM. The officers assigned to swing and graveyard shifts will be on duty from 8 PM to 8 AM. All officers will report to the Personnel Assignment Officer in the Patrol Office for their assignments.

D. The Patrol and Traffic Squad Rooms will be used as a place of assembly for all officers *after* they have reported to the Assignment Officer. After an officer completes an assignment, and if his tour of duty is not over and he is not immediately reassigned while in the field, he will again report to the Assignment Officer and then proceed to room 105 or 106 and wait for another assignment.

E. Members of the division whose duties allow the wearing of civilian clothing should report in uniform if possible for the purpose of ready identification in the field. If the officer does not have a uniform, he will dress commensurate with the nature of the duty, if known.

   Members of the Police Division and members of the Police Reserve that normally wear full uniform shall wear same when reporting for duty and will bring the foul weather gear.

1. Officers who are subject to outside participation should check foul weather gear and be sure that it is in good condition, prior to an emergency occurrence in order to prevent a last minute rush for equipment.

Officers must prepare themselves mentally, physically and materially prior to an emergency. They should know what they are going to do and how they are going to do it. Not only should a thorough study be made by each officer of this emergency plan, but he should also make his own plans at home so that he can do his job efficiently and effectively without worry for the safety of his family.

J. H. Avant
Chief of Police

Appendix: *Personnel Assignment and Records Procedure*

The Personnel Assignment Officer will set up his operations in Criminal Investigation Office, room 108. His staff will consist of an assistant and a ranking officer of the police reserve and such other personnel as are needed for clerical work and liaison within the building. Two large blackboards will be utilized on which to write assignments.

Prior to the occurrence of a hurricane or city wide emergency situation, a map of the entire city and the surrounding area will be prepared on which the city will be divided into blocks of various sizes. The blocks are numbered from 1 to 57. The Assignment Officer will keep ample supply of these maps in the Criminal Investigation Office and will give one to each unit when assigned to the field. He will keep this map in the car for reference.

The Personnel Assignment Officer will mark with black felt pen the unit number of the assignment on the block(s) which he assigned. When all units have been assigned, he will have several maps marked showing all known assignments and will send one to each of the following: (1) Radio Dispatch, (2) Police Liaison Officer, (3) Chief of Police, (4) Operations Coordinator, (5) Assistant Operations Coordinator, (6) Field Commander, (7) Food and Supply Officer.

More than one unit may be assigned to a block, and also more than one block may be assigned to a unit.

During the assignment period, notices of such assignments will flow constantly to the radio dispatcher so that he might fill in his *block* map. In the assignment office, a prepared sheet will be available showing the following: (1) Block Numbers, (2) Unit Radio Number, (3) Name(s) of officer assigned, (4) Vehicle Unit Number, (5) Time assigned and (6) Date.

A data card will be initiated at time of assignment for each officer and will serve as an *overtime* card. Information filled in on card at time of assignment will be as follows: (1) Name, (2) Activity Number, (3) Days Off, (4) Employee Code Number, (5) Date, (6) Time On and (7) Justification for Overtime.

When tour of duty is over, the officer signs his card, notes time and date and leaves card with Assignment Officer who initials card and after the emergency is resolved, sends cards to Operations Coordinator who will see that final approval is made on card. After approval, the cards are to be *keypunched,* sorted and a complete report printed on tabulating machine, and report then sent to Chief of Police.

The following suggestions are made for the purpose of better coordination between various functions:

1. All Supplies issued to units upon assignment are to be turned in at conclusion of emergency to Food and Supply Officer.

2. The Assignment Officer and Field Commander will convey assignments to each other when made, so that each can keep currently informed.

3. The officer going off shift will write location of vehicle on a tag and attach it to keys when turning them in at Assignment Office.

4. When time arrives near shift change, each unit will await for his call to come to station, so that all won't arrive at one time and cause congestion.

5. When emergency is over, the unit number of any police unit having driven in salt water will be given to automotive repair officer.

6. The importance of checking *in* and *out* with Assignment Officer *cannot be over emphasized* if the officer is to receive overtime pay.

7. When at station awaiting assignment, officers must stay in area of assembly in order that they can be contacted quickly. Do not wander around building.

8. A news letter will be prepared during shift indicating such items as (1) High water areas, (2) Closed streets, (3) Special assignments, (4) Special passes, (5) Shelter conditions, (6) Conditions already reported and (7) other vital information. A copy will be given to each unit going on the next tour of duty.

9. All officers will remain on assigned duty until relieved. If an emergency arises, the Field Commander or his assistants will make decision for any changes.

10. Contact Mr. Scarbrough, Public Works, to provide mechanic for 24-hour duty and make necessary supplies available such as: Jumper cables, batteries, tires, alternators, bulbs, etc.

11. Assignment officers to be provided with monthly mileage report for assignment of low and high mileage vehicles.

12. Consider arrangements for pot flares, barricades, Skid-O-Cans, repellant, etc., for *Check Points.*

CITY OF CORPUS CHRISTI
CIVIL DEFENSE
EMERGENCY OPERATION PLAN

(Revised 9-1-71)

The Hurricane Emergency Operation Plan is primarily designed to quickly marshal the full resources of the City of Corpus Christi for the purpose of protecting life and property and maintaining critical municipal functions immediately before, during and after a storm of hurricane intensity. This plan presupposes that each department and division head will maintain complete control over the operation of his department or division, except as specifically altered hereafter, and that each department head has made preparations to protect the property of his department and to gear his forces to meet the high winds and rising water typically associated with hurricanes.

The hurricane plan is built around five *conditions* which represent varying degrees of threatened emergency. These *conditions* and the action to be taken will constitute the basic outline of the City's emergency plan and/or as follows:

CONDITION NO. FIVE — This is a condition which automatically goes into effect annually on June 1 and remains in effect through November 30. It indicates that the hurricane season now exists.

Action — Each department head is expected to review or supplement his own internal emergency plan and update the general location and status of equipment likely to be needed in an emergency.

CONDITION NO. FOUR — This condition will be declared by the Director of Public Safety or Civil Defense Director when the course of a hurricane has been established and the National Weather Service predicts a likely landfall within seventy-two hours and within one hundred miles of the City of Corpus Christi.

Action — (a) The Civil Defense Office will be opened and maintained on a twenty-four hour basis. (b) Direct radio and/or telephone communication will be established with the local National Weather Service. (c) The City Manager will be notified and he will advise the Mayor and the City Council of the status. (d) The Director of Public Safety and/or Civil Defense Director will notify all emergency operating center department and division heads and all other persons who will man the emergency operating center in the event of a hurricane. (e) All primary EOC personnel will check the status of their operation and equipment and will be available to be reached by telephone.

CONDITION NO. THREE — This condition will be declared by the Director of Public Safety and/or Civil Defense Director when the National Weather Service indicates the possibility of a landfall within thirty-six hours close enough to cause damaging winds or tides in the City of Corpus Christi.

Action — (a) The Mayor, City Manager, Director of Public Safety, Director of Public Works, Director of Public Utilities, Director of Traffic Engineering and all of the division heads of the above mentioned departments, as well as the Public Information Officer and the Central Message Control Coordinator, will meet in the Emergency Operating Center with representatives of the National Weather Service, communication officer and Red Cross representatives to evaluate the path and nature of the hurricane. Briefing at this time will include a review of hurricane procedures and any amendments or modifications to the hurricane plan will be made in the light of existing circumstances. (b) The Director of Public Works and the Director of Public Safety shall be responsible for seeing that building inspectors and fire inspectors begin touring the city, during daylight hours, to enforce the building code provisions against loose material and construction sites. (c) The Public Information Officer shall open the Public Information Office and shall inform area news media that it is operational. (d) Telephones and other communications equipment will be activated and checked by the Director of Civil Defense. (e) All emergency operating center personnel will remain on one-hour call.

CONDITION NO. TWO — This condition will be declared by the Mayor or City Manager when the course of the hurricane has been established and the National Weather Service suggests a landfall within eighteen hours near enough to the City of Corpus Christi to cause damaging winds or tides.

Action — (a) Emergency Operating Center will be fully manned as described hereafter. (b) Each department will begin full hurricane operation. (c) The City Transit operation will be transferred from the Director of Public Utilities to the Director of Traffic Engineering. (d) The Mayor shall order evacuations of low-lying areas and other areas of special danger, if such evacuation has not been ordered before.

CONDITION NO. ONE — This condition shall be declared by the Mayor or City Manager when damaging tides or hurricane-force winds are imminent.

Action — All personnel shall immediately complete their hurricane preparedness operation, and all personnel exposed to tides and high winds, except those immediately engaged in the protection of human life, shall take cover until the storm has passed.

Emergency Operations Center

Since Civil Defense is municipal government operating promptly in an emergency, the concept of the EOC is to bring the decision-makers and key operational personnel at one point where information may be fed to them, a decision made and action dispatched to the field.

Figure 10 shows the physical location of key personnel in the EOC. Unless otherwise indicated, each department or division head shall control and operate his own department.

Communications Facilities. Rooms C and D will house the police communications equipment. Room K will have public works, public utilities and fire department radio communications. Room L will house the ham radio operators and the Citizen Band base station. The ham operators will have primary responsibility for communications with hospitals, Red Cross and local non-city essential services. They will also have primary responsibility for maintaining contact with out-of-city essential stations. The local Citizen Band operators will have primary responsibility for maintaining contact with shelters.

Room M will have a direct radio contact with the Weather Bureau as well as direct radio communication with the news media through a transmitter in Room N. Room J will have at least six additional telephones added at the declaration of *Condition Three*. Other rooms now have phones through the police switchboard.

Operations. It is imperative that each desk or groups of desks be manned at all times by the person mentioned or his designated representative. This will insure continuity of operation and reduce considerable confusion and possible bottlenecks.

Room I will contain the Civil Defense Coordinator (the Mayor) and the chief executive officer of the city (the City Manager). They will be assisted by the Assistant City Manager and one Emergency Administrative Assistant (station five and six).

The remainder of the operating center descriptions are self-explanatory with the following exceptions:

A. The Civil Defense Director (2) will be advised of all information of general conditions so he may post it on blackboards for the information of all EOC personnel.

B. The Message Coordinator function will be the responsibility of the City

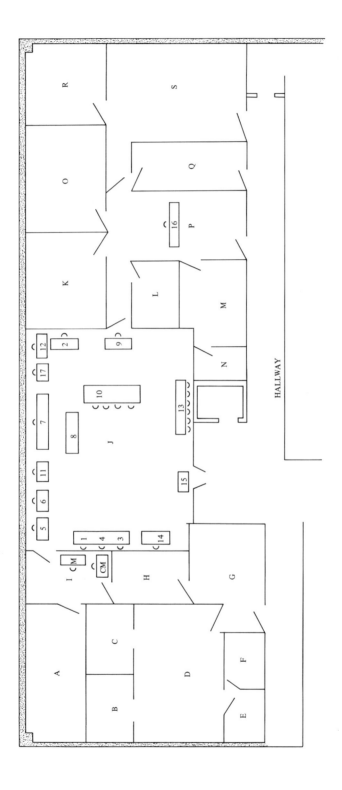

Figure 10: Civil Defense Emergency Operating Center: A = Police Radio Equipment; B = Police Communication Tape-Recording Room; C = Police Dispatcher; D = Police Communication Officers — Complaint clerks, tape-operated teletype; E = Restroom for communication Personnel; F = Telephone Switch Board; G = Police Command Watch; H = Police Command Watch; I = Mayor and City Manager — This room has plate glass wall so that the Mayor and City Manager may have over-all observation of the emergency operating center. J = Emergency Operating Center — Stations: (1) Director of Public Safety, (2) Director of Civil Defense — Chalk board behind Director of Civil Defense for the purpose of writing necessary messages for all EOC people to view. (3) Police Chief, (4) Fire Chief, (Note) Stations 1-3-4 will be a long table. If one must leave his station, one of the others will know his whereabouts. (5) Assistant City Manager, (6) Emergency Administrative Assistant, (7) Public Works, (8) Public Utilities, (9) Message Coordinators — will be responsibility of City Attorney and his assistants. This station will be manned by two city employees at all times. Written messages going out will go directly to the message coordinators, then to Civil Defense Radio. Civil Defense Radio will give all incoming messages to message coordinator. The message coordinator will direct the message to the proper person in EOC. Answers will come back through the message coordinator and be passed on to C. D. Radio. The message forms PS 4-5 are in triplicate — white copy must remain in the C. D. Radio Office for 1 year; yellow copy will remain with the message coordinator, and the recipient or sender keeps the pink copy. Message coordinator will maintain a log of all messages and will examine content for obvious error or possible conflicts. (10) Telephone Information — Four positions to be filled by Park and Recreation Department. Battery of outside line telephones to be installed. Personnel at this station to avoid unauthorized use of telephones. (11) Traffic Engineer, (12) Health and Welfare, (13) Messengers — Six positions to be filled by city personnel assigned by Personnel Department. Personnel at this station to be available for runners in order that key personnel may remain at their stations or with EOC. (14) National Guard — If necessary for National Guard to be called out, the C. O. or his designee will be stationed near the Director of Public Safety, Mayor and City Manager. (15) Control Point for EOC — Personnel at this station will attempt to minimize traffic in EOC. (16) Control Point for Rooms K-L & O — This station will be located in the Civil Defense Office. (17) Red Cross — Personnel from Red Cross to act as liaison between Red Cross and EOC. K = Fire, Public Utilities & Public Works Radio Communication; L = Corpus Christi Civil Defense Radio — Manned by Corpus Christi Amateur Radio Club. M = Public Information Officer; N = Emergency Broadcasting System — KEYS transmitter, also National Weather Service Teletype, located in this room; O = State and Federal Defense and Disaster Personnel; P = Civil Defense Office — Station 16 is also located in Civil Defense Office. Q = Civil Defense Storeroom; R = Conference Room — This room to be used for executive conferences. S = State and Federal Defense and Disaster Personnel.

Attorney and his assistants.

C. Telephone information personnel will be assigned by Park and Recreation Department.

D. The Traffic Engineer will assume control of the Transit System upon the declaration of a *Condition Two*. At the same time, all Park and Recreation heavy equipment will be transferred to the Director of Public Works. The Director of Park and Recreation shall provide the Director of Public Works with a complete inventory of such equipment when a *Condition Three* is declared.

E. Control points will be manned by police supervisory personnel who will not permit unauthorized personnel into the EOC. The Director of Civil Defense shall issue arm bands or other suitable identification to people authorized to be in the EOC. (Room J).

Press Relations

The Public Information Officer will be responsible for manning the Public Information Office (Room M) at all times. All public announcements will be issued on the News Media Teletype Network (Room G) and repeated, if possible, on the Civil Defense News Media transmitter (Room N). All public announcements and items of general news interest will be given to the Public Information Officer as soon as possible in order that he may, at all times, be able to provide all news media with current, accurate information. Interviews with EOC personnel will be coordinated through the Public Information Officer. Space will be provided in Room M for voluntary news media pools which may be organized and for the Regional Public Information Officer. The Public Information Officer shall also issue Civil Defense Press Passes to members of the working press who do not have State Department of Public Safety press cards. The state cards will be recognized as valid during an emergency.

Shelters

A list of shelters which will be open during a hurricane is attached. The primary list will not be made public until the decision is made to open them. The Red Cross liasion officer (17) may make adjustments in this list as may be justified by circumstances.

Primary Shelters   *Secondary Shelters*

Boys Club   Cunningham Jr. High School
3902 Greenwood   4321 Prescott

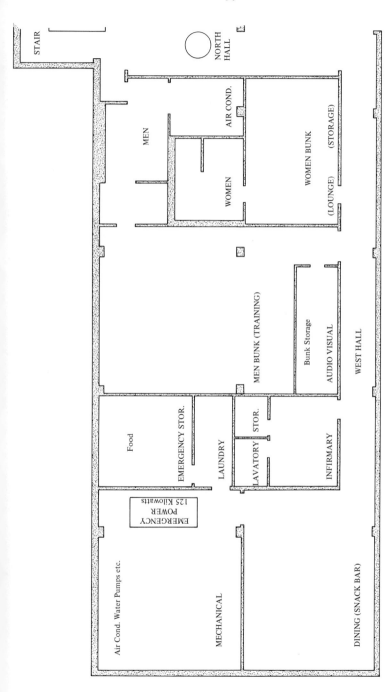

Figure 11: FLOOR PLAN — EMERGENCY OPERATIONS CENTER: Area marked *Infirmary* is being used as a storeroom. Mens Bunk (Training) — This room is usually held in reserve for other emergency agencies called in, such as Corp. of Engineers. Womens Bunk Room — This room can be used as a clerical pool as well as space for typewriters and tables for stenographic work.

Primary Shelters	Secondary Shelters
Primary Shelters	*Secondary Shelters*
W. B. Ray High School 1002 Texan Trail	Baker Jr. High School 3445 Pecan
Crossley Elementary School 2512 Koepke	Robert Driscoll Jr. High School 261 Weil
Wynn Seale Jr. High School 1707 Ayers	Menger Elementary School 2209 South Alameda
Barnes Jr. High School 3102 Highland	Zavala Elementary School 925 Francesca
Lamar Elementary School 2212 Morris	Roy Miller High School Cafe & Gym 515 Fisher
Washington Elementary School 1141 Sam Rankin	Oak Park Elementary School 3701 Mueller
Flour Bluff Jr. High School 2300 Waldron	Flour Bluff Ind. School District Administration Building 2300 & 2505 Waldron Road
Skinner Elementary School 1001 Bloomington	Molina Jr. High School 1115 Bloomington
Kennedy Elementary School 5040 Rockford	New West Oso High School 5202 McMullen
West Oso Independent School District Office 5050 Rockford	Carl Allen Elementary School 1101 Villareal
Tuloso-Midway Jr. High School 1925 Tuloso Road	Tuloso-Midway High School 9830 LaBranch

APPENDIX B

AMERICAN RED CROSS - DENTON COUNTY CHAPTER DISASTER PLAN

DALLAS COUNTY COMBINED SERVICE TERRITORY
DISASTER PLAN

A. *Types of Disasters:*

1. Fire
2. Flood
3. Tornado
4. Hurricane

5. Transportation accidents (plane, train, bus, etc.)
6. Civil Disorders
7. Famine, Earthquakes, etc.
8. Explosions

B. *Disaster Equipment Available:*

1. 1200 cots and 2400 blankets (in Dallas and Texarkana)
2. Three Handi-Vans (1 in Dallas, 1 in Longview and 1 in Texarkana)
3. Three Canteen Units (1 Van Type, 2 Catering Units)
4. One Mobile Headquarters (32 ft. Trailer)
5. Seven Station Wagons

C. *If a Disaster Occurs, IMMEDIATELY Do the Following:*

1. Report known facts to:

Disaster Services, The American Red Cross
Dallas County Chapter, Dallas, Texas

Telephone (office): 214 — RI 1-4421 (8:00 a.m. to 5:00 p.m.)
Telephone (night): 214 — RI 1-5435 (after 5:00 p.m.)

This report should include:
a. type of disaster
b. time it occurred
c. area affected
d. number of homes destroyed and damaged
e. number of injured and dead
f. what you are doing and assistance needed (personnel and/or equipment)

    2. Put chapter disaster plan into operation:
       a. provide food
       b. provide shelter
       c. provide First Aid, medical and nursing care as needed (Each shelter should have one nurse.)
       d. provide clothing

D. *REMEMBER,* the *affected chapter* must act *immediately* to care for the disaster victims. Equipment and personnel from the Dallas Combined Service Territory will be dispatched as *needed.*

American Red Cross
Disaster Organization
For Denton County Chapter
Address Rayzor Building — Telephone 382-6323

RED CROSS CHAIRMAN	BUSINESS	HOME
NAME Ben C. Ivey, Jr. ADDRESS 1817 Emerson	PHONE: 382-6321	387-6659

EXECUTIVE DIRECTOR

NAME Mrs. Katherine Rhyne ADDRESS 903 Denton	PHONE: 382-6323	382-3387

DISASTER CHAIRMAN

NAME Ray Boutwell ADDRESS 321 Pearl	PHONE: 387-6171	382-2258

DISASTER COMMITTEE MEMBERS

SURVEY CHAIRMAN

NAME Bill Coleman ADDRESS 2433 Kayewood		387-2049

FOOD CHAIRMAN

NAME Mrs. Howard Frank ADDRESS 1919 Mohican	PHONE: 387-1013	382-3355

| CLOTHING CHAIRMAN | BUSINESS | HOME |

NAME Jake Craven   PHONE: 382-5016   387-1595
ADDRESS 801 Live Oak
Co-Chairman
NAME James Russell   PHONE: 387-6121   382-5504
ADDRESS 1919 Maid Marion

SHELTER CHAIRMAN

NAME Tommy Turner   PHONE: 387-3551   387-6353
ADDRESS Ranch Estates

MEDICAL NURSING CHAIRMAN
                           HOSPITAL
NAME_Ewell Burkhalter, M. D. PHONE: 387-5861   382-2842
ADDRESS 1025 Alice

DISASTER HEADQUARTERS

1st CHOICE: First Baptist Church
2nd CHOICE: St. Andrews Presbyterian Church

American Red Cross
Denton County Chapter
Denton, Texas

Disaster Resources

Immediately Available, Any Hour, Day or Night

PERSONNEL:

FOOD SERVERS, CANTEEN WORKERS, SCHOOL CAFETERIA PERSONNEL, ETC.

How Many
Who to call to activate workers:
NAME Sarah Frank
ADDRESS 1919 Mohican
TELEPHONE 382-3355 or 387-1013

CLOTHING COMMITTEE

How Many
Who to call to activate workers:
NAME James H. Russell
ADDRESS 1919 Maid Marion
TELEPHONE 382-5504 or 387-6121

SHELTER WORKERS

How Many
Who to call to activate workers:
NAME Owen Griffin
ADDRESS Route #2
TELEPHONE 382-3288

NURSES

How Many
Who to call to activate workers:
NAME Miss Ann Burtis
ADDRESS 515 Malone
TELEPHONE 382-2746

Family Service case workers to interview and give personal assistance.

How Many
Who to call to activate workers:
NAME Frances Young
ADDRESS 1016 Ector
TELEPHONE 387-1888

COMMUNICATIONS

Denton County C-B Club — through Co. D Office — To handle all communications where telephones are still out.

FOOD SERVICE

Firemen's Auxiliary, Mrs. Howard Frank, Chairman

Unloading and placing of cots and blankets, Owen Griffin, Chairman

TRANSPORTATION

From danger area to shelter for those that are not injured, by church buses.

GROCERIES

Osborn Piggly-Wiggly chain will open at any hour
Jack Carlisle (7-3074), 2914 Croydon Street

Jays Grill at any hour — To help in any need.
Lamba Chi Alpha Fraternity, 907 W. Hickory (7-9677)

Cafe for sandwiches and coffee any hour — Jays Grill, Ft. Worth Hwy, L. T. Henslee, Owner

RED CROSS FLAGS

Shelter Chairman, Tommy Turner

FAMILY SERVICES

Case Workers Chairman, Francis Young

LONG DISTANCE COMMUNICATIONS

Ham Radio Club

SPECIAL EMERGENCY MESSAGES

Carried by Radio KDNT

Red Cross directors are to come to headquarters for any special assignments, unless they are already assigned to any special duty.

Survey Committee

PREPAREDNESS

1. Arrangements have been made with police, sheriff and fire departments to promptly notify disaster representative when disaster occurs.

2. Committee members have been appointed.

WHEN DISASTER STRIKES

At direction of disaster representative, survey chairman and committee will:

1. Make a personal on-the-scene preliminary survey of affected areas and report findings directly to the disaster representative.
2. Make progressive reports as directed.
   Purpose of preliminary survey is to determine immediately the general effect of the disaster – the amount and kind of help needed.

Survey report should include the following:

1. Estimate number of persons
   a. Injured
   b. Killed
   c. Hospitalized
   d. Homeless
2. Estimated Number of Homes
   a. Destroyed
   b. Damaged
3. Location and Kind of Immediate Relief Needed

CHAIRMAN	*BUSINESS*	*HOME*
Bill Coleman		387-2049
COMMITTEE MEMBERS		
Roy Gibson	382-6741	387-7168
Weldon McBride	382-8311	382-5275
D. J. Wagg		382-2029

Shelter Committee

PREPAREDNESS

1. Conduct survey of schools and churches to be used as shelters and/or feeding stations.
2. Arrange for 24-hour staffing of shelters. (Shelter manager and adequate number of assistants on 8 or 12 hour shifts.)

WHEN DISASTER STRIKES

Establish, staff and operate temporary mass housing for disaster victims who are unable to find shelter through own resources.

MASS SHELTERS:

Building	Location	Capacity Feeding	Sleeping	Who Has Key

(All these places have kitchens and can serve food when needed)

Building	Capacity	Who Has Key
First Baptist Church	75 persons	Dr. L.L. Armstrong 915 Edgewood Pl 2-6404 John Matt Howard 512 Mimosa Dr. 7-4485 Bill Shedd 703 Greenwood 7-2435 Mrs. Joann Dickson 2204 Foxcroft
First Christian Church	75 persons	Rev. R.S. Martin 1025 Kings Row 7-6200 John Littrell 1110 Boliver St 2-2708 W. K. Baldridge 2015 Locksley Ln 2-2905
Grace Temple Baptist Church	35 persons	R. O. Stiff Henry Powell Rev. Vernon Davis Mrs. J. D. Coffin
Immaculate Conception Catholic Church	50 persons	Father Johnson at Rectory
Fred Moore School	125 persons	C. B. Redd

Building	Location	Capacity Feeding	Sleeping	Who Has Key
				Sam Lawson
				Mrs. Eva Hodges
				Mrs. Annie Jones
Memorial Baptist Church		288 persons		Owen Griffin
				Melvin Hartline
				Olton Funderburk
Denton Baptist Temple	Hwy 35			Rev. Boyce Brannon
				Larry Bruce
				1607 Bernard St.
				Suzanne Collier
				Houston Hall TWU

SHELTERS OUTSIDE OF DENTON

SANGER: High School Cafeteria & Gym	Herbert Arledge
	Office: 458-7447
	Home: 458-3287
	Mrs. C. G. Bryson
	Home: 458-3440
	Norman Greenwood
	Home: 458-7813
PILOT POINT: 1) High School Cafeteria	Ben D. Smith
2) High School Gym	
3) Basement of Elementary School	Emory Close
	Marlin Bobo
	Don Holly
	Peggy Close
LEWISVILLE: 1) New High School Cafeteria	James M. Burkhead
2) Central Elementary	
3) Lewisville Middle School	Marshall Durham
4) College Street Elementary	
	William T. Bolin
	Ray Hopper

Building	Location	Capacity Feeding Sleeping	Who Has Key
			Ellis Thomas
JUSTIN: Elementary Cafeteria & Gym			Henry Davis
ARGYLE: Elementary Cafeteria & Gym			Wayne Vaughn 464-7278
			Mrs. Elmer Morgan 464-7349
	First Baptist Church (Parsonage (Carpenter)		464-7225
			Mrs. Sam Haynes 464-7454

Medical — Nursing Committee

PREPAREDNESS

1. Survey community medical resources and maintain current list of facilities and personnel available for disaster use.
2. Formulate understanding with local hospitals regarding basis of care for ill and injured in accordance with Red Cross policies.

HOSPITAL FACILITIES

Name	Address	Bed Capacity
Flow Memorial Hospital	1310 Scripture	256
Denton Osteopatic Hosp.	2026 University Dr.	22

WHEN DISASTER STRIKES

1. Provide medical and nursing care in Red Cross shelters.
2. Establish and staff aid stations and emergency hospitals if needed.
3. Furnish supplementary emergency medical and hospital supplies.
4. Augment local resources for transporting the ill and injured.
5. Provide additional nursing personnel when needed.
6. Assist hospitals and physicians with plans for the care of disaster patients.

CHAIRMAN	*Office*	*Home*
Ewell Burkhalter, M.D.	PHONE 387-5861	382-2842
Miss Ann Burtis	PHONE 387-6151	382-2746

Clothing Committee

PREPAREDNESS

1. Make arrangements with a store manager to open and furnish emergency clothing to disaster victims at night, if necessary.
2. Suggested committee personnel: clothing store operators and church groups.
3. Be ready to receive, sort and issue clothing.
4. Arrange with newspapers and radio stations in advance to clear all appeals for clothing with disaster representative, so that they may be controlled and based on actual *needs* and not *excitement* or *drama*.

WHEN DISASTER STRIKES

Provide clothing for disaster victims who are unable to obtain needed clothing through immediate resources.

CHAIRMAN	*Business*	*Home*
Jake Cravens	PHONE 382-5016	387-1595

CO-CHAIRMAN		
James H. Russell	PHONE 387-6121	382-5504

BIBLIOGRAPHY

American College of Surgeons: *Essential Equipment for Ambulances.* Chicago, 1970.

American Medical Association: *First Aid Manual.* Chicago, 1970.
Developing Emergency Medical Services – Guidelines for Community Councils. Chicago, 1970.
Bibliography: Medical Aspects of Civil Defense. Chicago, 1953.

American National Red Cross: *Community Involvement in Civil Defense.* Washington, 1967.
Disaster Manual. Washington, 1955.
Charter, By-Laws and Endowment Fund Regulations. Washington, 1928.

American Nurses Association: *The Role of the Licensed Practical Nurse in Disaster.* New York, 1966.

American Psychiatric Association: *First Aid for Psychological Reactions in Disasters.* Washington, 1965.

American Society of Anesthesiologists, Committee on Acute Medicine: *Community-wide Emergency Medical Services.* Pittsburg, 1970.

Baker, George W., and Cottrell, Leonard D., Jr.: *Behavioral Science and Civil Defense.* Washington, National Academy of Sciences, 1962.

Baker, G. W., and Chapman, D. W.: *Man and Society in Disaster.* New York, Basic, 1962.

Bates, F. L., Fogleman, C. W., Parenton, V. J., Pittman, R. H., and Tracy, G. S.: *The Social and Psychological Consequences of a Natural Disaster.* Washington, National Academy of Sciences, No. 1081, 1963.

Berry, F. B.: *Medical Organization of Combat Zones and Critical Areas of Civil Defense.* Washington, Walter Reed Army Medical Center, Army Medical Services Graduate School, 1952.

Bullard, F. M.: *Volcanoes in History, in Theory, in Eruption.* Austin, University of Texas Press, 1962.

Carson, R.: *The Sea Around Us.* New York, Oxford University Press, 1951.

Office of Civil Defense: *Example of a Local Government Civil Defense Emergency Plan for a Municipality of Approximately 20,000,* Part G, Chapter 1. Washington, U. S. Government Printing Office, June, 1968.
Law and Order Training for Civil Defense Emergency, Instructor Guide, Part A, IG10.1 A. Washington, U. S. Government Printing Office, August, 1965. Also Part B.
Law and Order Training for Civil Defense Emergency, Student Manual – Part A, SM-10.1 A. Washington, U. S. Government Printing Office,

August, 1965. Also Part B.

Civil Defense, MP-54. Washington, U. S. Government Printing Office, May, 1970.

Maintenance of Law and Order During Civil Defense Emergencies, Part E, Chapter 9. Washington, U. S. Government Printing Office, November, 1968.

National Civil Defense Program, Part A, Chapter 2. Washington, U. S. Government Printing Office, 1965.

Fire Prevention and Control During Civil Defense Emergencies, Part E, Chapter 10. Washington, U. S. Government Printing Office, June, 1969.

The Federal Civil Defense Act of 1950. As amended April, 1965.

Annual Report, 1970. Washington, U. S. Government Printing Office, 1971.

Actions for Increasing Local Government Civil Defense Readiness, Part G, Chapter 5. Washington, U. S. Government Printing Office, 1965.

In Time of Emergency: A Citizens' Handbook on Nuclear Attack and Natural Disasters, H-14. Washington, U. S. Government Printing Office, March, 1969.

Community and Family Service for Civil Defense, H-11. Washington, U. S. Government Printing Office, 1967.

The National Plan for Civil Defense and Defense Mobilization. Washington, U. S. Government Printing Office, 1958.

Danzig, E. R., Thayer, P. W., and Galanter, Lila R.: *The Effects of a Threatening Rumor on a Disaster-Stricken Community*, Disaster Study No. 10. Washington, National Academy of Sciences, 1958.

Department of Defense: *Rescue Skills and Techniques*. Washington, U. S. Government Printing Office, 1959.

Disaster Research Group: *Field Studies of Disaster Behavior*, Disaster Study No. 14. Washington, National Academy of Sciences, 1961.

Federal Bureau of Investigation: *Prevention and Control of Mobs and Riots*. Washington, U. S. Government Printing Office, 1967.

Flora, Snowden D.: *Tornadoes of the United States*. Norman, University of Oklahoma Press, 1953.

Form, William H., and Nosow, Sigmund: *Community in Disaster*. New York, Harper and Brothers, 1958.

Fritz, Charles E., and Mathewson, J. H.: *Convergence Behavior in Disasters*. Washington, National Academy of Sciences, 1957.

Garb, Solomon, and Eng, Evelyn: *Disaster Handbook*. New York, Springer Pub, 1969.

Healy, Richard J.: *Design for Security*. New York, John Wiley & Sons, 1968.

Healy, Richard J.: *Emergency and Disaster Planning*. New York, John Wiley & Sons, 1969.

Hodgson, J. M.: *Earthquakes and Earth Structure*. Englewood Cliffs, Prentice-Hall, 1964.

Ikle, Fred C., and Kincaid, Harry V.: *Social Aspects of Wartime Evacuation of American Cities.* Washington, National Academy of Sciences, 1956.

International Association of Chiefs of Police: *General Emergency Plan,* Unit 4A11, Supplement 1. Washington, 1971.

Guidelines for Civil Disorder and Mobilization Planning. September, 1968.

Janis, I. L., Gillin, D. W., and Spiegel, J. F.: *The Problem of Panic.* Washington, Federal Civil Defense Administration, Bulletin 18-19-2, 1955.

Johnson, G.: *The Abominable Airlines,* (airline crashes). New York, Macmillan, 1964.

Kahn, H.: *On Thermonuclear War.* Princeton, Princeton University Press, 1960.

Kearney, P. W.: *Disaster on Your Doorstep.* New York, Harper & Brothers, 1953.

Killian, Lewis M.: *An Introduction to Methodological Problems of Field Studies in Disasters.* Washington, National Academy of Sciences, 1956.

Killian, Lewis M.: *The Houston, Texas, Fireworks Explosion.* Washington, National Academy of Sciences, 1956.

Lamers, William M.: *Disaster Protection Handbook for School Administrators.* Washington, American Association of School Administrators, 1959.

Lane, F. W.: *The Elements Rage,* Chapter 5. New York, Chilton, 1965.

Leet, L. D.: *Earthquakes, Discoveries in Seismology.* New York, Dell, 1964.

Lowell, V. W.: *Airlines Safety is a Myth.* New York, Bartholomew House, 1967.

Momboisse, Raymond M.: *Store Planning for Riot Survival.* Sacramento, MSN Enterprises, 1968.

Moore, Harry Estill: *And the Winds Blew.* Austin, University of Texas Press, 1964.

National Association of Manufacturers: *Bomb Threats: Suggested Action to Protect Employes and Property.* Chicago, 1970.

A Checklist for Plant Security.

National Board of Fire Underwriters: *Fire Safe School Buildings.* New York, 1960.

National Education Association: *Checklist of Safety Education in Your School.* Washington, 1960.

Perry, Helen Swick, and Perry, Stewart E.: *Schoolhouse Disasters.* Washington, National Academy of Sciences, 1959.

Prince, S. H.: *Catastrophe and Social Change.* New York, Columbia University Press, 1920.

Raker, John W., Wallace, Anthony F. C., and Rayner, Jeannette F.: *Emergency Medical Cafe in Disasters.* Washington, National Academy of Sciences, 1956.

Robinson, D.: *The Face of Disaster.* Garden City, Doubleday, 1959.

San Francisco Police Department: *Civil Disobedience Demonstrations.* San

Francisco, 1963.

Serling, R. J.: *The Probable Cause* (airline crashes). Garden City, Doubleday, 1960.

Shames, Sally Olean: *Records Essential for Identification of Persons; An Inventory and Evaluation of Public Records Relating to Identification of Persons During Emergency and Post-Emergency Periods.* Washington, George Washington University Press, 1961.

United States Army Headquarters (Sixth): *U. S. Army Films for Public Use.* Presidio, San Francisco, 1971.

Tazieff, H.: *The Orion Book of Volcanoes.* New York, Orion Pr Grossman, 1961.

Texas Department of Public Safety, Office of Defense and Disaster Relief: *Emergency Operating Centers.* Austin, 1964.

Texas Division of Defense and Disaster Relief: *Civil Defense and Disaster Relief Planning – A Manual for Local Governments.* Austin, 1962.
Texans on the Alert for Civil Defense and Disaster Relief. Austin, 1956.
Civil Defense and Disaster Planning. Austin, 1962.
Curriculum Guide for Civil Defense and Disaster Relief Education. Austin, 1956.

United States Air Force: *Medical Planning for Disaster Casualty Control,* APM 160-37. Washington, U. S. Government Printing Office, 1962.

Wallace, Anthony F. C.: *Tornado in Westchester.* Washington, National Academy of Sciences, 1956.

Wallace, Anthony F. C.: *Human Behavior in Extreme Situations.* Washington, National Academy of Sciences, 1956.

INDEX

A

Aircraft disasters, 28
Alarm systems, 289
American College of Surgeons, 297
American Medical Association, 297
American Red Cross, 50, 51, 170, 270-276, 315
Anatomy of Disaster, 3-46
Andrews, Rex R., 71
Apprehension capability, 289
Arnwine, Major Henry B., 247
Auxiliary police unit, 70, 238

B

Beaufort Wind Scale, 11
Blackmon, Jack, 50
Bristow, Allen P., fn 240
Burbank Unusual Occurrence Control Plan, 68-162

C

Camille, the incredible, 46
Celia, hurricane, 47
Chronology of disaster, 3
Civil Defense System, 41, 70, 250-269
Civil disorder, containment of, 163-237
Colton, Chief Constable J. E., 249
Computer sciences in disaster situations, 294
Corpus Christi Hurricane and Emergency Plan, 299-314

D

Denton County Disaster Plan, 315

E

Emergency medical services, 296

Emergency operating center, 49, 69
Emergency Planning, Federal Office of, 277
Eng, Evelyn, fn 3
Evacuation Detail, 69
Explosions, 28

F

Fallout Shelter Program, 252
Fan out procedure, 69
Fault lines, 3
Federal Bureau of Investigation, fn 40, 294
Federal Government, role of in disaster, 277-285
Federal Reserve Bank, 290
Field command post, 69
Fires, 21
Floods, 21

G

Garb, Solomon, fn 3
Gates, Deputy Chief Daryl F., 163
General Operations, 241
Gourley, G. Douglas, 240
Guidelines for Civil Disorder and Mobilization Planning, 163

H

Healy, Richard J., fn 3, 11
Highland Park (Michigan) Reserve Force, 241
Hurricanes, 11, 14

I

International Association of Chiefs of Police, 51, 163, 247, fn 270, fn 288, fn 289

J

Jessup, Chief Jacob A., 239

K

King, Everett M., fn 240
Kingsbury, Arthur A., fn 291
Klimkowski, Major Adam, 163
Kobitz, Richard W., 163

L

Leonard, Glenford, fn 249
Leonard, V. A., fn 6
Lubbock (Texas) tornado, 49
Lund, Donald, fn 163

M

Man-made emergencies, 37
Mass Care Center, 70
Medical post, 69
Medical services, emergency, 296
Miami Police Department, 163
Mine disasters, 28
Missing persons post, 69
Mobile emergency headquarters, 286
Mobile Task Force, 241
Mob situations, 37
Modified Mercali Earthquake Intensity
Scale, 6
Momboisse, Raymond M., fn 40
More, Harry W. Jr., fn 6
Morgue post, 69

N

National Crime Information Center, 294
National Geographic Society, 10
National Sheriffs Association, fn 270
Natural disasters, 5
Newman, Frank, 6
Nuclear attack, 40

O

Office of Emergency Planning (Federal),
277

P

Perimeter of control, 69

Pilcher, Weyland, 50
Police hazards, 291
Police roadblocks, 291
Posse Comitatus, 70
Post, Richard S., fn 291
President's Advisory Commission on
Civil Disorder, 163

R

Railroad wrecks, 28
Red Cross, 50, 51, 170, 270-276, 315
Reserve Force Concept, 238-249
Richter, Dr. Charles F., 6
Richter Earthquake Magnitude Scale, 6
Riot situations, 37
Roadblocks, 291

S

Sagelyn, Arnold, 163
Schwartz, J. L., fn 292
Simpson, Dr. Robert H., 51
Smith, Dean, 163
Special Operations, 242
Steiner, Richard V., fn 291
Sunnyvale Department of Public Safety,
239

T

Tactical Unit, 241
Texas Department of Public Safety, 17,
fn 39
Texas Rangers, 39
Tornadoes, 11
Townsend, Marvin, 50
Trowbridge, Alexander B., 290

U

United States Coast and Geodetic Survey, 9
United States Weather Service, 41, 11

V

Volcanic eruptions, 26

W

When disaster strikes, 46-51
Winds, 11
Wood, Harry O., 6